D1558973

Between
Tradition and Revolution

The Hegelian Transformation of
Political Philosophy

Between Tradition and Revolution

The Hegelian Transformation of Political Philosophy

Manfred Riedel
Translated by Walter Wright

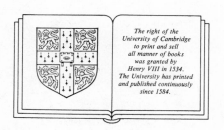

The right of the
University of Cambridge
to print and sell
all manner of books
was granted by
Henry VIII in 1534.
The University has printed
and published continuously
since 1584.

Cambridge University Press

Cambridge
London   New York   New Rochelle
Melbourne   Sydney

Published by the Press Syndicate of the University of Cambridge
The Pitt Building, Trumpington Street, Cambridge CB2 1RP
32 East 57th Street, New York, NY 10022, USA
296 Beaconsfield Parade, Middle Park, Melbourne 3206, Australia

© Manfred Riedel
English translation © Cambridge University Press 1984

First published 1984

Printed in Great Britain at the University Press, Cambridge

This book was originally published in German in 1969 (second edition, 1972)
by Suhrkamp Verlag under the title *Studien zu Hegels Rechtsphilosophie*.

Library of Congress catalogue card number: 83–20885

British Library Cataloguing in Publication Data
Riedel, Manfred
Between tradition and revolution.
1. Hegel, Georg Wilhelm Friedrich –
Political Science 2. Political science
I. Title II. Studien zu Hegels Rechtsphilosophie
English
320.5'0924   JC233.H46
ISBN 0 521 25644 5

N.P.

Contents

Preface

This study deals with the relation of Hegel's *Philosophy of Right* to modern revolution and the classical tradition of political thought in Europe. This presupposes an entirely different point of view from that offered by the history of this influential book during the nineteenth century and its varying influence on the global ideologies of Marxism, Liberalism and Fascism, a conception of Hegel which has become popular since K. R. Popper. Anyone who chooses not to follow the ideologies of contemporary history, but rather assumes as I do that it is an intellectual virtue to understand a philosophical author as he understood himself, is confronted, when interpreting the *Philosophy of Right*, by questions which were posed to Hegel by his predecessors and under the condition of being conscious of his own times. Thus, this study attempts to correct the distortions and flaws in the history of the book's influence by offering a point of view which allows Hegel's *Philosophy of Right* to be read within the context of Plato's *Republic* and Aristotle's *Politics*, Hobbes's *Leviathan* and Rousseau's *Social Contract*. Only when these amendments have been made can the importance of that conceptual revolution and the new perspectives offered by it be understood, a dramatic change which has determined the language of political philosophy since Hegel and Marx.

I am greatly obliged to Walter E. Wright for the fact that my book can now appear in English. Without his energetic initiative this translation probably would not have been made so soon. I should also like to thank Robert Pettit for reading the English manuscript and offering constructive suggestions. The text of Chapter 2 is based on a lecture I delivered at the University of Oxford in the Spring of 1978. The text of Chapter 3 was written for the book edited by Z. A. Pelczynski: *Hegel's Political*

Philosophy: Problems and Perspectives (Cambridge University Press, 1971). I want to extend my final thanks to the editor for allowing this study to be reprinted here.

Erlangen, August 1983   Manfred Riedel

PART I

The Structure of
Hegel's Philosophy of Right

Framework and Meaning of 'Objective Spirit': A Conceptual Change in Political Philosophy

Hegel's doctrine of objective spirit poses several difficulties which his interpreters must address before undertaking a closer examination of the philosophy of right which follows from it. There are three chief thematic issues: first, the problem of the concept's structure; second, the problem of its place in the philosophical system; and third, the particularly vexing problem of the history of its evolving role in the diverse periods of Hegel's thinking. The first problem coincides with the question of the concept's intrinsic ambiguity. Here I shall mention only a few of the most important elementary meanings which interact in Hegel's use of the term. Objective spirit is the *supra-individual trans-subjective spirit* which two or more subjects, and, in particular, unions of subjects (families, classes, associations, peoples, etc.) have in common. In this sense it is general spirit (*Encyclopedia of the Philosophical Sciences*, 1st edn (Heidelberg, 1817), par. 399), which – on the model of the general will as not merely the sum of individual wills, but rather a reality penetrating and spreading through them – contains individual 'subjective' minds in itself. However, general spirit, as 'objective', manifests itself in outward appearance, and is thus in contrast to the formula for the general will, which talks about an 'inner' connection of wills withdrawn from time and change. To this extent, it is for Hegel essentially *historical spirit*. Moreover, this outer appearance, as the objectivity or reality of objective spirit, includes further dimensions in which the complexity of the concept approaches equivocation. At one time it can mean the *objective*, that is, *real* spirit; at another time the *objectivizing*, *realizing* spirit; or finally the *objectified*, *realized* spirit. Following Nicolai Hartmann, who took offence at these equivocations, one might speak of 'objective' and 'objectified' spirit.[1]

1 *Das Problem des geistigen Seins*, 2nd edn (Berlin, 1949), pp. 196 f.

The problem of Hegel's systematic use of the concept and the history of its development can be limited to the following propositions. The concept of objective spirit is introduced initially in the *Encyclopedia* of 1817, in connection with the well-known distinction between subjective, objective, and absolute spirit. The distinction is missing from earlier writings. To be sure, Hegel's various early systematic ventures follow the common modern trichotomy of reason, nature, and spirit, as worked out by Descartes and Kant. In these early ventures, however, the philosophy of spirit had not yet been explicitly distinguished, and appeared under such diverse titles as 'the system of *ethical life*', or '*practical philosophy*'. 'Spirit', in this context, was always 'absolute', so that the only distinction which Hegel recognized concerned the 'absolute spirit' itself: in a people it is '*existing* absolute spirit'.[2] A differentiation is first worked out in the *Philosophical Encyclopedia* from the *Nürnberg Propädeutik* (1811–12), even though Hegel was not then in possession of the final concept. This text distinguishes the sphere of *spirit's realization* from that of its *fulfilment* (par. 128); however, it handles the first under the heading of 'practical' rather than 'objective' spirit (par. 173).[3] This is of decisive importance for the concept's structure and for the doctrine of objective spirit's systematic employment. Conceptually, the sketch of the *Nürnberg Propädeutik* still preserves an insight which was gradually lost to Hegel's view as well as to the view of the nineteenth-century tradition of philosophical, historical research shaped by him. This insight is that the 'objective spirit' grew out of and depended on what the tradition called 'practical' philosophy. The considerations which determine the concept's role in Hegel's *Philosophy of Spirit* are not adequate for understanding this connection. Indeed, one might say that they have been a disaster for the correct evaluation of practical philosophy's role in modern thinking. Objective and practical spirit, which were inseparable up to the time of the *Nürnberg Propädeutik*, come to be distinguished. In the encyclopedia system of 1817, the

---

2 Cf. *Jenenser Realphilosophie* (hereafter *JR*), Vol. II (1805–6), ed. J. Hoffmeister (Leipzig, 1931), p. 272.

3 Cf. Hegel, *Sämtliche Werke*, Jubiläumsausgabe (hereafter *WWG*), ed. H. Glockner (Stuttgart, 20 vols., 1927–30), Vol. III, pp. 200 and 215.

practical becomes a component of subjective spirit, i.e., the doctrine of will in psychology (pars. 368–99). Practical philosophy's slide to oblivion is undoubtedly due to the fundamentally psychological theory of the human sciences, which appropriates both this absorption of practical spirit by the subjective and also the opposition between the philosophy of nature and the philosophy of spirit in Hegel's system. Wilhelm Dilthey, who built his school on this issue, tried to demonstrate that, as early as the seventeenth century, the newly-discovered analysis of consciousness and the anthropological theory of emotions led to the replacement of the 'false dichotomy' between theoretical and practical philosophy by this same opposition.[4] Thus, an interpretation based on the organizational structure of the philosophy of spirit has frequently led to misunderstandings of the young Hegel's writings. On these premises, one cannot even ask why Hegel replaces practical philosophy with objective spirit. Nor is it plausible to ask what this conceptual shift means historically, or why it is only at a relatively late period in his development that Hegel first comes to it. To answer these questions one must travel in the opposite direction, moving from the reconstruction of the idea of practical philosophy in the early Hegel to its dissolution in the doctrine of 'objective spirit' which is based in the philosophy of right. First, I will locate Hegel's place in the quarrel between modern thinking and the tradition to determine the exact point at which he takes an active part in the progress of this continuing debate.

I

The distinguishing feature of practical philosophy as founded by Aristotle, and of its tradition in the Middle Ages and early modern period, was perhaps not so much its theoretical content as the particular form and historical significance which it possessed during these centuries. Hegel pointed this out in his lectures on the history of philosophy, and he also identified the cause of this importance. 'We will not', he says, 'find practical philosophy

---

4 Cf. *Einleitung in die Geisteswissenschaften*, Vol. 1 (1833), in *Gesammelte Schriften*, 1, 4 (Stuttgart/Göttingen, 1959), pp. 225–378.

conceived speculatively until the modern period.'[5] The stability of practical philosophy follows from its non-speculative nature, i.e., its independence from the premises of 'first philosophy'. For Aristotle and Aristotelian scholasticism, practical philosophy does not depend directly on metaphysics, although it employs metaphysical theorems. This situation changes with the 'modern period', of which Hegel speaks, that is, with the development of natural law during the seventeenth and eighteenth centuries. Here theory permeates the structure of practical philosophy, and practical philosophy advances the same claim to universal validity found in the modern notion of scientific method. Its task, according to Hobbes, is to know the relations of human actions with certainty equal to that in our knowledge of the comparative size of geometrical figures. Just like geometry, practical philosophy should become a deductive a priori science. According to Hobbes, its objects are uniquely suited to this end, since there can be an a priori science from 'first principles' for human beings only with reference to those things which they themselves have produced.[6]

This orientation towards a geometric epistemological ideal grounds the 'speculative' character of modern practical philosophy and is *the first step* towards the critique of its tradition. *The second step* comes from the 'scholastic' character of practical philosophy itself, which at the start of the eighteenth century assimilated the critical principle enjoined on it from without by the methodological claim of a priori demonstration. Christian Wolff's application of this method led to the division of practical philosophy into a 'rational' and an 'empirical' part. The first part, which demonstrates a priori the varieties of human action and the

---

5 *Vorlesungen über die Geschichte der Philosophie*, ed. Karl Ludwig Michelet, Vol. i, in *WWG*, Vol. xvii, p. 291. (Eng. tr. E. S. Haldane and F. H. Simpson, *Hegel's Lectures on the History of Philosophy* (3 vols., London, 1896).)

   Where available, English translations of German works are cited at the first occurrence in each chapter. They are cited subsequently and page references are given only where the translations are quoted directly. In all other cases, passages are retranslated for this work.

6 *Thomae Hobbes Malmsburiensis – Opera Philosophica Quae Latina Scripsit Omnia*, ed. W. Molesworth (London, 1839–45), Vol. i, Ch. x, p. 5. (Eng. tr. B. Gert, *Man and Citizen* (New York, 1972).)

principles of right and obligation, carries the title borrowed from Descartes's idea of the *mathesis universalis: philosophia practica universalis*.[7] The introduction of this new science prepares the *third step* (taken initially by Kant) in the debate between modern thinking and the tradition of practical philosophy. With the 'Propädeutik des berühmten Wolff vor seiner Moralphilosophie', Kant became clear just how far short the new science falls of being a critique of practical reason. This new science arose from the need for grounding the concepts and objects which were derived from the tradition and on which the *philosophia practica universalis* remained dependent with respect to both method and content. According to Kant, this is precisely why it does not break new ground. It does not do so because, as a general practical philosophy, it has taken for its guiding theme only the general concept of will, 'willing in general', and thereby has not considered the possibility of a will of 'a certain sort, in particular one free of all empirical determining grounds, wholly determined by a priori principles, which one might call a pure will'.[8] It was the discovery of this 'certain sort' of will freed from the nexus of natural activity which led Kant to replace a grounding of the discrete parts of practical philosophy, as found in the scholastic tradition, with the idea of self-grounding, an idea which renders impossible the recapitulation of the concepts and objects transmitted by the tradition, the strategy pursued by Wolff's *philosophia practica universalis*. The theme of Kant's *Critique of Practical Reason* (1788) is the deduction of the first principle of practical knowledge from the idea of that pure will which, in its freedom, is a law unto itself, rather than from the law of nature as the Wolffian propaedeutic still conceives it. The law of freedom explodes the coherence of the traditional system of practical philosophy as well as the relation between its 'universal' and 'particular' parts as reconstructed by Wolff.

7 *Philosophia practica universalis mathematico methodo conscripta* (hereafter *PPR*) (Leipzig, 1703). The Leipzig 'Disputationsschrift' which Wolff claimed to have written because Descartes had not handled the subject (*Ratio Praelectionem*, Ch. VI, par. 3) is the basis for the taxonomy of the *Philosophia practica universalis*, Vols. I–II (Frankfurt/Leipzig, 1738–9).

8 *Grundlegung zur Metaphysik der Sitten* (1785), (22 vols., Berlin/Leipzig, 1900–42) (hereafter Akademieausgabe), in *Kants gesammelte Schriften*, ed. Königlich Preussische Akademie der Wissenschaften, Vol. IV, p. 390. (Eng. tr. Thomas K. Abbott, *Fundamental Principles of the Metaphysic of Morals* (New York, 1949).)

Politics, economics, and ethics are excluded from practical philosophy as doctrines of prudence and pleasure; for Kant they are merely pragmatic, technical sciences which belong to the world of empirical experience, the field of activity of prudence and dexterity. To be sure, they borrow rules from the natural world in order, from time to time, to produce an effect which is possible according to the law of causality; but they never – as in the older doctrine of prudence – borrow the ends which generate the power of ethical obligation in moral and political action. The Kantian law of freedom terminates such borrowing. In so far as it contains the a priori ground for determining all actions, it is for Kant the object of a 'particular philosophy which is called practical', in opposition to those – in the Kantian sense – pragmatic and technical disciplines which have unjustly appropriated the title 'practical'.[9]

Hegel's critique of the scholastic tradition of practical philosophy, a critique which goes as far beyond it as possible, is carried out on the basis of this Kantian concept of freedom and its theoretical presupposition, the discovery of the spontaneity of self-consciousness in the *Critique of Pure Reason*. The dialectical method completes what was left undone by the geometrical, rational, and transcendental methods: the dissolution of the tradition. This follows less from the critical acuity and radicality of Hegel's thinking – in this respect Hobbes and Kant were certainly his superiors – but rather from the conditions under which it arose. The *first* has already been mentioned, namely, the Kantian idea of the autonomy of the will to which Hegel's philosophy directs itself, making his criticism of the tradition superior to that of Hobbes and Wolff, since for both of them there is no solution to the related Aristotelian problems of freedom and of lordship and bondage. The *second* is the inclusion of modern political economy in the design of practical philosophy in an attempt to connect the latter's traditional principles with the present historical experience of the societal and industrial world. The most important consequence of this is Hegel's speculative dissolution of the relation of production (*poiesis*) and activity

9 *Kritik der Urteilskraft*, Introduction, Akademieausgabe, Vol. v (1790), pp. 171 f. (Eng. tr. J. C. Meredith, *Critique of Judgement* (Oxford, 1952).)

(*praxis*). To be sure, the traditional demarcation of the two had already been relativized by Hobbes, but it had not been truly overcome, because this relativizing was limited to the sphere of politics and to the creation of the leviathan, produced by the human subject, without reaching into the sphere of economics. This recurs in Kant, who wants to exclude completely the science of 'political economy', newly established in the mean time, from 'particular' practical philosophy. Finally, the *third* condition, which is, to be sure, an achievement of Hegelian thought rather than merely a presupposition on which it relies, concerns the connection with history. This connection severs the categories of practical philosophy from the ahistorical rigidity of the scholastic tradition and locates them within that dialectical movement of 'the concept' which brings itself into a fundamentally different relationship with its content.

At the same time, the shift in the history of practical philosophy initiated by Hegel begins with a paradox which must be recognized and articulated if one wishes to understand the scope of the shift. The paradox is that from the outset Hegel found renewed and immediate access to the very tradition from which he separated himself most widely. This paradox distinguishes his struggle with the tradition from the critical steps taken in various ways by Hobbes, Wolff, and Kant. While these others are all related to Aristotle either at a direct historical distance (Hobbes) or simply obliquely (Wolff and Kant) because they base their work on a specific, relatively late, stage of Aristotelian scholasticism, the young Hegel was one of the first people in Germany to study the texts of Aristotle's *Ethics* and *Politics*,[10] thereby achieving a much more accurate picture of the tradition than did those critics for whom these sources were either completely unknown or at best obscure. But the decisive thing in this process was Hegel's

10 Hegel's involvement with Aristotle began during his time at the Stuttgart Gymnasium with a reading of the *Nicomachean Ethics*. Cf. K. Rosenkranz, *Hegels Leben* (Berlin, 1844), p. 11. His proper study of Aristotle (from the old Basel edition of the sixteenth century) goes back to the years in the Tübingen seminary. Cf. the testimony of Leutwein in D. Henrich, 'Leutwein über Hegel. Ein Dokument zu Hegels Biographia', in *Hegel-Studien*, Vol. III (1965), 58. The influence of the reading of the *Politics* shows itself repeatedly in the early writings of the Jena period. Cf. *WWG*, Vol. I, pp. 111, 114, 485 ff., 494 f., 511; *Schriften zur Politik und Rechtsphilosophie* (hereafter *SPR*), ed. G. Lasson (Leipzig, 1913), pp. 417 ff., 442 ff., 460 ff., 478 f.)

simultaneous application of Aristotle to his own thoughts and to the task of a practical philosophy as posed by contemporary historical experience, rather than a simple reconstruction of the essentials of the classical theory. Hegel worked on this basis in the writings of the Jena period. The applicability which he demanded from the classical tradition clarifies the forced nature of his attempts to submit a mass of material to concepts often not derived from the material itself and of contrary origin. Thus in the first phase of Hegel's employment of practical philosophy (1801–4), concept and reality, form and content are completely separate; and although he comes to understand the foundation of his own philosophy and its relation to the sphere of the practical in the second phase (1805–7), it is not until the third, the beginning of which could be dated from the appearance of the second volume of the *Science of Logic* and the *Encyclopedia of the Philosophical Sciences* (1816–17), that he succeeds in formulating the concept of 'objective spirit' which provides a framework for overcoming the traditional principles and systematic form of practical philosophy.

II

Hegel's return to classical political philosophy at the beginning of the Jena period is foreshadowed in the predominantly theological and historical studies of the 1790s, although it had a different meaning in that context. The paradox of the youthful writings lies less in the fact that Hegel found his way back once again to the classical ethical life of the *polis* than in the fact that at the same time he adapted it to the concepts of Kant's *Critique of Practical Reason* (freedom, autonomy, spontaneity, etc.). For Hegel, the individual who believes and acts according to practical reason and the ancient republican are both equally free; the former determines himself as his 'immortal, spiritual' rational essence demands, and the latter does his duty 'in the spirit of his people'.[11]

11 *Theologische Jugendschriften*, ed. H. Nohl (Tübingen, 1907), p. 70. (Eng. tr. T. M. Knox, *Early Theological Writings* (Chicago, 1948).) Cf. Ephraim, 'Untersuchungen über den Freiheitsbegriff Hegels in seiner Jugendarbeit', in *Philosophische Forschungen*, Vol. VII (Berlin, 1928, pp. 59, 63.) Recent edn I. Görland, *Die Kant-Kritik des jungen Hegel* (Frankfurt on Main, 1966), pp. 4 ff.

The appearance of Kant's *Metaphysics of Morals* (1797) put an end to this mixture, since it offered no foothold for transplanting the idea of autonomy into the sphere of politics. During the Frankfurt period (1798–9) Hegel criticized it. He proceeded from the substantive ethical life of the ancients, and from the unity of reason and nature in the fulfilled freedom of a popular religion. But the freedom of the ancients did not form the measure of his own political will, nor did he use it in his interpretation of Kant's concept of autonomy.[12] On the contrary, the critical intention of the young Hegel was directed *against* the insufficient scope which Kant (and with him Fichte) gave to the law of freedom by severing it from the law of nature and thus exposing practical reason itself to the 'difference'. Since Hegel placed the differentiation of freedom and nature in Kant and Fichte (a relation which he interpreted as one of compulsion and suppression) at the centre of his criticism and searched for a unification of the two in the idea of a political whole, he was driven back to the pre-Kantian tradition of practical philosophy.

This is the paradox with which Hegel's critique of Kant and Fichte begins in the early writings of the Jena period. Extending the concept of freedom to a political whole, which is to make 'free ideal activity' possible for individuals, has exacted a price: nature, suppressed up to now, is once again to attain its 'right' in the construction of the moral ideal. This perspective is the origin for the essay *Über die wissenschaftlichen Behandlungsarten des Naturrechts*, whose title expressly avows the systematic form of scholastic philosophy: its 'Stelle in der praktische Philosophie'.[13] In the first section Hegel discusses the crisis of this science which, following Hobbes, had lived by criticizing its own tradition. The fate of natural law, as well as the fate of the disciplines of politics and political economy (to which Kant denied the title 'practical philosophy'), has been that in the course of modern thinking 'the philosophical element in philosophy' has come to reside solely in metaphysics, so that these sciences 'were kept aloof in complete independence of the idea'.[14] According to Hegel, Kant's critical

12 *Theologische Jugendschriften*, pp. 221 ff.
13 See Ch. 2 in this volume. Hegel, *Natural Law* (hereafter *NL*) (Eng. tr. T. M. Knox (Philadelphia, 1975).
14 *WWG*, Vol. 1, pp. 437 f.; *NL*, p. 55.

philosophy could not negate either the emancipation from meta-physics of the sciences which rest on experience and technical application or the separation of these same sciences from the reality of the real in nature and history. Instead, it pushed them to an inescapable extreme. Because the critical philosophy opposed nature as an irrational manifold to reason as a pure unity, reason – and with it the moral 'pure will' – became for it 'a non-substantial abstraction of the one', while nature evaporated con-versely into 'a non-substantial abstraction of the many'. At this point Hegel referred to a form of the tradition historically ante-dating this dichotomy. And so we find a remarkable thing: in attempting once again to vindicate the emancipated sciences of practical philosophy, Hegel not only agrees completely with the old conceptual form, but even justifies 'the old altogether contra-dictory empiricism' on which it is based. Recalling those critics who subordinated the empiricism of practical science to the geo-metrical ideal of knowing and in so doing were compelled to find the former's conceptual form 'as incoherent as it was con-tradictory', Hegel states that a great and pure intuition 'in the purely architectonic method of its exposition, in which the context of necessity and the domination of form do not visibly appear' can 'express the truly ethical' – the 'ordering of the parts and self-modifying facets will betray the inner rational, though in-visible, spirit'.[15]

By returning to this intuition, in which it is easy to detect a characterization of the free architectonic of Aristotle's philosophy, Hegel contrasts the principle of modern natural law theory with that of classical politics. The point at which both must explicitly express the difference in their basic tendencies is the being of the individual. According to the ethical life of the *polis*, the individual is neither rooted in himself nor united with others in society through some particular property of his nature (instinct for society, fear of death, self-sustenance, etc.). The indi-vidual is one with the social whole by nature (*physei*) or, as Hegel has it, in a 'living' way, and not abstractly – through contract or subordination to a particular will. In contrast to modern natural law theory, which posits the 'being of the individual as the first

15 *WWG*, Vol. I, pp. 453 f.; *NL*, pp. 67–8.

and highest principle', classical politics holds that 'individuality as such is nothing, and simply one with absolute ethical majesty – which genuine, living, non-servile oneness, is the only true ethical life of the individual'.[16] The approach to the classical concept of politics manifested in Hegel's early conception of practical philosophy expresses itself directly in his evaluation of ethics. Although, as the doctrine of virtue, it must be individual ethical life, 'absolute' ethical life appears as a negation to the individual understood simply as negative. Not only is the reflexive morality of modern subjectivity a 'negative morality', but negative too are the superficially self-justifying individual virtues which this morality splices on to the context of the ethical whole, and which Hegel wishes to see interpreted in reference to the classical model as their natural description.[17] This constitutes the formal distinction between 'morality' and natural law, which is not to be understood as it is by Kant and Fichte 'as if they were separated, this excluded from that; rather, their content is wholly included in natural law'.[18]

The aporia of this fundamentally classical concept of natural law and of its place in practical philosophy is that it causes the being of the individual and the negative to disappear, a dissolving and transient moment. This aporia, which made it nearly impossible for Hegel to achieve a historically adequate understanding of modern theories of natural law, continued with his assimilation of Aristotle's doctrine concerning work and activity into his science of rights. The *preservation of ethical life* according to Hegel owes itself to those *individual virtues* whose activity has no object – Aristotle's *ergon* – but which immediately destroys the object in its determinateness; it is 'without purpose, without want, and without relation to the practical sentiments, without subjectivity, and has no relation to possession and acquisition; rather its purpose and outcome ends with itself'.[19] Virtuous action is the 'totally

16 *WWG*, Vol. 1, p. 452; *NL*, p. 67.
17 Cf. *WWG*, Vol. 1, p. 513; *NL*, p. 115.
18 See 'System der Sittlichkeit', p. 465; *WWG*, Vol. 1, p. 510. (Eng. tr. H. S. Harris and T. M. Knox, *System of Ethical Life and First Philosophy of Spirit* (Albany, 1979), p. 112.)
19 *SPR*, p. 467. Cf. also *WWG*, Vol. 1, pp. 463 and 466. Here also the 'firearm' quite suddenly appears as the specifically modern ('mechanical') discovery of a universal impersonal bravery and of 'impersonal death' (pp. 467 f.).

indifferent' activity of the 'politician and warrior' which Hegel in the 'System der Sittlichkeit' wishes to see entrusted to an 'absolute class'. One easily recognizes here the civil class in the traditional sense, the class of free-born valiant men. In opposition to it stand the 'different' accomplishments of the 'honest' class (connected with natural relations, i.e., 'economic'), which consist in the 'work of necessity, in property, in acquisition, and in owner-ship'. This is the citizen class in the modern sense, the peaceful bourgeois restricted to private life, a class which originated for Hegel with the disappearance of slave relations. Its 'immersion in possessions and individuality now ceases to be bondage to the absolute indifference (the 'absolute class' – M.R.); it is indifferent as much as possible, or formal indifference, the mere person, is reflected in the nation, and the possessor does not succumb to the whole community because of his difference, does not fall into personal dependency; instead, his negative indifference is thought of as something real and he is therefore a bourgeois citizen, recognized as universal'.[20]

On the other hand, however, Hegel is very far from wishing to invert the relationship between production (*poiesis*) and activity (*praxis*) as Adam Smith had done in *The Wealth of Nations* (1776).[21] According to the theoreticians of the new science of national economics, who proposed the model of the modern civil society freed from its feudal bonds, the activity of politicians, jurists, and soldiers, which from the perspective of classical political theory preserved the *polis*, is demoted to an unproductive valueless activity because it does not realize itself in a 'work', that is, in an enduring object or commodity. For Hegel, on the other hand, the relation of labour and action not only preserves its validity as such, but also forms the basis for the appropriation of modern national economics and for the organization of social classes (estates) in his first projected systems of practical philosophy. The majority of the contradictions and obscurities which are connected with these projected systems can be traced back to the fact that

---

20 *SPR*, p. 473.
21 Cf. *An Inquiry into the Nature and Causes of The Wealth of Nations*, ed. R. H. Camp-bell, A. S. Skinner and W. B. Todd (2 vols., Oxford, 1976), Vol. I, Ch. 10; Vol. II, Ch. 3.

Hegel adopted the classical political model as the guiding thread for his quarrel with national economics. So, on the one hand he assumed it as a pattern, but on the other he was forced to introduce a series of modifications and additions which did not follow directly from the model itself.

These contradictions once again manifested themselves with particular clarity in the essay on the *Wissenschaftliche Behandlungsarten des Naturrechts* (1802–3). The 'absolute class' of the 'System der Sittlichkeit' appears here, with reference to Plato and Aristotle,[22] as the 'class of free people' which by nature is independent or 'for itself', and is differentiated from 'the class of unfree people' which 'is by nature not its own but another man's'.[23] The 'work' of the former, so he continues, does not exhaust itself in single determinate products, but instead extends to the 'being and preservation of the entirety of the ethical organization' as whose 'living movement and . . . Divine self-enjoyment' it presents itself.[24] Thus Hegel joins with the traditional doctrine of the superiority of an action whose purpose is pure motion (*kinesis*) and activity (*energeia*) rather than the determinateness of the product (*ergon*).[25] The concept of spirit finds its fulfilment in this model and expresses precisely this self-returning ('immanent') movement of ethical action. 'The same spirit of the people', say the Jena lectures of 1803–4, 'must turn itself into *work*, or rather it exists only as an eternal development into spirit'.[26] But for Hegel that activity from which a work is periodically emitted also belongs to the spirit's 'being-at-work' in a people – work in the modern sense of the struggle with nature, in which the movement surpasses itself and ends in a product. Thus he grants a position within the self-organized ethical life, albeit a subordinate one, to the class of

22 Cf. *WWG*, Vol. I, p. 495; *NL*, p. 100.
23 A translation from Aristotle, *Politics* I, 5, 1254b20–3; cf. further I, 4, 1253b27–30; *Metaphysics*, I, 2, 982b25–6; *NL*, p. 101.
24 *WWG*, Vol. I, pp. 494 f.; *NL*, pp. 99–100. With direct reference to the political theory of Plato and Aristotle: 'The task that Aristotle assigns to this class is what the Greeks called *politeuein*, which means living in and with and for their people, leading a general life wholly devoted to the public interest or else the task of philosophizing. Plato, in keeping with his higher sense of life, wants these two tasks not to be separated but wholly linked together' (*WWG*, Vol. I, p. 495; *NL*, p. 100).
25 Cf. *Metaphysics*, IX, 6, 1048b18–36; 8, 1050a21–31.
26 *JR*, Vol. I, p. 232.

the unfree 'whose work concerns particular objects'. In Hegel's view this self-organizing ethical life appears necessarily divided – 'into one part which is absorbed absolutely into indifference [the action of citizens whose work is political activity, supportive of the *polis* – M.R.] and another wherein the real as such subsists and thus is relatively identical (the production of slaves, labourers, etc., who make a product) and carries in itself only the reflection of absolute ethical life'.[27]

The relative justification which Hegel's thinking grants to political economy's concept of work, in contrast to the systematic basis of modern natural law theory, becomes apparent in the new architechtonic of practical philosophy which the natural law essay presents. On the one hand, by constructing a 'law of ethical life', Hegel would like to cancel both the modern separation of natural law and politics, as well as the predominance of civil law categories (e.g., contract) which had taken possession of the 'domestic management of natural law', particularly in the constitutional and international fields.[28] Thus in his intended system of practical philosophy, natural law together with politics and ethics would fall under the concept of 'ethical life'[29] understood in fundamentally political terms. On the other hand, political economy is in the eminent sense a 'practical' science for Hegel. Therefore, it replaces the old economics as the basis for the system which, secondly, is followed by a related 'formal' law in which one essentially sees the older natural law dealing with civil legal matters; and finally, ethical life, separated from both, and, because it has become 'absolute', removed from all entanglements with economics and formal law: 'The concept of this sphere is the real *practical* realm; on the subjective side feeling or physical necessity and enjoyment; on the objective side work and possession. And this practical realm, as it can occur according to its concept (assumed into indifference), is the formal unity or the *law* possible in it. Above these two is the third, the absolute or the ethical.'[30]

There is no doubt that, with this classification, Hegel places

27 *WWG*, Vol. 1, p. 494; *NL*, p. 99.
28 *WWG*, Vol. 1, pp. 410 f.
29 *WWG*, Vol. 1, pp. 509–13; *NL*, pp. 112–15.
30 *WWG*, Vol. 1, p. 494; *NL*, p. 99.

himself simultaneously in the middle of the tradition and in opposition to it. His subdivision of the system into political economy, law (i.e., natural law), and ethical life (i.e., politics and ethics) has clearly achieved internal stability when compared with the attempted rearrangements of the material of practical philosophy in the eighteenth century. That surely fits in with the distinctively 'class-oriented' form of recognition which the system of political economy found in the natural law essay. To this extent the arrangement expresses in a most precise way the tendency, characteristic of Hegel's first version of a system of ethical life, to confound the 'idea of absolute ethical life' with the ethical appearance of a class of 'the noble and free' and to oppose it with the 'relativity' of a working class.

Hegel passes beyond this arrangement by freeing the sphere of labour from the limitation mentioned above. This occurs after the first, and in many respects inadequate, exposition in the 'System der Sittlichkeit' (1802) in the *Vorlesungen zur Realphilosophie* (1803–4 and 1805–6). In these lectures, work appears as a central moment in the constitution of spirit, together with speech and action (recognition). Spirit cannot, as the natural law essay still implies,[31] be identified with 'ethical nature', nor can the latter be identified with a 'people' in which it reflects itself, taking nature back into itself in the form of intellectual intuition. What matters is rather reflecting anew on the 'taking back' itself, so that the process of spirit's 'development' becomes a theme. Because Hegel recognizes that this process is tied to the struggle with nature and does not complete itself in ethical action, 'work' becomes a problem for him in practical philosophy. He lays out the basis for a theory of work and thereby gives proper stress to that portion of philosophy called poietics, whose discussion had not advanced a step since Aristotle and which remained as good as absent in modern natural law theory (Hobbes, Rousseau, Kant). The new poietics is the result of a connection between national economy and transcendental idealism which arose in the young Hegel's thinking and was completed in the Jena lectures. Work itself is

31 *WWG*, Vol. 1, pp. 509 f.; also 'Glauben und Wissen' in *WWG*, Vol. 1, p. 427. (Eng. tr. W. Cerf and H. S. Harris, *Faith and Knowledge* (Albany, 1977); *NL*, p. 111.)

a basic form of spirit and as such is no longer degraded to a subordinate position in practical philosophy.

In opposition to the philosophical tradition, Hegel limits practical behaviour neither to the concept of interaction with others nor, like Kant and Fichte, to the inner working of moral subjectivity which has as an object only its own sensuousness. Rather, he extends it into the dimension of the struggle of mankind with nature, or – expressed in the degree of abstraction appropriate to transcendental philosophy – subject with object, self with not-self. His new meaning of the concept of work permits a fundamental shift in the principles and structural forms of practical philosophy. It originates in the concept of the transcendental ego developed in the *Critique of Pure Reason* as the synthetic unity of apperception – the 'I think' which must be able to accompany all my presentations. (In this way Hegel finds himself totally contradicting his initial construction which, by including the conception of individual existence found in natural law theory and the class-oriented exclusion of 'particular' labour from the idea of morality, had cancelled the basic tendency of Kantian philosophy.) Of course, Hegel views the function of the 'I think' not with Kant's eyes, but with Fichte's, who interpreted the spontaneity and achievement of this accompaniment, which founds the unity of possible experience, as transcendental 'production' – which, at the turning-point between the eighteenth and nineteenth centuries, put philosophy on to the path of eliminating all previous dogmatic demarcation lines between the sciences. This path expresses itself in a new science, the transcendental 'history of consciousness', which, following Fichte and Schelling, the young Hegel worked out initially for the Jena lectures. Like Fichte, Hegel restricted himself to the acts and productions of the 'subject' of transcendental philosophy. The meaning of being is determined by these rather than by the presuppositions of substantive ontology which led, in the Cartesian tradition, to an endless controversy still unsolved in the Kantian school: whether matter or form, the thing or the self, being or consciousness, subject or object have independent existence. On the one hand, these mutually exclusive determinations arose from the destruction of the classical Aristotelian ontology, but they could by no means escape the power of the substantive ontological principle itself, the presupposition of some being, whether independent or dependent, passive or active. For Hegel, on the other hand, such determinations are metaphysical abstractions, which lack not only the developmental process of spirit but also its concept: to be a unity of these opposites. As Hegel remarks, there is 'truly nothing rational to say' concerning such an 'irrational dispute' as whether being grounds itself in the 'passivity' or in the 'activity' of consciousness. The realist asserts that passivity belongs to form or to consciousness, while the idealist assigns it to matter or being. In truth, however, the dispute 'really' centres on 'the self-opposed potency of the middle, in which the bare determinations and their relatedness are simultaneously posited both as unified and as distinguished'.[32] Hegel thinks of the two opposed sides not merely in their opposition, but as a unity of opposites; however, he conceives this unity on the basis of transcendental consciousness, which reduces the rigidity of metaphysical predicates and makes them flexible. This consciousness is not simply the, so to speak, natural unity of the 'I think' which 'accompanies' the flow of presentations, but rather is itself in a process which Hegel presents as its history: the mediation of the self with the other in speech, tool, and work.[33] Labour – the struggle of the subject with the object and the objectification of the struggle in work – becomes for Hegel one moment in the historical mediation of consciousness; and work – as tool and possession – becomes the medium between the polar opposites, form and matter, subject and object, activity and passivity, etc., in which consciousness, itself a medium in the process of the struggle, organizes and 'develops' itself. Work and development belong together.

With this approach Hegel inverts the basis of classical practical philosophy. He cancels the hidden aporia in its account of the relationship between labour and action. This aporia might be described as follows: if the agent's activity (*energeia*) exists as his own proper activity (as in the case of ethical–political *praxis*) it can never objectify itself – if on the other hand the activity is objectified, it is not in the agent but his work, where it is simul-

---

32 *JR*, Vol. 1, pp. 214 f.
33 *JR*, Vol. 1, p. 213.

taneously extinguished. On the classical model of *poiesis* there is no reflexive connection between the work and the worker, and certainly not that coupling and oscillating movement between worker and work, between subject and object, expressed by Hegel's concept of development. The reason for this lies in the hierarchy of activity itself, which identifies action as superior to labour. Prudent practical action is more complete because in its execution it reveals the wholeness of the actor, while labour, which loses the form in the matter, cannot for just that reason lead to the perfection of the workers: *non est perfectio facientis, sed facti.*[34] The outcome of the technical–practical struggle between *poiesis* and nature does not serve the producer *qua* producer so that he might share in the insight into practical human affairs in the process of his producing; instead the product serves the use which *praxis* makes of it. But it is on just this *use* – and that also means on the capacity of *phronesis*, or practical prudence, denied by definition to the producer – that the model of pre-industrial society, which Hegel destroyed with his analysis of the labour process in political economy, is built. The new model which he offers in place of the old rests on the transcendentally transformed onto-logical foundation, which comes to focus in Hegel's category of *externalization.* The labour process is nothing other than the implementation of *poiesis*, the struggle with nature, the shaping of things. But Hegel does not conceive this as a transference into external matter of a form alien to the worker himself; rather he conceives it as the worker's *externalization* in two senses: (1) as the externalization of desire which is 'deeply rooted inwardly' in the individual and to that extent is universal; and (2) as the externalization of the equally 'inward' form, namely, consciousness. Hegel defines labour as the 'self-objectification of consciousness'[35] in which consciousness loses the form of subject in order to regain it (that is, to see itself) on a higher plane in the objective nature of work. The process of labour externalizes the subject into the thing by accommodating itself to nature in its work. At the same time it is saved from externalization because it makes itself an object in the product. This doubly negative movement eliminates not

34 Thomas Aquinas, *Summa Theologiae*, I/II, 9 v. 57, art. 5.
35 *JR*, Vol. II, p. 214.

only the simple dichotomy of form and matter, but also the priority of utility, a concept which plays a central role in the structure of the classical theory. Briefly summarized, Hegel does not interpret the process of labour in terms of its outcome, as does Aristotle and the pre-industrial tradition of poietics (artisanship or technology) which follows him; instead he interprets it in terms of its origin. Work is that movement which derives from the negating of desire and, in its progress, remains oriented as much to desire as to the negation of the object on which it works: it is 'controlled desire' and as such is formative, the negation of negation.

From this perspective Hegel, in a famous chapter from the *Phenomenology of Spirit*, develops the dialectic of lordship and bondage, which in a certain sense can also be viewed as a dialectic of labour and activity. In terms of historical development, the chapter concerns the emergence of *polis* ethical life. In this ethics, the 'class of free beings' manifests its complete superiority over the working class and the latter's immersion in the particularity of existence by virtue of the 'free being's talent for death' or skill in martial matters. The extent to which Hegel has moved beyond his initial standpoint shows itself in the fact that in this analysis he sees the moment of particularity as both annulled and preserved in labour and justifies its existence in the object. For Hegel, the lordship of the master over the slave must dissolve precisely because the former is bound to an activity which creates no product. The moment of political action in the classical sense is not, however, at issue in this chapter. The *good life* is interpreted as *enjoyment* rather than use, and in this way Hegel retranslates the basis of his own model, the connection of desire and labour, into the Aristotelian perspective. Thus it happens that for Hegel the exact moment which grounds the superiority of action over labour in the classical model is here a defect on the side of the master: non-objectification in a product. The idea that the 'moment of the unessential relation to the thing' falls to the lot of the slave, because in work the thing retains its independence, reveals itself as a mere appearance to the dialectical analysis. For the master, the object disappears in enjoyment while, for the slave, the negative relation to the same object 'passes into the form of the object, into something that is permanent and remains, because it is just for the labourer that the object has independence'.[36] Labour is not exhausted in the object of work, but instead becomes a permanent movement *between* desire and object – a 'negative mediating agency' or 'formative activity' which is just as imminent to the labourer as action is to the actor in the classical view. 'This negative mediating agency, this activity giving shape and form, is at the same time the individual existence, the pure self-existence of that consciousness, which now in the work it does is externalized and passes into the condition of permanence. The consciousness that toils and serves accordingly attains by this means the direct apprehension of that independent being as its self.' And 'by the fact that the form is objectified, it does not become something other than consciousness moulding the thing through work; form is his pure self-existence which therein becomes truly realized. Thus precisely in labour where there seemed to be merely some outsider's mind and ideas involved, the bondsman becomes aware, through this rediscovery of himself by himself, of having and being a mind of his own.'[37] Put into a terse Latin phrase, this passage says: *factio perfectio facientis est.*

III

If one wants to understand the concept of objective spirit and its role in Hegel's philosophy, it is necessary to give an account of this shift in the relation between labour and action. His philosophical divergence with the tradition is so very radical precisely because in appropriating practical philosophy he is compelled to revise its foundations. This can be shown in detail in the Jena lectures of 1805–6, which in certain respects annul the earlier construction of 'ethical nature' and surrender, together with the label, all attempted divisions of practical philosophy. Between 1801 and 1804 the philosophy of spirit, which in essence belongs together with the theory of ethical life, did not differentiate itself internally. Spirit was the 'absolute' of a people and its other moments supple-

---

36 *WWG*, Vol. II, p. 156. (Eng. tr. F. B. Baillie, *The Phenomenology of Mind* (hereafter *PM*) (London, 1931).)

37 *WWG*, Vol. II, p. 157; *PM*, pp. 238–9.

mented the beginning or the end of the people's spirit. Even religion and philosophy belong to this level of morality. Following the Platonic-Aristotelian pattern, Hegel compared philosophy with a people's 'absolute work'. Just as the pure activity of ethical action proves itself in a sacrifice for the political whole, so this activity transforms the people's spirit into the 'spirit of natural and ethical universality',[38] by wholly negating its 'particularity'. On the other side, under the assumption that 'ethical spirit' and 'absolute spirit' are identical, the possibility of an independent analysis of individual (subjective) spirit is lost. Thus, according to Hegel, the individual belongs immediately to the ethical whole 'in an eternal fashion; his empirical being and doing is wholly general, because it is not the individual that acts but rather the universal absolute spirit in him'.[39]

In this context the new meaning of the concept of labour now causes a fundamental transformation in the systematic pattern of the philosophy of spirit. Here for the first time Hegel fully engages the idea, introduced in the lectures of 1803–4, concerning spirit's cultivation (*Bildung*), the 'development' of 'absolute ethical life' out of the levels of consciousness ('intelligence' and 'will') present in the self-active ego. This concept avoids the dichotomy which the natural law essay and the 'System der Sittlichkeit' draw between 'natural' or relative ethical life (economics) and 'absolute ethical life' (politics which restricts 'political' economy in class terms). Essentially it does this in two ways: (1) together with the concept of labour in political economy, it preserves the justification for the moment of 'particularity' in the process of action, a moment which is connected with the reciprocal recognition between free and equal individuals,[40] and (2) it allows Hegel to deal with the concept of right as a moment of 'ethical life in general' proceeding from the 'movement of recognition', instead of treating it as a purely 'formal' unity of the economic-practical sphere. This outcome binds together the parts of the system which previously have been separated. Of course Hegel has not appropriated this central concept of natural law in the traditional way

38 See Rosenkranz, *Hegels Leben*, p. 133; further, *WWG*, Vol. 1, pp. 495 ff.; *SPR*, p. 467.
39 *SPR*, p. 465.
40 Cf. *JR*, Vol. 1, p. 230; 11, pp. 210 ff.

(as the result of a contract which facilitates the transition from a state of nature to 'civil society'). Instead he draws an analogy, comparing the categories of natural law with those of political economy. He discovered what neither he nor the natural law theoreticians had seen previously: that the concept of a subject of rights, as well as the individual freedom and equality contained in the 'individual' will's renunciation of itself in the 'general will', presupposed liberation from nature by labour. Hegel interpreted the general will of Rousseau and Kant as a bare abstraction because it ignored labour and as such lacked objective relatedness and enduring being. To be sure, the movement of recognition orients itself to the self-knowledge of the other and not to a thing,[41] but the content of the recognized will is mediated through labour and property. Initially this is how the general will becomes 'real spirit', and will and intelligence are related just as labour and action are. What, primarily and initially, are included under the general will are not conceptual constructs like the unification of wills and contract, which are equally abstract socially and historically, but rather these moments which originate in the mediative process of man with nature: labour, work, and property, which are presupposed by every relation involving will. 'Spirit is real neither as intelligence, nor as will; but instead, as a will, which is intelligence [...]. In this latter the abstract will must annul itself or, as annulled, it must produce this spiritual reality within the element of recognition. Thereby property converts itself into right, just as labour previously converted itself into the universal; what formerly belonged to the family [...] becomes the universal work and pleasure of all.'[42] The general will is 'real spirit' only in relationship to a work where its concept, the unity of intelligence and will ('I'), is born. This 'real' is not yet the 'objective spirit' which the *Encyclopedia* (1817) introduces into the system, but it is certainly a step towards it. Hegel completes the step by distinguishing between externalization as the *cultivation of existence* (also complete externalization or objectification) and as *alienation from the existing world itself*. This distinction is basic to the lectures of 1805–6, which no longer end with the elevation

41 *JR*, Vol. II, p. 210.
42 *JR*, Vol. II, p. 113.

of ethical life to religion, but instead with *art, religion, and science* as particular stages of the 'absolutely free spirit', drawing into itself the previous determinations and bringing forth 'another world'.[43] While the differentiation from 'absolute spirit' seems fully attained here, a clear demarcation of 'real' from 'subjective' spirit is still lacking. Hegel's ignorance of this term is closely connected to the phenomenological tendency which characterizes the philosophy of spirit as it is presented in the plan for the Jena lectures. Of course the lectures do develop 'real spirit' from the concept of consciousness, which is taken to include both knowledge (theoretical self) and will (practical self). However, as a result of the connection between consciousness and an object which is required phenomenologically, elements of both of what will later be called 'subjective' and 'objective' spirit continually intermingle: imagination corresponds to free will, memory to the tool, the symbol to technical cunning.[44] Therefore no genuine synthesis has yet been made between the theoretical and practical subject. The latter is developed in an extremely unclear way during the analysis of the family[45] only to be reintroduced as a new concept in the battle for recognition.

The same obscurity reoccurs in the *Nürnberg Propädeutik*. There the 'science of spirit' is divided into the following sections: (1) spirit in its concept; (2) practical spirit; and (3) spirit in its pure expression. The first division examines the spirit as (theoretical) intelligence and concludes with 'rational thinking' (pars. 170–2). No synthesis unites the latter with 'practical spirit' (will), rather this latter itself contains the whole science of ethical life, which paradoxically is located in the system of psychology.[46] This

43 *JR*, Vol. II, pp. 263 ff.
44 See *JR*, Vol. II, p. 212, n. 2. Cf. also J. Habermas, 'Arbeit und Interaktion: Bemerkungen zu Hegels Jenenser Philosophie des Geistes', in *Natur und Geschichte, Karl Löwith zum 70 Geburtstag* (Stuttgart/Berlin/Köln/Mainz, 1967), pp. 132 ff., 154, n. 3, although he overlooks the phenomenological tendency of the Jena philosophy of spirit.
45 *JR*, Vol. II, pp. 199 f.
46 *Philosophische Propädeutik*, Vol. III, Part 2, section 3, pars. 128–9, pars. 173 ff. Cf. R. Falckenberg, *Die Realität des objektiven Geistes bei Hegel. Abhandlungen zur Philosophie und ihrer Geschichte*, Part 25 (Leipzig, 1916), p. 62. The obscurity remains even if one begins with the assumption that Rosenkranz did not see the connections and disfigured the text with emendations. Cf. F. Nicolin, 'Hegels Arbeiten zur Theorie des subjektiven Geistes', in *Erkenntnis und Verantwortung* (Düsseldorf, 1960), p. 367 (Festschrift Th. Litt).

indecisive tendency, clearly congruent with Hegel's attempted analysis of the doctrine of the individual soul during the 1790s,[47] is finally eliminated in the (1817) Heidelberg *Encyclopedia*'s conceptual scheme which creates a synthesis, defining 'objective spirit' as the 'unity of theoretical and practical spirit'.[48] The phenomenological concentration on the 'I' of consciousness is eliminated. Spirit is the comprehensive unity incorporating thinking, will, and object, a unity whose development is tied solely to the path of the *Logic*.[49] From this derives the fundamental difference distinguishing the arrangement of the paragraphs in the *Encyclopedia* from that in the chapter on Spirit in the *Phenomenology of Spirit* of 1807. In the latter work the first level of 'spirit' (which is still not called 'objective') is the *substantial ethical life* of the ancient *polis* which excludes from itself the moment of individuality. The first step of 'objective spirit' is the *abstract right* of the 'person', in which 'objective spirit' finds its absolute justification through the logical concept itself, a unity of universal and particular. The phenomenological title agrees with the meaning of 'objective spirit' in so far as 'spirit' here means the 'universal work which produces itself through the doing of all and each, as their unity and equality',[50] and not merely the unity of thinking and will, or the 'general will'. Spirit is not, however, contained in a unitary concept [the objectivization of free will] but rather is divided into various 'worlds' of consciousness. It has substantiality in the ancient *polis*, external existence in the modern kingdom of culture, and is finally the self-certainty of knowing and will in the *general will* and in ethical life, although it does not find fulfilment there in a positive work.

The treatment of objective spirit in the *Encyclopedia* takes the opposite path. It begins with the moral concept of will, which is the 'general' will (or the will which grasps self in thought), as the ground of freedom itself. To that extent this discussion is based on the modern philosophy of right and the state, de-

---

47 See F. Rosenzweig, *Hegel und der Staat* (Munich/Berlin, 1920), Vol. II, pp. 83f.
48 Par. 400; *WWG*, Vol. VI, p. 281.
49 *Wissenschaft der Logik*, Part 2, ed. G. Lasson (Leipzig, 1951), pp. 219 ff. (Eng. tr. A. V. Miller, *Hegel's Science of Logic* (London, 1969).)
50 *WWG*, Vol. II, p. 336.

veloped by Rousseau, Kant, and Fichte. But for Hegel the general will is neither the origin nor the aim of the doctrine of objective spirit. It is not the origin, because it grows from the process of the struggle with nature, and it is not the aim, because it must fulfil itself in a work. Because Hegel defines free will as the self-determining spirit which gives its determinations external reality,[51] he reinserts it into the sphere of objective existence from which Kant and Fichte had released it. But he does so in such a way that this existence – human nature and history (right, state, etc.) – seems to be 'posited' by and penetrated with free will. Freedom can be conceived as the 'idea of right' only on the assumption that it has been realized historically and is immanent in positive law and the state. Law – the central category of objective spirit – is generally the sphere of existence which will gives itself in its free self-determination – the kingdom of realized freedom, or the world of spirit produced outside itself.[52]

This is the point at which Hegel's doctrine of objective spirit surpasses its eighteenth-century predecessors as well as the traditional understanding of practical philosophy. The concept of free, self-objectifying will brings together what remains separated there: the relationship of individual wills to one another in ethical action and the relationship to human needs and to their mediation with external natural objects through labour.[53] Finally this same unification of action (*Handlung*) and activity (*Tätigkeit*)[54] reveals the conceptual structure of spirit itself. Although, as a principle of philosophy, spirit is absolutely primary and presupposed by nature, Hegel interprets its mode of being with categories which are drawn from the sphere of our opposition to nature.

51 Cf. already *Nürnberger Propädeutik*, par. 173; *Enzyklopädie der philosophischen Wissenschaften*, 1st edn (Heidelberg, 1817), par. 400; 3rd edn, par. 484.
52 *Rechtsphilosophie*, par. 4, in *WWG*, Vol. VII, p. 50. Cf. par. 1, Addition, in *WWG*, Vol. II, pp. 38 ff.
53 See *Enzyklopädie*, 3rd edn, par. 483: 'The free will finds itself immediately confronted by differences which arise from the circumstance that freedom is its inward function and aim, and is in relation to an external and already subsisting objectivity, which splits up into different heads: viz., anthropological data (i.e., private and personal needs), external things of nature which exist for consciousness, and the ties of relation between individual wills ...' Cf. *Enzyklopädie*, 1st edn, pars. 403–5, 2nd edn, pars. 488–91. (Eng. tr. W. Wallace and A. V. Miller, *Hegel's Philosophy of Mind* (hereafter *PM*) (Oxford, 1971), p. 241.)
54 See *Nürnberger Propädeutik*, par. 176.

Spirit has no static being, but instead is process, activity, labour: 'But spirit exists only in that it annuls its immediate being. If it merely is, then it is not spirit; for its being resides in this: that it is mediated explicitly through itself as spirit which is for itself.'[55] 'Labour of the spirit' is no metaphor for Hegel, but rather names its essence: to be the production of itself, self-objectification and work. Spirit, Hegel asserts in the lectures on the philosophy of history, 'acts essentially. It makes itself what it is implicitly: its own act, its own work. Thus it becomes its own object, and it has itself objectively as an existent.'[56]

Interpreting objective spirit through the model of labour's unity with action leads to an essential alteration in the valuation assigned to practical philosophy. In his systematic work which followed the *Phenomenology of Spirit*, Hegel began by developing the *Logic* (1812–16). Thereafter, as an outline of the whole, he published *The Encyclopedia of the Philosophical Sciences* (1817). The final work to be published by him personally, *The Outlines of the Philosophy of Right*, appeared in 1821. It is the authentic fulfilment of the doctrine of objective spirit. In this last work Hegel referred explicitly to the intention of connecting with the traditional division of the system into theoretical and practical philosophy: 'I have', he says in the Foreword, 'developed the nature of speculative knowing in my *Science of Logic*.' The philosophy of right is not simply based on the dialectical method of logic, but rather is its counterpart, since it unfolds the nature of 'practical knowing'. Not without some justification, Hegel was still able in the Berlin period to explain their relation as the 'common division' into theoretical and practical philosophy.[57] At the same time, however, such a statement does not coincide with the conceptual meaning and structure of the Hegelian system. For Hegel, the logic is not just a 'theoretical' discipline of philosophy like the old metaphysics, but instead, as 'pure science', forms its first part. It *precedes* both of the other parts of the system (the philosophy of

55 *Vorlesungen über die Philosophie der Religion*, ed. G. Lasson (4 vols., Leipzig, 1925–9), Vol. I (1925), p. 70. (Eng. tr. E. B. Speirs and J. B. Sanderson, *Lectures on the Philosophy of Religion* (3 vols., New York, 1962).)
56 *Die Vernunft in der Geschichte*, ed. J. Hoffmeister, 5th edn (Hamburg, 1955), p. 67; cf. pp. 55 f., 12, and 135.
57 See *Nürnberger Schriften*, ed. J. Hoffmeister (Leipzig, 1938), p. xxiv.

nature and the philosophy of spirit) so that the parallelism of logic and natural law is lost. In fact, natural law has its systematic location as one element in the philosophy of spirit. For Hegel, the concepts and contents of 'practical philosophy' appear under the title of 'objective spirit'. The old name is surrendered in favour of the new because 'practical philosophy' corresponds neither to labour as the basis of the modern world and its society nor to the ontological necessity of the objectification of spirit in its products. Its themes are the actions of the human world in the spheres of right and morality, family and society, state and history. The doctrine of objective spirit, which retroactively presupposes subjective spirit (anthropology, psychology) and is surpassed by absolute spirit, encompasses those human actions which have their foundation and purpose in the humanly produced world. Actions of this kind cannot transcend themselves even in their meaning, but instead are inseparable from the human world, their 'objective spirit'. Hegel includes under the new title all of what school philosophy called ethics, economics, and politics, as well as what it connected with natural law. He thereby posited the system's difference from those sciences which, like the old ontology, psychology, cosmology, and natural theology, are 'pulled up root and branch' by the transcendental revolution in philosophy.[58] For objective spirit, which by its activity realized Kant's concept of 'pure will' and of freedom in contrast to the realization of the free acts following from natural law in the scholastic tradition, has already overcome the bondage to nature (of human beings *and* of the non-human world).[59] For Hegel that spirit is 'objective' which, by realizing its actual implicit freedom, makes nature itself, rather than just natural law (however one understands it), into an object posited by and filled with itself: freedom is being with itself in another.[60] The deeper reason why objective spirit has

---

58 Cf. *Wissenschaft der Logik*, Foreword; *WWG*, Vol. IV, p. 13.

59 See *Enzyklopädie*, 1st edn, par. 299: 'For us spirit has nature as its presupposition, while it is nature's truth. In this truth, nature has disappeared in its concept and spirit gives itself out as the *idea* whose object as well as *subject* is the concept' (*WWG*, Vol. VI, p. 227).

60 *Enzyklopädie*, 3rd edn, par. 24, Addition 2; *WWG*, Vol. VIII, p. 87; *Einleitung in die Geschichte der Philosophie*, ed. J. Hoffmeister, 3rd edn (Hamburg, 1959), pp. 110 ff., 223 f.; *Die Vernunft in der Geschichte*, ed. Hoffmeister, pp. 54 f.

a history, as well as itself being essentially historical, lies in this independence from nature. Thus, in reference to the concept of freedom, Hegel could say that whole regions of the world such as Africa and the Orient have never possessed it. The same principle applies to the history of philosophy: 'the Greeks and Romans, Plato and Aristotle, even the Stoics, did not have it; rather they knew only that a person might be genuinely free by birth (as an Athenian, Spartan, or other citizen) or by strength of character, culture, or philosophy. The former idea entered the world through Christianity.'[61]

With this insight into the historicity of the idea of freedom, so influential for his doctrine of objective spirit, Hegel has put aside the whole traditional structure of practical philosophy. Indeed, this insight may have been much richer for modern thinking than the destruction of the foundations of practical philosophy with which Hegel began. In any case, nineteenth-century interpreters read the theory of objective spirit from the perspective of the philosophy of history, thereby necessarily overlooking both its origins and the context in which it grew. Today philosophy is once again very close to clarifying these origins. This also means that it is learning from the tradition which Hegel thoroughly destroyed. But no instruction, no matter how one assimilates it and how far one can go with it, can avoid coming to terms with Hegel's critical destruction of the tradition. His arguments are not merely perspicuous and largely convincing; they also establish the very point at which the practical philosophy of the schools was only too clearly bound up with the power relationships of old European society. The question is, how is a theory of practical experience possible under the conditions of the contemporary social–historical world? No one would wish to say that Hegel's answer will do, but he must certainly be credited with raising the question – which is as fitting for our times as it was for his own.

61 *Enzyklopädie*, 3rd edn, par. 482, n. (Compare *PM*, pp. 239 f.); *WWG*, Vol. v, p. 380.

2

Dialectic in Institutions.
Historical Background and Systematic
Structure of the *Philosophy of Right*

Hegel's *Philosophy of Right* is neither a theory of jurisprudence
nor a theory of natural law confronted with the task of cataloguing individual human rights. It does not deal with any
historical or ahistorical system of rights at all, but rather with
right itself, or, more precisely, its 'concept' and the 'being' or
'realization' of the concept (par. 1). Hegel talks about the 'Idea
of Right', because philosophy, as is stated at the beginning of
the book, is concerned only with Ideas, and hence not with what
are often referred to as 'mere concepts' – 'On the contrary, it
exposes such concepts as one-sided and false, while showing at
the same time that it is the concept alone ... which has actuality,
and further that it gives this actuality to itself.'[1]

Hegel's language here presupposes an understanding of some
basic terms developed in the *Science of Logic*. According to Hegel,
'being' means 'determinate being', which in the determination
of its respective 'forms' and 'existences' does not correspond to
what is ordinarily called 'reality'. Hegel calls these determinations
'forms of the unmediated' which 'pass over into another'.
Examples of such determinations would be historically developed
positive laws such as the laws of a country or state which exist
and are valid; in Hegel's words, they 'exist historically'. The term
'existence', introduced in the *Logic* as the 'unmediated unity of
being and reflection', does not, however, define the structure of
actuality, but of *appearance*. And although right must appear,
although the 'world of ethical appearance' has a prominent place

---

1 Hegel, *Grundlinien der Philosophie des Rechts* (hereafter *GPR*), par. 1, Remark, in *Sämtliche Werke* (Jubiläumsausgabe (hereafter *WWG*), ed. H. Glockner (20 vols., Stuttgart,
1927–30), Vol. VII, p. 38. (Eng. tr. T. M. Knox, *Hegel's Philosophy of Right* (hereafter
PR) (Oxford, 1942), p. 14.) Page references will be given to both the Glockner edition
and the Knox translation, from which all important quotations will be taken.

in the conceptual structure of the *Philosophy of Right*, methodologically the language of appearance plays a subordinate role.
Every appearance is unmediated: it arises out of the ground, as
Hegel puts it, and disappears into the ground. Only the ground
which is no longer 'a passing over into another', 'mediates' the
logical with the historical. This ground, suitable to the form of
what is mediated, is called 'actuality' in Hegel's terminology:
'Actuality is the positing of that unity, the relation which has
become identical with itself; it is thus removed from transition ...; its determinate being is the manifestation of itself alone,
not of another.'[2] The subject of the *Philosophy of Right* is the
actuality of right, and according to Hegel this lies in the 'Idea
of Freedom', constructed in the unity of opposing determinations.
What posited right 'manifests' is that 'concept' which gives itself
its actuality, and thus – with reference to natural law – forms,
according to the normative principle of freedom (of the 'will,
which is free' (par. 4)), the starting-point for a 'philosophical
science of right'. The philosophy of right does not, however,
derive a system of ahistorical norms of right from the concept
of freedom, but representing a new methodological beginning
takes the path to the idea as the dialectically contradictory progress of the historical *formation of institutions* and recognizes this
indirect method of reconstruction as a necessary condition for
knowledge of the dialectic of the logical concept itself.

I

The word 'institution' is not defined in the *Philosophy of Right*,
but taken from and used according to common usage and the
particular context. We can distinguish a narrower and a broader
meaning. The narrower meaning follows features of Roman law,
which Hegel (historically incorrect) interprets as civil law.
Examples of 'institutions', in the original legal sense of the word,
are the 'Roman patriarchal power and the Roman state of matri-

---

2 Hegel, *Enzyklopädie der philosophischen Wissenschaften*, Part I: *Wissenschaft der Logik*, par.
142, in *WWG*, Vol. VIII, p. 320. (Eng. tr. W. Wallace, *The Logic of Hegel* (Oxford,
1892).)

mony' as the basis of the concepts of Roman civil law.[3] Beyond
the context of these examples, which encompasses the realm of
so-called 'abstract right' where property and contract are fundamental institutions, the word does not appear in the systematic
progress of conceptualization in the philosophy of right. The idea
of freedom is only 'actual' for Hegel after the critique of the
historically limited right of these institutions (in the section
'Morality') and their incorporation in the concept and being of
ethical life. Ethical life, 'in that on the one hand it is the good
become alive – the good endowed in self-consciousness with
knowing and willing and actualized by self-conscious action –
while on the other hand self-consciousness has in the ethical realm
its absolute foundation and the end which actuates its effort' (par.
142) also must assume a historical form.[4] The language of ethical
life is simply 'the serial exposition of the relationships which are
necessitated by the idea of freedom and are therefore actual in
their entirety, to wit in the state'.[5] It is in the linguistic context
of ethical life and its relation to the 'right of the state' – constitutional law – that the concept of institutions gains its broader meaning. Hegel does not in fact use the Latin term here, but replaces
it with the German equivalent, *Einrichtung*. The 'stable content'
of ethical life, the 'ethical powers' (par. 145), which are beyond
the subjective preferences and opinions of the individual are the
'absolutely valid laws and institutions'.[6]

The historical and logical element in right is, we had indicated,
mediated through the concept of actuality in the *Logic*, which
also forms the basis of the relationship between natural law, positive right and politics and is therefore the origin of the dialectic
of institutions, to which we shall now turn. Unfortunately, Hegel
failed to obviate obvious misunderstandings concerning the
ambiguity of a word as familiar to everyone and open to so many
usages as 'actuality'. It is true that the Preface of the *Philosophy of
Right* refers to the logically restricted meaning of the word in its
famous and infamous dictum about the rationality of the actual and

3 *GPR*, par. 3, Remark, p. 43; *PR*, p. 17.
4 *GPR*, par. 142, p. 226; *PR*, p. 104.
5 *GPR*, par. 148, pp. 229 ff.; *PR*, p. 107.
6 *GPR*, par. 144, p. 227; *PR*, p. 105.

the actuality of the rational. But because Hegel at the same time alluded to the non-philosophical and vulgar usage, he created the false impression that he was justifying the positive state, in particular the existing 'Prussian' state, as well as rejecting the principles of natural law. Hegel's conception of philosophical right has in fact little in common with that of his predecessors in modern natural law theory. However it has even less to do with the idea of a restorational 'philosophy of the state', which is how both his followers and his critics wanted to interpret it.

According to the definitions given in the *Logic*, 'actuality' means the 'unity of essence and existence, or of the internal and external, which has become immediate'.[7] This usage, which defines the structure of actuality as mediation, corresponds to two moments in the *Philosophy of Right* belonging to the dialectic of the concept of right and also to its realization in ethical institutions. We shall call them, departing somewhat from Hegel's terminology, the moments of the *reflexivity* and *positivity* of right. The term 'reflexivity' signifies the relation to the 'foundation' of right, making up part of the actuality of right. Hegel is referring here to the self-relation of a 'bearer of mind' constituting the foundation of right, that is, the legal subject who, knowing himself to have duties, recognizes and adheres to norms and laws. A fundamental expression of this reflexivity is the Hegelian concept of the 'free will' which wills itself in the other and thus wills the 'free will' (par. 27) according to the dialectic of actuality as the unity of 'externalization' and reflexion-in-itself. The 'free will' – man's universal capacity for right – is the elementary concept of 'right' in the sense of modern natural law; but, as the dialectical reconstruction revealed, the contents of that will are the historical formations of institutions. The philosophy of right denies the possibility of deriving determinate legal contents from a universal, normative principle of right; the idea that 'there could be a system of right and a legal situation which would be purely rational – only rational' is rejected by Hegel as an abstract postulate of natural law.[8] The content of the law at a particular stage in the development of institutions – e.g., of Roman law or medieval feudal law

7 Hegel, *Enzyklopädie der philosophischen Wissenschaften*, par. 142, Remark, p. 320.
8 *Philosophie des Rechts* (6 vols., Stuttgart, 1973–), Vol. II (1974), p. 89.

– is the product of contingent historical formation. Although it is not only to be described and explained historically, but also to be judged on the basis of man's capacity for right as a 'free agent', the philosophy of right consistently rejects the idea of deduction from the principle of natural law.

The key to understanding the dialectic of 'philosophical right' lies in the concept of 'positivity'. This term, which, as is well known, plays a central role in Hegel's early writings, is used here to express the relation of the concept of right to its concrete form in institutions, the way in which moral and legal norms are made positive in laws, a relation which Hegel considers to be constitutive for 'right in general'. It follows to a certain extent analytically from the concept of right that it should be positive, should appear in external forms of existence and have validity as 'that which is legal', i.e., the law. Philosophical and positive right are different from one another, but Hegel regards the antithetical view, that natural and positive law are opposites, as a 'gross misunderstanding'. Drawing a parallel with Roman law again, he compares their reciprocal relationship to the relationship between Institutes and Pandects: both belong together to the Corpus Juris Civilis, to the positivity of a system of right.[9]

Right is necessarily positive by virtue both of its *form*, which is to be valid only in the state, and of elements of its *content*, that is to say, national particularities and the historical stage of development of a state as well as the organization and use of the particular legal system, all of which cannot sprout from any principle of right (par. 3). The relationship of 'natural law' to 'political science' which is fundamental for Hegel's philosophy of right and contained in the work's programmatic title results from the fact that right is necessarily positive. From a historical point of view the title refers to two distinct philosophical disciplines. The first – natural law – was developed in modern times, whereas the second has its roots in the ancient world, in

9 *GPR*, par. 3, Remark, p. 42; *PR*, p. 16. Hegel's comparison is not very good, because the elementary textbook of law, Justinian's *Institutes*, is not constructed as systematically as is his own *Grundlinien* (*Elements*). Cf. F. Schulz, *Geschichte der römischen Rechtswissenschaft* (Weimar, 1961), pp. 187, 194, *inter alia,* who more correctly compares the *Institutes* to Aristotle's *Metaphysics* with its looser construction.

the Greek theory of the *polis*. Classical political philosophy is of course characterized by the fact that it does not separate natural law from political science. The political idea of an optimal constitution – an idea of reason – developed by Plato's *Republic* and *Laws* or Aristotle's *Politics* is conceived of as a manifestation of natural law and a legally founded 'civil' society (*koinōnia politikē*, *societas civilis*) which is identical with the state (*polis*, *civitas*, *res publica*). Following this unchallenged traditional form of political science, the young Hegel had initially seen the task of a scientific treatment of 'natural law' as consisting in constructing the 'law of ethical nature' within a political whole, thereby establishing the 'state' as the basic institution.[10] He soon had to recognize, however, that under the conditions of the specific historical form of the modern state the application of a non-dialectical concept of politics, by burying the activity of the individual in institutions and depriving him of the possibility of opposition, could only lead in practice to *political absolutism* – the position of Machiavelli. The opposing position of individualism was developed in natural law theory from Hobbes to Kant. Natural law theory postulates the right to contain within fixed limits the 'unlawful' incursions of the state against civil society and to revolutionize the state with a new concept of freedom and right once the policy of the state has ossified into the naked exercise of power. In this way the antithesis of natural law and political science began a movement of political enlightenment and a transition to revolution which it was to accompany in its progress from then on. Hegel's conceptual dialectics presupposes this antithesis and is a philosophical attempt to resolve it. The philosophy of right understands itself as such, because it seeks to mediate the antithesis between prepolitical natural law and positive law in the dialectic of the idea of right. The idea of right, Hegel says, is freedom (par. 1, addition) and in order to be properly understood it must be possible to recognize it in its concept and in its concrete existence,

10 See Hegel, 'Über die wissenschaftlichen Behandlungsarten des Naturrechts, Seine Stelle in der praktischen Philosophie und sein Verhältnis zu den positiven Rechtswissenschaften' (1801) in *WWG*, Vol. 1, pp. 435 ff. (Eng. tr. T. M. Knox, *Natural Law* (Philadelphia, 1975) as well as Chapter 4 in this volume.)

i.e., in the process of the historical formation of institutions and the legal actuality belonging to them.

Once the concept of right has been related historically and dialectically to the existence of institutions, then the idea of natural law becomes problematic. As early as the Heidelberg *Encylopedia of the Philosophical Sciences* (1817) Hegel says: 'The expression "natural law", which has hitherto been common in the philosophical theory of right, is ambiguous as to whether the law is as it were *implanted* directly by nature or whether it exists because of the *nature of things*, i.e., because of the concept. The former sense has always been intended; with the result that at the same time a *natural condition* has been invented in which natural law is supposed to be valid.' The 'concept' of things is for Hegel: right, to the extent that it and all its determinations are founded on the 'free personality', rather than nature – 'a self-determination which is ... the opposite of natural determination' (par. 415). The actuality of right is not nature; it is the 'world of mind brought forth out of itself' – a 'second nature' which Hegel calls the 'realm of freedom made actual'.[11] It is created in those institutions shown in the outline of the *Philosophy of Right*, from the first forms of abstract right to the historical formations of family, civil society and state. It goes without saying that 'natural' relations play a role in all of this; the question is, whether they produce a law governing those forms. Hegel firmly rejects the possibility of an affirmative answer to this question and the idea of a 'natural law'. The necessity which, for example, the institution 'state' acquires in relationship to the individual no longer means that it is a law of nature for the individual to live in the state; the ethical necessity of the state rests instead on the law of freedom, given not by an immutable 'nature', but by the concept itself – dependent in its dialectic on the historical realization in institutions. Self-realization of the concept – that, for Hegel, is the principle of natural right behind man's universal capacity for right, enabling him to law behind man's universal capacity for right, enabling him to through the illusion of naturalness which had hitherto concealed the basis of right: freedom.

11 *GPR*, par. 4, p. 50; *PR*, p. 20.

II

Thus for Hegel, 'philosophical right' differs just as much from positive law as it does from natural law. The philosophy of right stands in the middle between the two extremes of the rational (Kant, Fichte) and 'organic' (Savigny) conceptions of law. Hegel agrees with Savigny and the historical school in the rejection of the state based solely on reason found in theories of natural law. But in his case, the historical explanation does not just serve to substantiate and justify positive law, but constitutes the 'derivation from the concept' (par. 3). The dialectical development of the concept is itself historical – the progress of freedom in world history – and the task of the philosophy of right is to give the historical–positive right of each respective epoch its 'absolutely valid justification' (par. 3).

This is crucial for an understanding of the work and its basic historical attitude. Hegel's starting point is the modern revolution which incorporated natural law in its constitutional legislation and legal codes. The rationality of the state is no longer a postulate for him, but the actuality of recent history which is given proper recognition in 'philosophical right'. To the then popular 'philosophy of the state' and its aim of outlining a new and special theory, as if 'no state or constitution had ever existed in the world at all or was even in being at the present time, but that nowadays – and this 'nowadays' lasts for ever – we had to start all over again from the beginning',[12] Hegel opposes a concept of philosophy in which the 'exploration of the rational' is linked with the 'apprehension of the present and actual'. He takes up its traditional task, 'to comprehend what is', that is, to be speculative knowledge of Being, in order to give it an interpretation which seems to turn it into the opposite: to think *Being* in the framework of the events of *Time*. Philosophy, as knowledge of what is, is therefore 'its own time apprehended in thoughts'; it can no more go beyond its present world than the individual, as 'a child of his time', can jump over Rhodes.

Hegel's definition of the 'Idea of Rights' as the unity of *concept* and *existence* rests on this interweaving of time and being. By

12 *GPR*, Preface, p. 23; *PR*, p. 4.

recognizing freedom as this idea, the philosophy of right avoids the one-sidedness of both natural law and positive law, which adhere either to the abstract *concept* of a 'natural' law or to the *existence* of positive right. 'If it is to be truly understood [the idea] must be known both in its concept and in the determinate existence of that concept' (par. 1, Addition). It is this which *relates the idea to history*. Freedom can only be understood as the idea of right if it has already come into existence and is immanent in positive law. This happens in the state of the modern world which has adopted the revolution's principle of freedom and is obligated to preserve the individual as a free and legally responsible person. The state is defined by Hegel as an 'actuality' in the speculative sense of the *Logic*, as an immediate unity of inner essence and external existence: it is the 'actuality of the ethical idea' (par. 257), the 'actuality of the substantial will' (par. 258), and the 'actuality of concrete freedom' (par. 260). So for Hegel, as distinct from the idealistic theory of natural law from Rousseau to Fichte, the idea of right is not simply a possibility of thought, but a historically mediated actuality making it necessary for philosophy to relinquish its position of abstract natural law and 'to apprehend and portray the state as something inherently rational'.[13] It is this modern state, not the Prussian one of 1821, that Hegel's dictum in the Preface is referring to: 'What is rational is actual and what is actual is rational.' To recognize his 'progressive' intention, it is not necessary to play off the first sentence against the second; then both say the same thing: that in the modern state the *concept* of right has found *existence*, the rational – the idea of freedom – is actual, and the actual – the modern state – is rational. This does not exclude a partial lack of rationality. In the last lecture he gave on the philosophy of right, just a few days before his death, Hegel says in a lapidary note on the dictum: 'What is actual is rational. But not everything which exists is actual, what is bad is insubstantial and broken in itself.'[14]

In Hegel's examination of the revolution's principle of freedom, there arises the problem of the realization of philosophy. The concept of right which in the French Revolution turned against

13 *GPR*, Preface, p. 34; *PR*, p. 11.
14 *Vorlesungen über Rechtsphilosophie*, in *WWG*, Vol. IV, p. 923.

and overthrew the existing feudal regime, the 'old scaffolding of injustice' bereft of mind and reason, comes from philosophical thought. This is what makes the event so exceptional and unprecedented, and for Hegel it is an event of world-historical significance: 'As long as the sun has stood in the firmament and the planets have circled around it, it has never been known for man to stand on his head, that is on his thoughts, and construct reality in accordance with them. Anaxagoras was the first to say that νοῦς rules the world; but only now has Man come to realize that thought should rule spiritual actuality.'[15] The realization of philosophy does not mean its dissolution, the sacrifice of thought to a historically changed actuality, but rather just the opposite: philosophy is needed to comprehend the reason for the change. Thus philosophy becomes the theory of its age, something it never was in its history up to Hegel. It now has the task of saving the revolution's principle of freedom, firstly from itself, from capsizing into despotism, and secondly from the restoration, which is antithetically opposed to the principle of freedom and so denies the very continuity of history it would like to re-establish.[16] In this sense, Hegel's philosophy is the philosophy of the revolution and not of the restoration or the Prussian state. It faces time and its 'actuality' not with a will to change things, but with a will to know, with which it establishes the principle of the existing legal order. It is not without reason that Hegel says, alluding to a statement by Francis Bacon, that half a philosophy (and here you would have to include the romantic–restorationist theories of Haller and Schlegel, de Maistre and Bonald) leads away from the state, but the true one leads to it.[17] It may well be that the fault of this 'true philosophy' is that it offers only knowledge whereby to 'reconcile' oneself to the world, not to change it. Its advantage lies in the fact that it gives an account of a changed actuality – in terms of the same concept immanent in completed history.

15 *Vorlesungen über die Philosophie der Weltgeschichte*, ed. G. Lasson (4 vols., Leipzig, 1917–1920), Vol. IV (1920), p. 926.
16 See J. Ritter, *Hegel und die Französische Revolution* (new edn, Frankfurt on Main, 1965), pp. 24 ff.
17 *GPR*, Preface, p. 36; *PR*, p. 12.

The *Philosophy of Right* is therefore an instructive example of that 'comprehended history' which the young Hegel had made into the programme of his philosophy in the *Phenomenology*. The dialectical grounding of right in the self-development of the concept, which for Hegel is the human will in its freedom — feeedom constitutes for the will 'the substance of right and its goal' (par. 4) – is related both to the categories of classical political theory and natural law theory as well as to the process whereby the actuality of mind achieves historical form, giving those categories a new content. This is apparent from the outline of the system (of the institutions of 'right') with its division into *abstract right* (I) *morality* (II), and *ethical life* (III). *Abstract right* is the *natural law* (*jus naturale absolutum et hypotheticum*) of the eighteenth century, which was primarily concerned with matters of civil law (property, contract); it is the right of the abstract individual, emancipated from all governmental and corporative connections, which Hegel, in accordance with natural law theory, places at the apex of the philosophy of right and develops independently of the presuppositions of the 'substantial ethical life' (family, state), a modification of his initial position which cannot be overlooked. The basis of the concept of right and property is not man 'treated as possessing a certain *status*', a citizen as opposed to a slave, serf, or a stranger enjoying citizen's rights, but the legally responsible 'personality itself' (par. 40). The section entitled 'Morality' contains the concepts and subjects classified under *ethics* in scholastic philosophy – the doctrines of virtue and duty in the old sense, though Hegel introduces into them the principles of moral reflection first developed by Kant in his explication of the moral dimension of subjectivity. Hegel agrees with the scholastic tradition in his understanding of abstract right (natural law) as the doctrine of what is 'lawful' and of morality (ethics) as the doctrine of the 'moral will'. In both of these, it is man as an individual, thrown on his own resources by the modern philosophical and political revolution, who realizes and expresses himself, on the one hand in relation to the external world, both natural and human, in the forms of property (pars. 41–71), contract (pars. 72–80), and wrong (pars. 84–6); and on the other hand in relation to his inner world, with regard to purpose and responsibility (pars. 105–18), intention and welfare (pars. 119–28), good and conscience (pars. 129–41). Although Hegel recognizes these categories and uses them in his deduction, he regards them as abstractions with only limited validity in the system of the philosophy of right. Incorporated into the civil sphere and designated specifically as 'abstract right', natural law is the law of any person to whom law and property can apply, just as the subjective and reflective ethics which Kantian–Fichtean philosophy developed is the morality of the subject related to its own objectivity.

Whereas a clear parallel can be drawn between *abstract right* and *morality*, and the modern categories of natural law and subjective morality, applying the comparison to the third part of the *Philosophy of Right* creates some difficulties. They arise not only from the way in which it is structured into family, civil society and state, but from the title 'Ethical Life' itself. For in the seventeenth and eighteenth centuries, natural law was also divided into individual and social domains, whereby the former covered family (*societas domestica*) and civil society (*societas civilis*) or state (*civitas*), and the latter covered property and contract. Nevertheless, Hegel's theory of ethical life is equivalent to the re-introduction into the philosophy of right of a category which goes back to classical political theory. For modern natural law, customs do not have validity as an independent form of practical life and are in general subordinated to the rationality of the concept of right.[18] This is also true of Kant's legal philosophy, which is of course a part of what he calls the *Metaphysics of Morals*. In contrast, the category of ethical life, in which the discovery of 'moeurs' by eighteenth-century French writers (Montesquieu), the reconstruction of the Platonic-Aristotelian theory of the *polis* and the early romantic idea of the 'organic' unity of the 'national spirit' all intertwine, places Hegel in the old *tradition of morals*. 'Ethical life' means for Hegel the unity of the individuals with the 'ethical

18 Cf. N. Bobio, *Hegel und die Naturrechtslehre* (1966), reprinted in M. Riedel (ed.), *Materialien zu Hegels Rechtsphilosophie* (2 vols., Frankfurt on Main, 1975), Vol. II, pp. 81 ff.

powers' (par. 145) and 'necessary relationships' (par. 148) in any particular, historical nation and state. In this way it represents the same connection between morality and politics which was essential for the traditional doctrine of the ethical–legal constitution of the state and its unity with civil society (*civitas sive societas civilis*). Hegel can therefore with good reason point to the identity of 'the doctrine of duty in moral philosophy', which is 'objective' and not 'contained in the empty principle of moral subjectivity', with the 'systematic development of the circle of ethical necessity which follows in this third part', the ethical relationships and institutions within the state (par. 148).

But the linking of the doctrine of institutions and the tradition of morals only touches one aspect of the Hegelian theory of ethical life. The other is that the same category of the legal-philosophical system, which in form and content goes beyond modern natural law, registers the fundamental changes in the structure of the socio-political world which came about at the turn of the eighteenth and nineteenth centuries. The systematic reconstruction of institutions does indeed follow the conceptual dialectic of the *Logic* which Hegel presupposes everywhere in the *Philosophy of Right*. The trinity of logical moments in the 'concept' (the individual, particular and universal) already underlay the division of ethical life in the *Encyclopedia* of 1817. But there, the basic institution of 'nation' is a static unity, which is not yet differentiated into the moments of particular and universal, but is taken as a whole to represent the category of individuality.[19] Hegel abandons this position in the *Philosophy of Right* where he subjects the substantial ethical life of the 'individual nation' to the dialectic of the concept for a second time: ethical life splits up into *family* (individuality), *civil society* (particularity), and *state* (universality).

Even in this division of the third part of the *Philosophy of Right*, Hegel is taking up a long and venerable tradition in order to dissolve it by means of dialectics and to overcome it in his thought. One of the most important reasons for the dialectical dissolution

---

19 *Enzyklopädie*, Part 2: *Der objektive Geist, C. Die Sittlichkeit*: 1. Das einzelne Volk, 2. Äusseres Staatsrecht ('Besonderheit' in the sense of the (many) 'particular' states which confront one another in times of peace and war), 3. Allgemeine Weltgeschichte ('Allgemeinheit' in the sense of the 'universal' mind which develops out of the dialectic of the particular 'national minds'). Cf. *Enzyklopädie*, pars. 430–52.

of traditional categories lies in the *introduction of a new conception of society* which is epoch-making in the history of political theory. With this conception of society, as valid now as it was then, Hegel created an awareness of nothing less than the historical result of the modern revolution: the formation of a depoliticized civil society, resting on the freedom and equality of individuals and whose focal point shifted with the English Industrial Revolution from the form of political organization to economics.

Whereas political economy had been considered only inadequately or not at all by the liberal political theory of natural right, it provides Hegel with a frame of reference for a completely altered conceptual deduction. In natural law theories, 'societies' are formed on a personal basis. They are associations of people who, by means of rational discussion and action, form a common will which, for all those bound by it, is the will of one 'legal individual'. Speaking and acting are of public relevance here, because as a legal figure every 'society' (and not just the state) constitutes a public medium, in which both are carried on. For Hegel, on the other hand, 'society' consists by definition in private persons bound together by need and labour. Labour is a specific mode of action, need is the natural basis of man as a 'private person'. Hegel's philosophical achievement in this field consists above all in his having seen the 'private' frame of reference of individuals as publicly mediated and grasped their natural basis as a social constant. The theory of civil society is not oriented around the contract, the union of rational, articulate individual agents, but the 'system of needs' – a network of relations between 'private persons' resulting from need, the means of satisfaction and labour that is constantly reproducing itself (par. 187).

What Hegel understands as a reciprocal dialectical relationship between private and public ends forming the basis of a 'social connection' which encompasses 'personal' activity is something which had already been dealt with in Anglo-Scottish moral philosophy (Hume, Smith, Ferguson) and in the theory of interest developed by the French *encyclopédistes*. Already here we find that the contract schema gains a function over and above its formal legal one, in that private ends (the protection of the individual's life and property) are declared to be public affairs. The theory of utility and interest, which Hegel had studied as a young man, dominated the late European Enlightenment. It proclaimed that private citizens should have dealings with one another free from the constraints of estates and power, social relations being regulated by 'interêt personelle' (Diderot, Helvétius, Holbach) or 'self-interest' (Franklin, Bentham).

The harmonious picture of society is now interpreted as a model of conflict. Hegel is ambivalent in his attitude towards the logico-historical problems arising with this system of activity which is no longer synonymous with other concepts (state, civil society). On the one hand, 'society' is a legal structure and right is the existence of rational (free) will. On the other hand, the will engages in contract only in the private legal sphere – society as a natural historical institution, realized in family, civil society and state, does not rest on the legal obligations of contract.[20]

Although 'civil society' also appears as a legal structure, what Hegel wants to show in grounding and justifying it dialectically from the idea of the rational ('free') will is precisely that this institution is not touched upon in the traditional account of the genesis of 'societies' given by natural law theory. On the one hand, it goes beyond the institution of the family both systematically and historically, while on the other, it fails to reach the institution of the state. The rational will, generalized by Hegel to the 'Idea of Right' and fitted into the dialectic of objective mind, 'particularizes' itself on this level into a heterogeneous multiplicity of persons, who 'as such do not have absolute unity, but have their consciousness and their end in their own particularity and Being-for-themselves – the system of atomism'.[21]

What arises out of the dialectic of this institution, distinguishable from the state, is a continually self-reproducing fabric of relations between 'private persons', which grows out of need and labour – 'society' in the modern sense of the word. As civil society, it takes up a central position in the *Philosophy of Right* and its political theory, where it revitalizes the categories handed down by classical political theory and modern natural law. This can

20 *GPR*, par. 181, pp. 261 ff.; *PR*, p. 122. The schema of the contract is also rejected
    for the family (pars 75, 163) and the state (par. 258) as being conceptually insufficient.
21 *Enzyklopädie*, Part 3, par. 523, p. 401.

be seen first of all in the fact that 'civil society' does not remain fixed in its prescribed place, but encroaches on other institutional domains. For civil society is many things for Hegel: the 'determinate existence' of *abstract right* (pars. 209 f.); a field of activity for subjective *morality* in the alleviation of poverty (par. 242); the substantial ground of the *family* with power over it (par. 238); the stage of difference in the *state* (par. 182). In a particular historical way it has become a 'means' of developing *ethical life*. Here civil society forms a connecting element between the institutions of the 'family' and the 'state', which did not exist in the tradition of classical political theory nor in the modern theory of natural law.

As a 'middle', civil society does not just mediate by balancing and reconciling opposites. More importantly, it draws all institutions into its field of influence and alters their traditional structure. This begins with the institution of the 'family', the basic element of civil society, which, in the traditional conception of natural law and political science, was the mediating element with the political state. Hegel denies it this mediating function, not only because civil society and state are separate and distinct, but also because the family itself, according to its concept, cannot be an element in what makes up the state. Its relationship to the state is limited to being 'material' (par. 262), i.e., to prepare individuals as well as the 'mass' for the natural reproduction of life and the immediacy of ethical feeling and consciousness by educating them (pars. 173–5). In a word: whereas before Hegel the institution of the family, as 'the whole domestic unit' (*oikos*), was itself a part of the state as a whole, in his theory it is the individual, raised and educated in the private sphere of the family, who is so. This corresponds to a parallel historical dialectic in the construction of institutions. While on the one hand the relationship to the state moves from the family into the institutional domain of civil society, which Hegel has now added to the system of ethical life, on the other hand civil society and family must 'posit' themselves in a different institutional relationship. For Hegel, the family is not a 'society', the members of which enjoy different status, nor does it consist of smaller 'societies' (man–wife, parents–children, master–slave), but forms one 'person', who has his reality 'in some property', but not in the legal–economic unity of the house (par. 169). The original idea of the family as an economic unit has been replaced by the modern, sentimental one based on 'private' relationship and feelings which began to establish itself at the end of the eighteenth century. 'The family', according to the definition in par. 158, 'as the immediate substantiality of mind, is specifically characterized by love, which is mind's feeling of its own unity. Hence in a family, one's frame of mind is to have self-consciousness of one's individuality within this unity as the absolute essence of oneself, with the result that one is in it not as an independent person but as a member.'[22] It is the modern concept of the family, no longer tied to the economic cell of the domestic unit, which Hegel articulates in full knowledge of the alterations in the traditional form of economics due to the fundamental position given to civil society in the philosophy of right. Compared to previous theories of *societas civilis* found in classical political science and modern natural law which based civil society on 'domestic' society, the *family* plays a subordinate role in 'civil society' as conceived by Hegel and only lays the foundations; its effective range is no longer so comprehensive. Given the conditions under which modern society reproduces itself economically, whereby the boundaries of the 'whole domestic unit' are permeated, the individual is 'torn out' of the family and becomes, in Hegel's words, a 'son of civil society'. Civil society therefore assumes an ever-increasing economic function; 'for the paternal soil and the external inorganic resources of nature from which the individual formerly derived his livelihood, it substitutes its own soil and subjects the permanent existence of even the entire family to dependence on itself and contingency'.[23]

Just as the Hegelian concept of civil society points to the changed structure of the family, so it relates also to the altered position of the *state*. If one compares the third section of Hegel's theory of ethical life with the traditional doctrine of political theory, one will see that as a consequence of its premises, it can no longer be a theory of 'civil society' and its political constitution (government), but forms a 'theory of the state' distinct from

22 *GPR*, par. 158, p. 237; *PR*, p. 110.
23 *GPR*, par. 238, pp. 314–15; *PR*, p. 148.

this. The state and civil society, which had traditionally been linked by the relational concept of *societas civilis*, must first 'posit' themselves in a relationship which is one of division or 'difference' (par. 182, Addition). So Hegel rejects the 'old classification of constitutions', because he recognizes that given 'difference' the 'substantial unity' of social and political constitutions on which it was based is not 'rational', or, what is the same thing given the logical premises of the *Philosophy of Right*, it is no longer 'actual'. Consequently, this classification is reduced to a historical phenomenon which is valid only for the 'ancient world': 'The ancient division of constitutions into monarchy, aristocracy and democracy, is based upon the notion of substantial, still undivided, unity, a unity which has not yet come to its inner differentiation to a matured internal organization and which therefore has not yet attained depth and concrete rationality. From the standpoint of the ancient world, therefore, this division is the true and correct one ...'[24]

However, the break the *Philosophy of Right* makes with tradition is shown not only by the fact that because of the difference between state and civil society, the concepts and content of earlier theories have ceased to be rational and have become a thing of the past. It is really brought out far more by the reciprocal relationship between the state and *history*, which is fundamental to Hegel's theory of ethical life. The Hegelian concept of the state, which looking backwards presupposes the dissolution of the 'substantial unity' found in traditional society and the difference which comes into being with modern civil society, moves forward into the broader sphere of world history. Civil society stands under the state, as, in a complementary way, history stands above it. If one looks at the position accorded to history in earlier theories of politics and natural law, one can say that both agree in resolving the problem of right or of the 'good life' by means of an 'optimal constitution', i.e., the setting up of the 'state' (*civitas*). To both ancients and moderns this meant the arrangement of 'civil society' (*societas civilis*), lawfully constituted so as to permit the practice of virtue. For this purpose one simply has to refer to 'prior' sciences like metaphysics, anthropology, psychology and also

24 *GPR*, par. 273, pp. 371–2; *PR*, p. 176.

ethics as the doctrine of virtues and duties; all these sciences just formed the beginning, however, or the basis of the doctrine of the state as civil society. The unity of these sciences in practical philosophy dissolves in the eighteenth century with the rise of new disciplines such as political economy and the philosophy of history. Even Kant, who first established the connection between the problem of a doctrine of right and the state and the problem of a philosophy of history, still formulates the theme in terms of traditional natural law: as the problem of 'the achievement of a universal civil society which administers law among men'.[25] With the theory of 'civil society' Hegel has freed the philosophy of history from the context of natural law. At the peak of its perfection, the Idea of the state breaks down into the particularity of the 'many states' which stand opposite to one another in the movement of history. The Idea of the state is the Idea 'as a genus and as an absolute power over individual states – the mind which gives itself its actuality in the process of *World-History*' (par. 259). In Hegel, the state is no longer the traditional concept of political status nor a static, ahistorical model based on nature or a contract as was the case in classical political theory and modern natural law. History stands above it now – as a new instance of practical philosophy – so that 'the ethical whole itself, the autonomy of the state, is exposed to contingency' (par. 340), just as was the ethical totality of the family. The dimension of history, which Hegel introduces at the end of the *Philosophy of Right*, is the actuality of that idea of the natural condition, which the theorists of natural law placed at the beginning of their systems. The movement which in their case runs from nature to civil society (in the sense of *societas civilis*) and ends there, begins for Hegel when the state does not relate any more to civil society, but to *other states*. This natural condition is a real and not a fictitious one – the movement of history, which the philosophy of right incorporates and whereby it frees itself once more from the abstract natural theory

25 Kant, *Idee zu einer allgemeinen Geschichte in weltbürgerlicher Absicht* (1784), in *Kants gesammelte Schriften*, ed. Königlich Preussische Akademie der Wissenschaften (23 vols., Berlin, 1902–55), Vol. VIII, p. 22; (Eng. tr. L. W. Beck, *Ideal for a Universal History from a Cosmopolitan Point of View*, in *On History*, ed. L. W. Beck (New York, 1963), p. 16).

of law and society. The element in which 'universal mind' exists, from which the self-development of the concept of right proceeds and in which it ends, is the 'actuality of mind' in world history, in which the 'nature' of man and of things is not an unshakeable '*law*', but the concept, thought of as *freedom*, which develops itself 'in its whole compass of internality and externality alike'. In the face of this universal movement, which corresponds to the end of the philosophical system of right and the beginning of the philosophy of history, family, civil society and state are 'only ideal, and the movement of mind in this element is the exhibition of this fact' (pars. 341–2).

IV

The structure of Hegel's *Philosophy of Right* could be summarized by saying that the principles of its logical construction are based on historically situated conceptual forms. The logico-historical paradigms are the institutions of ethical life, in particular the concept of 'society', and the final concept of 'world history'. Both at the same time change the constitution of *family* and *state*, which for centuries had been presented as conforming to one another by both classical political and natural law theory. Just as the family stands *between* the individual who belongs to it as a member and civil society, so likewise the state moves *between* civil society and history. It is this gap in the structure of the traditional political institutions which results in the weaving dialectical development of the concept of right in Hegel and the ingenious structure of his system. And it is also for this reason that the philosophy of right acquires its peculiar richness of historical substance, which radically distinguishes it from modern works of natural law theory.

The new elements which the *Philosophy of Right* as a system of institutional dialectics brought into the political theory of the modern world also became the starting point of the theories which were to alter the system after Hegel's death and break through its mediations. Criticism of the *Philosophy of Right* was directed at precisely those elements which Hegel himself thought of as mediating the logical and the historical in the philosophical reconstruction of the actuality of right: the relationship between state and history and the relationship between civil society and state. For Eduard Gans, the first editor of the *Philosophy of Right* (1833), its prime value consisted in the 'tremendous spectacle' which Hegel places before us at the end of the work: the fact that he makes the state 'plunge into the ocean of history'. Gans makes the justifiable point that Hegel's short, sketchy account of the transition to history contains 'only an intimation of the more important interests' which devolve upon this ground.[26] Gans is here anticipating the criticism which was to be levelled against philosophy by historicists and which prevailed throughout the nineteenth century. Gans himself, and later Hegel's pupil Ferdinand Lassalle, pays tribute to the historical method of thought in his book *The World-Historical Development of the Right of Succession* (1824–35). The essence of historicism is to see the state not as its own *actuality*, but as a *product* of history. Arnold Ruge also criticized Hegel's *Philosophy of Right* from this position. According to Ruge, it takes no interest in the progressive movement of time and history because it defines the state in the above sense. In fact the state is not a universal *actuality* at all, but an individual historical *existence* – like the Prussian state of 1840, which Ruge then criticizes historically. The state of the *Philosophy of Right* does remind us of 'the present one' – indeed, Hegel names it explicitly – but he does not allow it to arise out of the '*historical process*', which is why he has according to Ruge failed to influence the development of the way people think about political life and times.[27]

The second point of critical departure is the relationship of civil society to the state, something which the young Marx deals with in his commentary to paragraphs 261–313 of the *Philosophy of Right* (1841–3). Marx puts an end to their mediation by reversing Hegel's speculative interpretation of their relationship: it is the state that is a *form of appearance* of civil society, and the latter, which Hegel could relegate to the position of 'the world of ethical appearance' (par. 181), is actually the *reality of political economy*, which is far more concrete, because it is comprehended completely unspeculatively, and provides Marx with the key to

26 Foreword to *GPR*, in *WWG*, Vol. VIII (1833), pp. viii–ix.
27 *Die Hegelsche Rechtsphilosophie und die Politik unserer Zeit*, in: *Deutsche Jahrbücher* (1842), pp. 762 ff.

an understanding of the state and history. Here too, the state is reduced from an actuality to a product – in this case, of economics. The problem for a critique of political economy no longer consists in the mediation of the 'private' principle of civil society with the political principle of the state, but in the critique of this society itself and of its private, individualist principle. Though he turned away from the *Philosophy of Right* and towards the political economy of the English and French, this did not stop Marx from relating his critique to the dialectic of *poverty* and *wealth* which crops up on the edge of Hegel's theory of civil society (pars. 243–5). These extremes and their basis – the sphere of civil society discovered by Hegel – become independent and in Marx's dialectic move beyond the conceptual movement of the *Philosophy of Right*, i.e., from the individual via the family and civil society to the state. The form of thought called 'sociology', which links Marx to Saint-Simon and August Comte, John Stuart Mill and Herbert Spencer, regards the state as a product of social movement, and not the actuality of the ethical 'Idea' which Hegel had imparted to it.

To this extent then, the *Philosophy of Right* marks an end, and the notion of the 'dying state' which arose in the early stages of industrial society is not to be found in it. It did, however, prepare the way for this idea by separating the state and civil society from one another, though without being able to focus in on it clearly. Hegel's conception of philosophy, which originates in the wisdom of self-limitation, makes it impossible for him to do so. For philosophy seeks neither to teach the world what it should be like nor to prophesy how it will be. As the thought of the world, it does not appear until the process of historical formation is complete and 'finished'. So the *Philosophy of Right* restricts itself to an 'old' form of life, which can be understood, but not *rejuvenated* or changed. It is this obligation to be knowledge which ties philosophy to the boundaries of its own epoch. The owl of Minerva, Hegel says at the end of the Preface to the *Philosophy of Right*, does not begin its flight until dusk is falling. That does not mean that philosophy belongs to the past and has itself become 'historical'. One reason why the work is currently being studied just as much in the East as in the West is because in the reality of the industrial society the state has not died as Saint-Simon and Marx said it would, their ideas hurrying ahead of society's development, but rather has remained very much alive. As modern society has formed, the state has become something mythological, a repository of power and wisdom depriving the individual of the possibility of opposition and hence the freedom which Hegel held to be the origin of thought. The age of ideologies and great prophesies did not check the mythology of the political rule it turned against, but promoted it. The return of the leviathan represents a challenge to philosophy which it must accept in order to find again its classic vocation: the destruction of myth through the power of reason. Hegel's *Philosophy of Right* bears witness to this power, and it is not fortuitous that the discussion of the relationship between freedom, right and the state on the basis of a society 'potentially' emancipated from political rule has once again begun with Hegel; today, more than ever, elucidating this relationship is a matter of urgency.

PART II
The Hegelian Conception of Natural Law Theory

3
Laws of Nature and Laws of Right: Problems in the Realization of Freedom

In the Preface to the *Philosophy of Right*, Hegel contrasts the theory of the ethical world developed in that work with the philosophy of nature. Everyone is prepared to agree that philosophy has to understand nature as it is; that nature is inherently rational, and that science has to explore and grasp the actual reason present in nature as her immanent law. On the other hand the ethical–historical world created by man, in so far as it is brought forth by his will and is subject to chance and caprice, is supposed to be devoid of law and reason.[1] In the second edition of the *Philosophy of Right* (1833) prepared by Eduard Gans, there is a lengthy footnote taking up this distinction, which is a very old one in the history of philosophy: it concerns the difference between natural and normative laws, a topic which Hegel did not deal with in the text of the work itself but only in his introductory lectures given during his time in Berlin.[2]

According to the distinction drawn in this addition, there are 'two kinds of laws, laws of nature and laws of right'. The laws of nature simply exist; their existence renders them valid, and we naturally think of the whole of nature as being determined by laws. In the sphere of laws of nature, being and validity are

[1] *Grundlinien der Philosophie des Rechts* (hereafter *GPR*) in *Sämtliche Werke*, Jubiläumsausgabe (hereafter *WWG*), ed. H. Glockner (20 vols, Stuttgart, 1927–30), Vol. VII, pp. 23 ff. (Eng. tr. T. M. Knox, *Hegel's Philosophy of Right* (hereafter *PR*) (Oxford, 1942), p. 4.) The paragraphs of this edition are the same as in Knox's translation. Gans's footnote mentioned below is printed as Addition 1 in Knox's translation.
[2] The basis of this remark, which Gans edited, is a passage from the lecture notes of H. G. Hotho taken in the Winter term of 1822–3. The notes are among the Hegel documents in the Staatsbibliothek der Stiftung Preussischer Kulturbesitz, Berlin (referred to afterwards as 'Hegel documents'). They are catalogued as 'Philosophie des Rechts. Nach dem Vortrage des H. Prof. Hegel, im Winter 1822/23, Berlin', Ms. 2, pp. 1–4. Cf. also 'Vorlesungen über Philosophie des Rechts WS 1824/25, Nachschrift von Griesheim', Ms. Germ. quart. 545, pp. 13 ff.

identical: 'These laws are true, only our view of them can be false. The measure of these laws lies outside us, and our knowledge adds nothing to them, does not modify their existence in any way; only our knowledge of them can be extended.'[3] So far they are not distinguishable from normative laws, which we likewise come to know from without as something given; and the jurist necessarily maintains this objective standpoint according to which the laws are valid precisely because they are laws. But it becomes apparent from the variety and mutability of normative laws that they are not as absolute as the laws of nature, that in their case being and validity diverge. Normative laws are laid down ('posited', *gesetzt*), they originate with man and depend upon his will and consciousness. Thus, while laws of nature directly determine the essence of things and are essentially immutable, positive laws, because of their dependence on man, are in a state of constant change. They have a history and for this reason man does not automatically recognize and accept them as valid, but mediates their existence and validity through himself, through the subjectivity of his will and consciousness. We cannot submit to power and authority stemming from laws issued by a law-giver in the way in which we bow to the necessity of natural laws which regulate the course of non-human things, for the measure of these human laws no longer lies outside ourselves but within our own breasts. A law of nature receives its highest confirmation from the simple fact of its existence, while in the sphere of right a law does not derive its justification from its mere existence but from the fact that it is known and willed. And for this reason it is only with laws of this latter kind that the conflict between being and obligation (*Sein und Sollen*) is possible.

The most important viewpoint which emerges from this contrast between laws of nature and normative laws is not, however, this dualism in the fundamental concept of natural law, which has been apparent since the time of Hobbes and Kant. What interests Hegel is a dualism that goes far deeper, the contrast between nature and spirit, which resolves the conflict between being and obligation by penetrating to its very root. Hegel's juxtaposition is sharpened into the following contrast: 'If we con-

3 See 'Hegel documents', p. 1 and *GPR*, Preface, p. 24.

emplate the difference between these two kinds of laws, and ask what is the basis of laws of right (*Gesetze des Rechts*, that is, norma- ive laws), we will conclude: right proceeds solely from the Spirit, or nature has no laws of right. And so there is a world of existing 1ature, and a spiritual world of nature, each opposed to the other.'[4] With this in mind, Hegel says in par. 4 of the *Philosophy of Right* hat the basis of right is 'spirit' and that its starting point is the free will' that wills itself and possesses in the system of right he 'realm of realized freedom' – 'the world of spirit brought orth out of itself as a second nature'.[5]

I

The world of spirit as a second nature is not the *deutera physis* of Aristotle, the native custom and morality of the *polis* based on law (*nomos*) and tradition (*éthos*), but rather a nature produced and set to work by man, and therefore closer to Hobbes' *Leviathan* han to Aristotle's *Nicomachean Ethics* or his *Politics*. In fact, lmost all the adjectives used by Hegel to distinguish laws of 1ature from normative laws are to be found in the classical contrast between 'natural' and 'artificial' societies, which Hobbes, at the beginning of modern natural law theory, insinuated into both he Aristotelian theory of the natural character of the *polis* and the raditional sophist alternative between law and nature (*nomos* and *hysis*). Concord in 'natural' societies – according to both Hobbes and Hegel the concord of animals – is 'the work of God by way of nature'. On the other hand, 'concord amongst men is artificial, and by way of covenant'.[6] And Hobbes, too, in agreement with Hegel, regards the things of nature as permanent and necessary vhile the artificial structure of laws and contracts created by men, precisely because of its dependence on human will, is held to be rbitrary and inconstant. In the background the old conceptual problem of law and nature (*nomos* and *physis*) still stands out quite

4 *Ibid.*, p. 2.
5 *GPR*, Introduction, par. 4., *PR*, p. 20.
6 *Elements of Law*, Part 1, Ch. 19, sect. 5; *De cive*, Part 2, Ch. 5, sect 5; *Leviathan*, Part 2, Ch. 17. *The English Works of Thomas Hobbes*, ed. W. Molesworth (17 volumes, London, 1836).

clearly: what is natural is independent of contracts and deeds (in Hegel, of will and consciousness), while what is artificial *is* thus dependent. But Hobbes draws from this contrast a conclusion which diverges from the sophist alternative and its solution in Plato and Aristotle. He no longer wishes to show that only natural society, that is, a society ordered according to nature's yardstick, can impose obligations on individuals while an artificial society leaves them free. On the contrary, he wants to demonstrate that only a society which is in the strict sense 'artificial' can place an obligation of obedience on its citizens, for in connection with nature the concept of obligation can no longer be used meaningfully. And so as between the alternatives of *nomos* and *physis*, the idea of obligation attaching to the concepts of 'natural' and 'artificial' has shifted from the one to the other.[7]

What this shift means for the theory of modern natural law may be seen from the function of the biblical God of the Creation who, in reducing nature to the merely created, empties her of autonomy, and bases her existence in the divine will. This has the following consequences for the concept of obligation: if the natural is still to have some binding power on men, then the basis of this obligation can no longer reside in nature, but separated from her, in the will of God. This model allows of a further transformation: an entirely new basis of obligation is now opposed to the binding power of nature, and in the process its derivation from the will of God is renounced.[8] In Hegel's view this new step was taken not by Hobbes but by Rousseau, whom he commends in par. 258 of the *Philosophy of Right*: 'by adducing the will as the principle of the state, he is adducing a principle which has thought both for its form and its content, a principle indeed which is thinking itself, not a principle, like gregarious instinct, for instance, or divine authority, which has thought as its form only'.[9] Rousseau made the 'innermost part of man', freedom as 'oneness with oneself', the foundation of right, thereby conferring on it an infinite strength *vis-à-vis* nature or the will

---

7 Cf. F. O. Wolf, *Die Neue Wissenschaft des Thomas Hobbes. Zu den Grundlagen der politischen Philosophie der Neuzeit* (Stuttgart Bad Cannstatt, 1969), pp. 82 ff.

8 *Ibid.*, p. 84, where this viewpoint is explicitly developed.

9 *GPR*, par. 258, Addition; *PR*, pp. 156 f.

of God working through nature.[10] All the same, the contrast between nature, freedom, and right already occurs in the work of Thomas Hobbes, with whom, in Hegel's view, the real history of modern natural law begins. For he was the first to try to 'trace the framework of the state and the nature of its supreme power back to principles within ourselves, which we recognize as our own'.[11] Hobbes breaks with the assumption of a teleological law of nature (*lex naturalis*) which stands above the human will and rules over the world of natural things, a law which reason need simply reflect or copy if it is to be 'right' (*recta ratio*) and lead to 'righteous' action. With Hobbes the theory of right and of society still depends on the concept of nature, only in so far as the 'law of nature' contains conditions which necessitate the abandonment of natural law. Through Hobbes an 'ambiguity' arises in the traditional expression 'natural law' which is of the greatest importance to Hegel, and he draws attention to it in his lecture on Hobbes: 'The expression "nature" is ambiguous in the sense that the nature of man is his spirituality and rationality; but his natural state is that quite other condition wherein he behaves in accordance with his brute naturalness.'[12]

According to Hegel, this ambiguity is sharpened in Rousseau, who widens Hobbes's initial breach with traditional natural law theory. Rousseau conceives of the 'spirituality' and 'rationality' of man as his freedom, which removes him from nature and is the essential mark of distinction between man and beast. While Hobbes allows the 'natural' bond of authority of the master–slave relationship to subsist side by side with the institutional or 'artificial' bond of authority which rests on the contract, Rousseau inquires into the ultimate justification of authority itself. And he makes neither positive law nor the fundamental natural laws of Hobbes the ultimate principle of justification – but freedom. Without regard for his predecessors of the seventeenth century – whom he places on a footing with Aristotle the apologist of

0 *Vorlesungen über die Geschichte der Philosophie*, in *WWG*, Vol. xix, p. 527. (Eng. tr. E. S. Haldane and F. H. Simpson, *Hegel's Lectures on the History of Philosophy* (3 vols, London, 1896).)
k Cf. *ibid.*, p. 442.
e *Ibid.*, p. 443.

human oppression and servitude, and Caligula its practitioner and without regard for the current laws of contemporar European states, 'he replies to the above question as follows: Tha man possesses free will, and freedom is what is qualitatively uniqu in man. To renounce freedom is to renounce being human. No to be free is to renounce all duties and rights.'[13] Rousseau' principle that man is free, and that the state built on the foundatioi of the 'general will' is the realization of freedom, must, so Hege says, be 'deemed correct'. 'Ambiguity' occurs in Rousseau onl when he allows the general will to be 'composed' of the separat wills of individual men, their natural inclination towards freedom The 'freedom of nature' – the spontaneity of the individual wi – cancels 'thereby freedom as the utterly absolute' as it is con ceived by Rousseau in his concept of the general will.[14] Yet fo all that, he makes us fully aware that freedom is the utterly absolute the very 'concept of man': 'Thinking itself is freedom; whoever rejects thinking and speaks of freedom knows not what he says The unity of thought with itself is freedom, the free will . . . Onl the thinking will is free. The principle of freedom arose and ha conferred on man, who conceived of himself as infinite, thi infinite strength.'[15] What the will is in itself can be grasped neithe by analogy with nature and her 'laws' nor through its simple cor trast with nature or naturally determined caprice. The will – an Rousseau's appeal to the 'general will' as the fundamental principl of the state reminds us of this – must break out of these opposite: It is only free when it 'wills nothing else, nothing external an nothing foreign – for then it would be dependent – but onl itself; when it wills the will. To will to be free is the absolut

13 *Ibid.*, p. 527. Hegel quotes the well-known section of *The Social Contract*, Book Ch. 4 (see the edition by Charles Frankel (New York, 1947)). Cf. also Chs. 1, 8, Book III, Ch. 9. Cf. *Discours sur l'origine de l'inégalité parmi les hommes*, ed. K. Weigax (Hamburg, 1955), pp. 106 ff. Cf. also *Vorlesungen über die Philosophie der Weltgeschichte*, e G. Lasson (4 vols, Leipzig, 1917–20), Vol. IV (1920), pp. 920 ff.

14 *Vorlesungen über die Geschichte der Philosophie*, in *WWG*, Vol. XIX, p. 528. 'These principle expressed in this abstract way, must be deemed right; yet ambiguity soon arises. Ma is free, and indeed this is the substantial nature of man. Not only is freedom n surrendered in the state, but in fact it is established there for the first time. The freedo of nature, the propensity for freedom, is not yet true freedom, for only the sta is the actualization of freedom.' Cf. further *Enzyklopädie*, par. 163; *GPR*, par. 25 PR, pp. 155 ff.

15 *Vorlesungen über die Geschichte der Philosophie*, *WWG*, Vol. XIX, pp. 528 ff.

will.' With this notion of the free will Rousseau completes the
inversion begun by Hobbes of the teleology of nature – which
is the basis of the *lex naturalis* of traditional natural law – into
the subjectivity of the individual who thinks and wills himself.
In place of the binding power of nature and the ambiguous
recourse to the will of God, we are given the binding power
of the will become absolute. This transformation of the Hobbesian
model by Rousseau was recognized by Hegel as the most important
presupposition of his own concept of right.

The absolute will consists in the will to be free. The will that wills
itself is the basis of all right and of all obligation, hence of all positive
laws, moral duties, and imposed obligations. Freedom of the will itself,
as such, is the principle and substantial foundation of all right, is indeed
itself absolute, eternal right, and the very highest, in so far as other,
specific rights may be placed beside it; it is indeed even the essence
of what makes man truly man, that is, the fundamental principle of
spirit.[16]

It is from this point that Hegel deduces the transition to the
Kantian philosophy. Kant puts an end to the 'ambiguity' still
present in Rousseau's concept of natural law by making a radical
distinction between the laws of nature and those of freedom,
between the 'empirical' and the 'free and pure will'.[17] From the
viewpoint of transcendental philosophy the 'concept' of the will
attains to an understanding of itself. The 'simple unity of self-
consciousness', the 'ego' dissolved from all preceding natural
causes, is the

unassailable, utterly independent freedom and source of all general
determinations of thought – theoretical reason; and likewise the highest
factor in all practical determinations – practical reason as free and pure
will; and the reason belonging to the will aims simply to maintain itself
in a state of pure freedom, to will nothing but this in all specific instances,
to will right only for the sake of right, duty only for the sake of duty.[18]

'Consciousness of the spirit' thereby becomes the foundation of
the philosophy of right. It discovers 'a principle of thought for
the state . . . which is now no longer some principle derived merely

16 *Vorlesungen über die Philosophie der Weltgeschichte*, pp. 921 ff.
17 *Ibid.*, pp. 529 ff., 552, 590.
18 *Ibid.*, p. 22.

from opinion, like the social instinct, the need for security of property etc., nor of piety, like the divine institution of authority, but the principle of *certainty*, which is identity with my self-consciousness . . .'[19]

II

This characterization of the principle of right as it occurs in Hobbes, Rousseau, and Kant must be kept in mind if one wishes to grasp the relationship between nature and freedom in Hegel's *Philosophy of Right*, and to understand the peculiarly ambivalent position of this work at the close of modern natural law theory. Hegel stands on the ground of natural law theory prepared by Hobbes, and does so in two ways: on the one hand he adopts the concept of nature which constitutes this theory, and on the other the presupposition of a will emancipated from given natural and historical forces, a will which, through its own movement, must first come into relations with things and then adjust them to itself. The *Philosophy of Right* shares with the natural law theories of the seventeenth and eighteenth centuries an essentially restricted definition of nature from which is absent the notion of 'natural' ends and their organization towards the realization of an 'ultimate' end. As a part of the philosophy of spirit, the *Philosophy of Right* knows of no graduated scale of nature each of whose members occupies a natural position on it, and which, according to the scholastic notion, has its continuation in the 'realm of grace' (*regnum gratiae*). It further knows nothing of the doctrine of pre-established harmony between the 'kingdom of nature' and the 'kingdom of ends', which both obey various causal laws and in which, by virtue of this harmony, the paths of nature lead automatically to the state of grace.[20] The realm of the spirit, whose realization this work presents, presupposes a teleology which is immanent in the free will itself and constitutes that movement of the 'concept' which pervades all reality and therein wins its freedom. The graduated scale of the spirit does not fall into the

19 *Ibid.*, p. 924. Cf. in this connection my essay 'Hegels Kritik des Naturrechts' in *Hegel-Studien*, IV (1967), 178 ff., and see Ch. 4 of this volume.
20 Leibniz, *Monadology*, tr. P. G. Lucas and L. Grint (Manchester, 1953), par. 88.

category of natural concepts; it rests upon its own essence, and for Hegel this means: on freedom which only exists as a continuing liberation from nature and the production of a 'second nature', of the world of spirit. The realm of spirit is the realm of freedom, and as such no natural hierarchy or otherworldly kingdom of spirits, but the 'world of the spirit brought forth from within itself'.[21] Within this world – this 'second nature' – nature and freedom stand to each other as does spirit to nature – in an antagonistic relationship. 'The nature of spirit may be understood from its most perfect opposite. We oppose spirit to matter. Just as weight is the substance of matter, so we are moved to say that freedom is the substance of spirit.'[22]

It is the same antagonism which affects the concept of nature as it occurs in natural law theory. This concept, which in the doctrine of the state of nature plays both a fundamental and fateful role, contains for Hegel an

important ambiguity which can lead to absolute error. On the one hand nature means our natural existence, us as we directly know ourselves in our various facets, the immediate aspect of our being. But over against this determination, and different from it, nature is also the concept. The nature of a thing is the concept of a thing, what it is from the point of view of reason, and this can be something quite other than merely natural.[23]

If nature designates the concept of a thing, then right in the state of nature must be conceived of as that form of right 'that is fitting for man according to his concept, the concept of spirit'. But this must not be confused with what the spirit is in its natural state, the state of servitude and dependence on nature. For this reason Hegel says with Hobbes and Spinoza: 'Exeundum est e statu naturae.'

The ateleological character of this utterance, seen against the backdrop of modern natural science, takes on a curious sharpness and pointedness. When nature was defined as an order moved by final ends, freedom could be related to it, and human action

21 GPR, par. 4; PR, pp. 20 f. Enzyklopädie, par. 387.
22 Die Vernunft in der Geschichte, ed. J. Hoffmeister, 5th edn (Hamburg, 1955), p. 55; Enzyklopädie, par. 381, Addition.
23 Die Vernunft in der Geschichte, p. 117.

thought of as its continuation or imitation. With the transformation of nature into a mathematically describable and mechanically conceived causal system, this reference back to nature becomes impossible. The idea of freedom – and Kant's *Critique of Pure Reason* makes this abundantly clear for the whole modern era – can no longer find in nature the analogy of natural ends, and therefore turns in upon itself. This is also of decisive importance for Hegel's *Philosophy of Right*. It is true that Hegel finds in the concept of gravity a kind of natural analogy for the basic concept of freedom, but here we have a category which itself has only made its mark on the conception of nature since the advent of Newtonian physics. Freedom of the will is best understood, so we are told in the Addition to par. 4 of the *Philosophy of Right*, by 'reference' to physical nature. Freedom and gravity are 'fundamental properties' of the will and of bodies, that is, properties which are not contingent but necessary and essential, conditions of their very existence:

When one says that matter is heavy, one might suppose that this predicate is only incidental: yet it is not incidental, for it is not as though there were something about material which is heavy: material is rather gravity itself. Gravity constitutes a body and is the body itself. And the same goes for freedom and the will, for what is free is will. Will without freedom is an empty word, just as freedom is only real as will, as thinking subject.[24]

In the case of weight, natural bodies strive towards a central point, the centre of gravity of the system formed by the relative position of these bodies in space. But this centre remains permanently outside them. In the case of freedom as the fundamental determination of the will, the will refers permanently to itself. Indeed, such self-reference is precisely the essence or substance of will, which likewise strives towards a centre, but a centre which it already possesses in itself: 'It does not have unity outside itself; it finds it constantly within itself, it is in and with itself (*in und bei Sichselbst*). Matter has its substance outside itself; spirit on the other hand is self-contained being (*Beisichselbstsein*), and this precisely is freedom.'[25]

24 *GPR*, par. 4, Addition; *PR*, pp. 225 ff.
25 *Die Vernunft in der Geschichte*, p. 55.

The second presupposition which Hegel shares with modern natural law theory concerns the movement of the will. It is on this that the *Philosophy of Right* rests, rather than on the teleological structure of social and political institutions arranged in complex tiers one above the other, as we know it from Aristotelian–scholastic natural law theory. Although Hegel expressly distances himself from the theoretical extremes of Hobbes, Rousseau, and Kant, the overall position of the *Philosophy of Right* remains in an important respect one of natural law: its conceptual development begins with the 'individual will of the subject' in its relations with the things of nature (property) and with other individual wills (contract).[26] It begins with a form of 'abstract' right which reproduces the pre-political condition of natural law theory. The impulse issuing from the individual will – and this is often overlooked – permeates the whole system, stretching even to the derivation of the will concentrated in the 'state' which, according to Hegel, must likewise be an 'individual' will, that of the monarch.[27] Admittedly this individual will is not 'free' in the sense of natural law, it is not the chance individual whim and impulse of each and all from whose reciprocal restriction right, the concept of the general will, arises. It is because Hegel first introduces the will as the object of the *Philosophy of Right* only after he has, in his doctrine of subjective spirit, purged it of all incidental causal determinations, that the movement of the work stems from the 'general' will already contained in the individual will. And so the free will for Hegel is the 'unity of the rational will with the individual will, which latter is the immediate and peculiar element of the activity of the former'.[28]

Yet this does not mean any retraction of the idea of natural law; on the contrary, it means in reality an enormous intensification of it.[29] For it is no longer the individual as such, in his naturalness, who is the object and point of departure of the doctrine of right,

---

26 Cf. *Enzyklopädie*, pars. 400 ff.; *GPR*, pars. 34 ff; *PR*, pp. 27 ff. Hegel repeatedly emphasized the moment of individuality which belongs to the immediacy of the free will, as for example in pars. 13, 39, 43, 46, 52.

27 See *GPR*, par. 279 with the Remark to par. 281; *PR*, pp. 181 ff. in addition, cf. par. 190, and *Enzyklopädie*, 2nd edn, par. 514.

28 See *Enzyklopädie*, 2nd edn, par. 485; also *GPR*, pars. 2, 4.

29 Cf. F. Rosenzweig, *Hegel und der Staat* (Munich/Berlin, 1920), Vol. II, pp. 106 ff.

but the individual as a rational being. While Kant and Fichte restrict the concept of freedom revealed by them to the field of ethics, and take as a basis for natural law the naturally determined free whim and impulse of each and all, Hegel makes use of this concept in his doctrine of right as well. Right is not the restriction of the free will but its very 'being' – 'freedom as Idea'. This new twist means for Hegel that freedom is no longer a postulate (an 'idea' in the Kantian sense), but reality, something actually given in the historical–social world, and not just something yet to be achieved. The dialectic is necessary in order to grasp this reality, and in the introduction to the *Philosophy of Right* Hegel applies it to the natural law 'concept' of the will. According to Hegel, Kant does discover in the principle of the transcendental ego the fundamental basis of the self-determination of the will, the moment of 'pure indeterminacy or of the pure reflection of the I into itself', in which all limitation and every content 'given' by nature is dissolved. But freedom of the will, considered in itself, would be merely negative. In the political sphere it would lead – as did indeed happen during the French Revolution in accordance with Rousseau's theory – to the 'destruction of all existing social order' and the 'annihilation of all organization striving to re-emerge'.[30] The ego as the pure concept of the will thus necessarily contains a second moment, the 'determining and positing of something definite as content and object', whereby it posits itself as determined, that is, comes into existence. This something specific which determines and limits the will is not a given external limitation, but – according to Hegel, this is a point overlooked by Kant and Fichte – is immanent in the very act of self-determination. In the unity of these two moments, the undetermined universality and the determined particularity of the will, freedom is realized as the third moment. 'It is the *self*-determination of the ego, which means that at one and the same time the ego posits itself as its own negative, that is, as restricted and determinate, and yet remains by itself, that is, in its self-identity and universality. It determines itself and yet at the same time binds itself together with itself.'[31]

30 *GPR*, par. 5; *PR*, p. 22.
31 *Ibid.*, par. 7; *PR*, p. 23.

III

This dialectical movement of the free will which combines the moment of the universal and the particular, and reconciles both with itself into 'concrete' individuality, into the 'existence of the free will' (par. 29), is that 'nature of the thing' which we encounter in Hegel's *Philosophy of Right* as the 'concept'. The concept contains within itself the full sense of nature; it designates nothing other than that form of right which, along with all its determinations, is based on the 'free personality', on 'self-determination which is the very opposite of natural determination'.[32] The dialectical 'person' who is free from all 'natural' determinations. It begins with the infinite 'concept' of the free will unlimited by anything external to itself as the sole principle of right.

This connection between concept (= nature), freedom and right was repeatedly discussed by Hegel in the Berlin lectures on the philosophy of right. The first lecture given in the year 1818–19 – before the appearance of the work itself – goes into this question in par. 3:

The principle of right does not reside in nature, at any rate not in external nature, nor indeed in the subjective nature of man in so far as his will is naturally determined, i.e., is the sphere of needs, impulses, and inclinations. The sphere of right is the sphere of freedom in which nature, in so far as freedom externalizes itself and gives itself existence, does indeed appear, but only as something dependent.[33]

Manifestations of freedom are all aspects of the objective, historical–social reality of man as they are represented by the *Philosophy of Right*, beginning with the outward forms of abstract right and leading to the family, civil society, and the state. It need scarcely be said that, in all of these, 'natural' relations and forms of existence play a part. The question is whether they produce out of themselves a law which rules over those forms.

---

32 *Ibid.* Cf. also the *Nürnberger Propädeutik*, in *WWG*, Vol. III, pp. 55, 71, and especially *Propädeutik*, Part 3, sec. 2; *Enzyklopädie*, Part 3, par. 181: 'The spirit as a free, self-conscious being is the self-identical I, i.e., that I that is first of all utterly exclusive in its absolutely negative relations, a single free being or person.'

33 'Hegel documents', Ms. Germ. quart. 1155, p. 9; 'Natur und Staatsrecht nach d. Vortrag des Professors Hegel im Winterhalbjahr 1818/19 von G. Homeyer'.

The necessity ascribed, for example, to the existence of the state in relation to the being of the individual no longer means in Hegel that for the individual it is a law of nature to have to live in the state. The necessity of the state rests much more upon that law which freedom prescribes to itself. On this point Hegel's elucidation of par. 3 is unambiguous:

This paragraph is prompted by the term 'natural law'. The unification of freedom and necessity has been brought about not by nature, but by freedom. Natural things remain as they are and have not freed themselves from law in order to make laws for themselves. But spirit breaks away from nature and produces for itself its own nature and its own laws. Thus nature is not the basis of right.

As for Kant and Fichte,[34] so too for Hegel, the term 'natural law' is 'merely traditional'. Indeed, it is even wrong from the point of view of the 'concept' of right itself, because 'by nature' is to be understood as (1) the essence, the concept; (2) unconscious nature (the proper meaning). The 'proper' name of the subject should be 'philosophical jurisprudence'.[35]

Thus at the time when he was working out the system of the philosophy of right, the development of Hegel's thought leads straight back to that philosophy of freedom which the early essay on natural law ('Über die wissenschaftlichen Behandlungsarten des Naturrechts') sought to overcome by the construction of a law of 'ethical nature'. But at the end of a long process of coming to understand the basic concepts of 'philosophical jurisprudence' – a process which at the same time clarifies its historical relationship to traditional natural law theory – there can be no question of resort to this solution. Nature and freedom, the law of nature and the law of right, have parted company in Hegel too. He thus emphatically rejects the traditional view that the 'law of nature', in so far as man is willing to recognize and follow it, might serve him as a 'model' of law. The only law which governs the historical existence of man is the law of freedom, which is not given by

---

34 See Kant, *Reflexionen zur Moralphilosophie* 7084, in *Kants gesammelte Schriften*, ed. Königlich Preussische Akademie der Wissenschaften (22 vols, Berlin/Leipzig, 1900–42), Vol xix (1934), p. 245; Fichte, *Grundlagen des Naturrechts*, in *Sämtliche Werke*, Vol. iii, p. 148. (Eng. tr. A. E. Kroeger, *The Science of Rights* (Philadelphia, 1870).)

35 'Hegel documents' as n. 33.

'nature' but by the 'concept' itself.[36] The concept becoming its own legislator means for Hegel the eighteenth-century idea of man's universal eligibility for rights,[37] with which philosophy rose against the existing state of affairs and broke down the façade of naturalness behind which the idea of law, that is, freedom, had until then been hidden. Positive law now becomes inseparable from the knowledge of this idea.

Admittedly, as is pointed out in the introductory lecture of 1824–5, in 'conventional natural law', which has nature, natural needs, goals, etc., as its basis, the idea of freedom is not consciously excluded, but 'in effect it is neglected, for both principles are taken up without due assessment of their characteristic features'. Freedom cannot be thought in the form of nature but must be thought in the form of the 'concept', which reconciles freedom with itself and nature. And if freedom comes forward with the claims of the 'concept', which assert that it is only freedom 'that is at stake in matters of law and ethics, then the term "natural law" begins to totter'.[38] One could only retain it by conceding that freedom is the 'nature of the thing' postulated by natural law, i.e., the 'concept'. But the expression is nevertheless 'inappropriate', for nature, in contrast to freedom, is 'basic, not opposed to anything else. Freedom on the other hand appears to be polemical, it has opposites, and the first of these is nature itself.'[39]

IV

This opposition of nature and freedom decisively shapes the system and concepts of Hegel's *Philosophy of Right*. It determines not only the demarcation of 'philosophical jurisprudence' and 'natural law' in the double title of the work,[40] but also the doubling

---

36 *Ibid.*, p. 3; 'The concept of the thing does not come to us from nature.'

37 *Ibid.*, p. 5; 'We must find something lofty in the fact that now man, because he is man, must be regarded as possessing rights, so that his human essence is higher than his status.'

38 'Hegel documents', 'Nachschrift von Griesheim', pp. 9 ff. (see n. 2).

39 *Ibid.*, p. 10.

40 Hegel expressly refers to this in his lectures of 1824–5. Cf. Griesheim as above, p. 3; and my essay: 'Tradition und Revolution in Hegels "Philosophie des Rechts"' in *Zeitschrift für philosophische Forschung*, XVI (1962), 206 ff. (Reprinted in my *Studien zu Hegels Rechtsphilosophie*.)

which the last and most important section of the system undergoes with the introduction of the concept of 'civil society' beside family and state. For the difference between civil society and state has its basis in the separation of the concepts of nature and freedom, a separation which historically is thought through to an end in Hegel. True, in the course of the development of modern natural law the identity of state (*civitas, res publica*) and civil society (*societas civilis*) is dissolved. This identity of state and civil society was the characteristic hallmark of the traditional ('feudal') theory of state and society, and received philosophical legitimation from the teleology of the *lex naturalis*, which made the natural ends (impulses, needs, etc.) of separate individuals coincide with the ethical end of the whole. But the dissolution of this identity does not lead to a permanent distinction; it is overcome time and time again.

Paradoxically, the cause of this lies in the natural law doctrine of contract, which is the catalyst both of this separation and of its overcoming. The view that the teleological order of nature transcends the individual and civil society is abandoned, but nature nevertheless enters the construction of the contract, at the point of departure of natural law theory, as the caprice (*Willkür*) of the many. It is the needs, instincts and inclinations which, contained in the category of 'free caprice', must be restrained by the concept of law so that the capricious will of each can harmonize with the will of all under a universal law, which replaces the now discarded natural law. Here is to be sought the real motive for the polemical separation of the principles of law and freedom as against Kant and Rousseau, on which Hegel sets great store in his philosophy of right. At the same time he is also fully aware in this context of the differences between Rousseau's and Kant's conceptions of nature, and that of the older natural law theories. The traditional mode of treatment in which 'the two meanings' of the concept of nature are still unseparated takes as its basis the 'natural being' of man, his inclinations, needs, impulses: first, his physical needs and the necessity of their satisfaction, but then also the 'impulse towards sociability and society which is connected on the one hand with relations between the sexes, and on the other is extended into universal civil society' which in

LAWS OF NATURE AND RIGHT

turn 'develops into the state'.[41] But it is precisely at this point that for Hegel the 'unsatisfactory nature of this connection' appears. There is no teleology of nature to reconcile the instincts and needs of individuals with the ethical–historical existence of the 'state'. All determinations deduced from the instinctual nature of man remain 'abstract' in comparison with what the state and civil society are according to the 'concept':

If we are to say that civil society and the state arise out of instinctual impulse, then at once the unsatisfactory nature of this connection, of the state arising from impulse, is apparent. The impulse towards sociability which philosophy formerly accepted as the basis of the state is something indefinite and abstract which can only furnish some of the necessary conditions for the vast and highly structured state, and which appears excessively thin beside the phenomenon it is meant to explain.[42]

To this natural principle which was first abandoned by Hobbes, Rousseau, and after him Kant and Fichte, oppose the principle of freedom. But, as Hegel says in the lectures of 1824–5, this is done 'in a manner which is not ours, and which did not permit jurisprudence to develop into a complete and coherent system'.[43] Hegel agrees with Kant that freedom under the laws of nature is impossible since nature and freedom are opposed to one another. For this reason he rejects, like Kant, the question posed by the traditional teleological conception of nature concerning the 'historical origins of the state',[44] or, to use the traditional terminology of politics and natural law, the question of the 'beginning of civil society'. For the philosophy of right is only concerned with the 'Idea of the state', with the 'thought as concept' (*gedachten Begriff*). But in Kant and Fichte, and in Rousseau before them, the principle which they make the basis of jurisprudence contradicts their exposition of it. On the one hand the principle of the state – that principle 'which is not just thought in its form, like the social instinct or divine authority, but thought in its content' because 'thinking itself' is will – excludes nature from itself. And

41 Cf. Griesheim as above, pp. 5–8. Cf. *Philosophie des Rechts*, Introduction, par. 19.
42 Cf. Griesheim, p. 8.
43 *Ibid.*, p. 11. Cf. 'Hegel documents', Hotho, pp. 7 ff. (see n. 2).
44 Cf. *Philosophie des Rechts*, par. 258.

yet on the other hand, Rousseau, Kant and Fichte reintroduce nature by placing, in the forefront of their theories, will in its specific form as the 'individual will',[45] the 'particular individual'. As a result of this they conceive of the 'general will' of the 'concept' of the state, not as the 'absolutely rational part of the will, but only as the common good (*das Gemeinschaftliche*) which emerges from this individual will'. And hence the more recent natural law theory, and with it the classical liberalism of the nineteenth century, retreat to the viewpoint of older natural law theory, in their attitude to the 'concept' of state and civil society. The construction of the contract, which in Hobbes, Rousseau and Kant presupposes the dissolution of the classical identity of *civitas* and *societas civilis*, repeats that confusion of two separate conceptual spheres which Hegel uses in par. 182 of the *Philosophy of Right* as an objection to the natural law view of the state.[46]

The fact of such an objection presupposes that Hegel had drawn for himself the conclusions that follow from the approach of modern natural law theory. By radicalizing the contrast between laws of nature and laws of freedom, Hegel relinquishes, along with the traditional term 'natural law', the term 'civil society' (*societas civilis*). The abandonment of the latter was to prove incomparably the richer in results. With Hegel's separation of state and civil society, a whole new perspective of problems concerning human life and will was opened up. The relations of individuals with one another and with nature were given theoretical independence and set in relative isolation, and could now be conceived of and studied as 'social' relations. The naturally determined individual will, the 'particular individual' and his needs, impulses and inclinations, is no longer directly and fundamentally related to the universal will manifest in the state. Precisely because of this it becomes possible for Hegel to discern in that 'system of needs' the economic basis of modern society which had been concealed from the liberal followers of the natural law theory by

---

45 Cf. *ibid.*, pars. 258; 29, 182, Addition; *Die Vernunft in der Geschichte*, pp. 111 ff.
46 *Philosophie des Rechts*, par. 182, Addition: 'If the state is represented as a unity of different persons, as a unity which is only partnership, then what is really meant is only civil society. Many modern constitutional lawyers have been able to bring within their purview no theory of the state but this.'

the model of the social contract and its political implications. It is therefore apparent that the problem of the relationship between nature and freedom finds no satisfactory solution in the philosophy of right; on the contrary, it re-emerges on a new level. The 'freedom as Idea', which demands the conceptual liberation of civil society from the state, descends, on this new level, from reality to appearance – 'the world of ethical appearance', in which ethical identity cannot be thought of as freedom but only as necessity.[47] The cluster of concepts centred on the sphere of the free will is here on the verge of being transformed into the law of development of society, a law which has as its basis nature, instead of the freedom presupposed by the concept. This is the 'element of inequality' which gives expression to the objective right of particularity of mind, and not only fails to cancel the inequality given by nature, but indeed 'produces it out of spirit'.[48] Here lies one of the seminal points in Hegel's philosophy of right against which the dialectic of the concept of will strikes as against a barrier – a barrier which Hegel's most important and historically most influential pupil, Marx, sought to surmount by the 'material-ist inversion' of this dialectic into the development of relations of production.

47 *Ibid.*, par. 186. Cf. pars. 184–5.
48 *Ibid.*, par. 200. A minimum reference to nature which is indispensable to the concept is further to be found in the deduction of hereditary monarchy (pars. 280 ff.) and in the justification of war (par. 324).

4

Criticism of Natural Law Theory

Hegel scholarship has made widely divergent judgments about particular passages of Hegel's essay in the *Critical Journal of Philosophy* (1802–3) – a work which develops his first major critique of the previous 'scientific modes of dealing with natural law' – but a nearly unanimous judgment as to the whole. Briefly summarized, the claim is that, if one disregards the obscurities of some of its particular passages, the essay on natural law already contains the outlines of the *Philosophy of Right* (1821). As in so many other cases, the source of this view is Karl Rosenkranz. According to him, Hegel, in his mature philosophy of right, simply repeats all the same concepts more distinctly and in greater detail within a more ingenious systematic structure; the 'immature form' of the journal essay, on the other hand, shows up the concepts' initial originality and gives them a 'more beautiful, fresher, indeed partially truer' expression.[1] Rosenkranz's judgment is echoed in the presentations of Hegel by Theodor Haering and Hermann Glockner, both of whom are representative of the neo-Hegelianism of the period between 1910 and 1945. Glockner goes the further, saying simply that with the natural law essay Hegel appears as a 'complete' moral philosopher,[2] even before the final shaping of his dialectical method. We ask: is this the case? Unquestionably, the essay outstrips all the earlier works of the young Hegel in the richness of its content and its relatively perspicuous systematic arrangement. But it remains debatable whether, and to what extent, Hegel ever does better in the employment of basic concepts. Neo-Hegelianism ignored this question in favour of a substantive interest in the concept of 'absolute ethical life' (the people, govern-

1 *Hegels Leben* (Berlin, 1844), pp. 173 f.
2 *Hegel*, 2nd edn (2 vols., Stuttgart, 1958), Vol. II, p. 308. Also compare Th. Haering *Hegel, Sein Wollen und Sein Werk* (2 vols., Leipzig/Berlin, 1938), Vol. II, pp. 398 f., 404 f

ment, etc.). To decide the issue one must reflect on basic theoretical concepts which ground the ethical–political categories of the Hegelian concept of natural law. First and foremost among these is the concept of 'nature'. That this essentially obvious problem has not been pursued up to now in the Hegel literature is even more surprising since Hegel himself believed that the connection between 'natural' and 'law', as it is expressed in the title of this essay, required reflection. Working from this problem, it is possible to trace the development of Hegel's philosophy of right and, what is more, to understand the place which it occupies in the history of modern natural law theory. It will become obvious that both these aspects are dependent on the insight which Hegel achieved in the ontological foundation of his philosophy; and, hence, that he appears before us as a 'complete' moral philosopher only when the grounding of the dialectical method has advanced far enough to provide a guide for settling accounts with the traditional concepts in the field of natural law as well.

I

It is crucial for the systematic and historical importance of the journal essay that in its critical sections it is limited to a debate with modern theories of natural law. According to Hegel, in the history of natural law theory two mutually opposed scientific methods had been developed for dealing with the concept: the 'empirical' method of the seventeenth century and the 'formal' method of the late eighteenth century. The former abstracted singular aspects, such as the drive for self-preservation, sociability, or unsociability, from the multiplicity of natural and ethical relationships, which it took as comprising the essence of practical empirical experience, gave them the form of unified concepts, and elevated them to the rank of fundamental principles within the scientific system. The latter distinguished the form of unity, which it took to be the essence of practical reason, from empirical experience, fixed it in the concept of the intrinsically pure will, and opposed it to the multiplicity of empirical relations. Although the two methods differ specifically in the fact that the principles of one are 'the relations and mixtures of empirical perception with the universal (while the principle of the other is absolute opposition and absolute universality)', for Hegel both the 'ingredients' of the systems and their mode of handling them are identical: intuition and concept, separation and fixing of particular determinations, the opposition or incomplete connection of the latter.[3] The systems have a common basis in the separation of moral law (*lex moralis sive naturalis*) from empirical nature, a separation on which the 'recent definition of the concept of natural law and its relation to the whole science of ethics' depends.[4] To clarify this, Hegel uses the example of the 'empirical' method of the seventeenth century. In trying to subordinate practical experience to conceptual unity, the pure empirical experience in which each aspect of nature stands on equally basic grounds with the others is methodically destroyed; and 'chaos', a negative concept of nature, becomes the system's point of origin. Instead of positive nature as it is grasped in 'pure' empirical experience, without disturbing the 'position of the manifold', we find a negative concept of nature – either in the 'representation of existence in fantasy' as a *state of nature*, or in the 'form of potentiality and abstraction' as a list of given anthropological capacities, i.e., of the *nature of man*.[5] From the negative unity of these determinations – the state of nature on the one side and human nature on the other – it is not possible to deduce the positive unity of the ethical state from which they have been abstracted. The empirical method must therefore either presuppose other natural properties (such as a gregarious instinct and a fear of death) as a basis for the transition or else have recourse to positive historical explanations (like the subjection of the weak by the strong).[6]

According to Hegel, the *negation of nature*, as the characteristic

---

3 See 'Über die wissenschaftlichen Behandlungsarten des Naturrechts' (hereafter 'Naturrecht'), pp. 328 ff., 332. The page references to this work as well as to 'Glauben und Wissen' and to 'Differenz des Fichte'schen und Schelling'schen Systems der Philosophie' are to Hegel's *Werke*, ed. P. Marheineke *et al.* (18 vols., Berlin, 1832–45) (hereafter *Werke*), Vol. 1 (This includes Hegel's *Sämtliche Werke*, Jubiläumsausgabe (hereafter *WWG*), ed. H. Glockner (20 vols., Stuttgart, 1927–30), Vol. 1 (1927), since in this case the pagination of the two editions is the same.) The English text is cited from Hegel, *Natural Law* (hereafter *NL*), tr. T. M. Knox (Philadelphia, 1975), p. 59

4 *WWG*, Vol. 1, p. 359; *NL*, p. 83.

5 *WWG*, Vol. 1, pp. 333 f., *NL*, p. 63.

6 *WWG*, Vol. 1, p. 337; *NL*, p. 65.

systematic basis for natural law in the seventeenth century, reached its culmination in the philosophies of Kant and Fichte. While Hegel recognizes here that – in the systems of Hobbes, Spinoza, and Pufendorf – the ethical whole achieves a kind of 'harmony', if only a 'formless and external' one, it is his intention to show how the idealistic theory of natural law in its formalism 'vainly attempts to achieve a positive organization'.[7] The incomplete separation of nature and concept, which makes it possible within the empirical method to recover particular aspects of the natural, gives way to a complete 'absolute' antithesis; nature appears in the idealistic systems as an unsubstantial abstraction of the many opposed by an equally unsubstantial abstraction of the one: practical reason.[8] Hegel has already pointed out the consequences for the principles of natural law and the construction of 'human society' which follows from this beginning in the essay 'Die Differenz des Fichte'schen und Schelling'schen Systems der Philosophie' (1801). The results achieved there, which are pre-supposed rather than recounted in the journal essay, actually complement the critique of the empirical method for dealing with natural law. According to Hegel, nature has meaning in Kant (but more so in Fichte) to the extent that it is dependent on concepts. Fichte exacerbates this dependence to the point that the concept dominates nature, and nothing about this is altered by the fact that nature, the implicitly unconscious product of the ego, is itself ego. As outer nature (determinateness) it is formally derived in Fichte's natural law theory only for the purpose of clarifying the 'determinate nature' of the ego, its instinctual character.[9] Hegel sums up his criticism in these words: 'The actions of intelligence in [Fichte's] *Natural Law* only produced nature

7 See *WWG*, Vol. 1, pp. 329 and 337; *NL*, pp. 59, 64.
8 *WWG*, Vol. 1, p. 345; *NL*, p. 71.
9 See 'Die Differenz des Fichte'schen und Schelling'schen Systems der Philosophie' (hereafter 'Differenz'), pp. 226 ff.; *The Difference between Fichte's and Schelling's Systems of Philosophy* (hereafter *DFS*), tr. H. S. Harris and Walter Cerf (Albany, 1977), pp. 135 ff. The particular relevance of the concept of nature in Hegel's criticism results from its philosophical origin in the method of objective positing by the transcendental imagination taken over from Schelling. Cf. p. 226 (*DFS*, p. 135): 'The ego remains a subjective subject object because the subjectivity of transcendental intuition is held fast. This is most strikingly apparent in the *relation of the ego to nature*. We can see it both in the deduction of nature and in the sciences founded on that deduction.'

as modifiable material; so it was not a free, ideal action; it was the action of intellect, not reason.'[10]

Hegel counters nature's fragmentation at the hands of the concept, a fragmentation which is expressed 'in all its harshness' in Fichte's system,[11] by developing a notion of natural law which tries to restore the original relationship between nature and law. He takes the task of natural law theory to be the construction of 'the true positive (which) belongs to natural law as is implied in its name' – that it 'is to construct how ethical nature attains its true right'.[12] The positive element, which is incorporated in the name 'natural law', leads Hegel to the method of positing nature and morality absolutely which characterizes the first phase in the development of his philosophy of right.[13] But this only

10 *WWG*, Vol. I, p. 247; *DES*, p. 153. Cf. also 'Glauben and Wissen', pp. 140 ff. (Eng. tr. W. Cerf and H. S. Harris, *Faith and Knowledge* (Albany, 1977).)

11 Cf. 'Differenz', p. 234; *DFS*, p. 142. 'In the exposition and deduction of nature, as it is given in [Fichte's] *System of Natural Law*, the absolute opposition of nature and Reason ... [reveals itself] ... in all its harshness.' As nature is what is 'posited by the Ego' (p. 226; *DFS*, p. 136), so freedom is 'purely negative'. It is the absolutely undetermined whose determination is possible only in perennial self-limitation – 'this concept of limitation constitutes a realm of freedom where every truly free, reciprocal relation of life, every relation that is infinite and unlimited for itself, that is to say, beautiful, is nullified; for the living being is rent into concept and matter; and nature goes into servitude' (pp. 236 f; *DFS*, p. 144). Hegel repeatedly brings up the fact that Fichte does not conceive nature as living, independent and effective as the 'expression of the inner fullness and force of bodies' (p. 248; *DFS*, p. 153). Cf. p. 230 (*DFS*, p. 139): 'It follows that both in the theoretical and in the practical respect *Nature* is something essentially determined and lifeless'; p. 232 (*DFS*, p. 140): for Fichte reason remains as nothing but the '*idea* of the independence of the Ego and of the absolute determinacy of nature, which is posited as something to be negated, something absolutely dependent'; p. 233 (*DFS*, p. 141): 'The transcendental standpoint ... extracts the subject-objectivity from what appears as nature, and there remains nothing to nature but the dead shell of objectivity'; and p. 235 (*DFS*, p. 142): the 'basic character of nature' is to be 'an absolute opposite'. Cf. 'Glauben und Wissen', pp. 136 f., 140, 142.

12 'Naturrecht', p. 397; *NL*, p. 113. This passage was overlooked by H. Glockner. He erroneously reports that in the journal essay Hegel calls the philosophy of right the science of natural law only because it had no other title in the eighteenth century and not 'because perhaps he himself advocates the standpoint which we today call the natural law tradition'. Cf. Glockner, *Hegel*, Vol. II, p. 304.

13 See *WWG*, Vol. I, p. 372: to determine the true concept of natural law and its relation to the practical sciences, the 'aspect of infinity' must be stressed, i.e., the 'positive element' must be presupposed, that 'the absolute moral totality is nothing other than a people'. Cf. further 'System der Sittlichkeit' (Eng. tr. H. S. Harris and T. M. Knox, *System of Ethical Life and First Philosophy of Spirit* (Albany, 1979)), pp. 415, 406 f., 462 (pagination according to Hegel, *Schriften zur Politik und Rechtsphilosophie*, ed. G. Lasson (Leipzig, 1913)), 'Differenz', p. 242.

means that, struggling against the negative concept of nature assumed by current systems of natural law, he is compelled to revert to an earlier time's natural theory of law and society. Here lies the significance of Hegel's terminological and substantive connection with Schelling, evidenced in the writings of the early Jena period. The concept of nature, borrowed from Schelling's *Naturphilosophie*, is the traditional teleological one, which Hegel attempts to renew as a fruitful basic principle for natural law.[14] This theory of nature is distinguished by its engagement with the system of ethical life as a whole rather than in the form of particular determinations. It stands neither in opposition to some absolute concept (I, freedom, reason) arbitrarily understood, nor as a negative theory of the state of nature opposed to the positive power of the legal order. It is not the former because 'the ethical order' unites the concept (of pure individuality and universality) in itself;[15] and it is not the latter, because this same nature also incorporates both 'majesty and the state of nature as simply identical' – for Hegel, the majesty of the legal order is 'nothing but absolute ethical *nature*'.[16] Consonant with the classical theoretical tradition, natural and moral law are directly interconnected. Here too *status civilis* is the realization and not the conquest of nature's being. Alluding to the theory of the *status civilis* in Hobbes and his successors, Hegel says, 'But the natural, which would have to be regarded in an ethical relation as something to be sacrificed, would itself not be ethical and so could least of all represent the ethical in its origin.'[17]

This is precisely the point at which Hegel brings in his critique of current natural law theories: thinking of a concept of nature not as something 'to be given up' but rather as itself 'ethical',

---

14 Cf. 'Glauben und Wissen', pp. 141, 148, where Hegel calls 'obedience to the eternal law of nature and to holy necessity' the principle of true morality. Nature here means 'living itself which at the same time posits itself universally in the law and becomes genuinely objective in the people' (p. 149). Cf. 'System der Sittlichkeit', pp. 460 f.

15 'Naturrecht', p. 395; *NL*, p. 111.

16 *WWG*, Vol. 1, p. 338; *NL*, p. 66.

17 *WWG*, Vol. 1, p. 338; *NL*, p. 66 – the concept of nature as in principle teleological also motivates the equating of the mentioned 'moral nature' with the concept of 'organization' (or reason in the context of nature) and its contrast with the concept of the 'machine', the 'rational state' (*Verstandesstaat*) of natural law theory. Cf. 'Differenz', p. 242.

an 'ethical nature'.[18] Thinking of the ethical as 'nature' means, according to Hegel, conceiving the existence of all its potencies, and thinking of their reality and unity with necessity. For 'the uniqueness of the individual is not primary, but rather the living- ness of ethical nature, its divinity; and the single individual is too poor to encompass this latter's nature in its total reality'.[19] This ambiguous turn of phrase should, therefore, express both the priority of the ethical whole with respect to its parts (indi- viduals) and the self-sufficient existence of all the aspects which constitute the whole. Thus the concept of nature is employed in two ways: (1) as totality in the sense of Spinoza's 'God or nature', and (2) as 'essence' in the sense of Aristotle's doctrine that the *polis* is 'according to nature prior' to the individual. In the natural law essay he parallels this point, saying that it 'cannot express itself in the individual, unless it is his soul, and this it is only in so far as it is a universal and the pure spirit of a people. The positive is prior by nature to the negative, or, as Aristotle says, "The state comes by nature before the individual." '[20] This double formulation of the basic principle shows that Hegel appeals simultaneously to Aristotle and Spinoza in the construction within natural law theory of what he calls 'ethical nature'.[21] Spinoza's general doctrine of the essence of the finite[22] as the negative element which is not able to exist by itself is equated with Aristotle's relatively specialized political thesis that the separate individual is not self-sufficient but is 'by nature' subordinated

18 This phrase occurs repeatedly in the 'System der Sittlichkeit' and in the journal essay, and can be viewed in some respects as constitutive for Hegel's early understanding of natural law. Cf. 'System der Sittlichkeit', pp. 443, 471, 473, 478; 'Naturrecht', pp. 338, 347 f., 369, 393, 397; *NL*, pp. 66, 73 f., 92, 110, 113.

19 'System der Sittlichkeit', pp. 470 f. For Hegel, the individual can express the ethical only 'momentarily', i.e., in time and particularly; the negative which the individual is, is posited by negating time, so that the unity ('indifference') of the ethical is for him 'formal' and not 'real'; its identification with nature follows from this: 'the ethical must encompass itself as nature, as the existence of all potencies, and each in its living pattern; it must be one with necessity and exist as relative identity' (p. 471).

20 'Naturrecht', p. 396; *NL*, p. 113.

21 We are indebted to K.-H. Ilting for stressing this important and heretofore insufficiently noticed source of the legal and political theory of the young Hegel. Cf. Ilting, 'Hegels Auseinandersetzung mit der Aristotelischen Politik', in *Philos. Jahrbuch*, LXXI (1963–4), 38–58.

22 See *Ethics*, ed. James Gutmann (New York and London, 1949), Part I, Prop. 8, Schol. 1, p. 45. Hegel cites this passage in 'Glauben und Wissen', p. 64.

to the *polis*. The grounds which suggest or motivate such an equation ontologically are of no interest to us here. Rather, it is important that Hegel's reiteration of Spinoza does not take into account his theory of natural and civil law, divergent from Aristotle's in significant ways, but only considers those doctrines from his metaphysics which can be compared to some extent with Aristotle's *Politics* or Plato's *Republic*. Indeed, one can say that Hegel makes use of Spinoza's metaphysics in constructing his criticism of natural law chiefly for working out more purely the construction of 'absolute ethical life', the structural parts of which he borrowed from classical political theory.[23] At the same time, he gives the doctrine of an infinite substance, which is 'by nature prior'[24] to its modes, a political–practical meaning which it possesses for Spinoza no more than does the doctrine of the *amor Dei intellectualis*, which Hegel understands here as an 'intellectual intuition' of 'absolute ethical life'. Obviously, alluding to Spinoza, Hegel says that 'philosophy's view of the world and of necessity, according to which all things are in God and no individual exists, is fully realized for empirical consciousness since this individuality of action, thinking, or being has its meaning and essence solely in the whole . . .'[25] The inclusion of Spinoza in the criticism of current natural law theory makes the basic principles of classical politics, the criteria for this criticism, more potent. The 'positive' element, that is, the absolute priority of the ethical whole to its parts and the concept of nature expressing the necessity of this relation, which Hegel makes the foundation for his concept of

---

23 The idea which underlies the borrowing and does not become very clear in Hegel is given by Schelling in the *Vorlesungen über die Methode des Akademischen Studiums* (1802): 'The scientific construction of the state will not, as concerns its inner life, find any corresponding historical elements in later times', *Werke*, ed. Schröter [8 vols., Munich, 1927–56), Vol. III, p. 335. Cf. also p. 315. Apparently, this passage already takes into account Hegel's attempted reconstruction or relates to Schelling's conversations with Hegel. At the same time we should not rule out the possibility that Hegel's exposition has also been influenced by Schelling. For further points of agreement compare Schelling, *Werke*, Vol. III, p. 314 ('Über die Prinzipien der Differenz zwischen antikem und modernem Staat') with Hegel's 'Naturrecht', pp. 383 ff; *NL*, pp. 104 ff.

24 See *Ethics*, Part I, Prop. I; Defs. 3 and 5, p. 42.

25 'System der Sittlichkeit', p. 465, with the preceding sentence, 'In ethical life the individual exists also in an eternal way; his empirical being and doing is something unconditionally universal; for it is not the individual who acts but rather the Universal absolute spirit that acts in him.'

natural law, renders it impossible to impute anything but a wholly 'negative' significance to the individual's role.[26] Thus it is that in the first phase of his developing philosophy of right, Hegel submits modern natural law theory to devastating criticism from the standpoint of classical politics. The employment of Spinoza's metaphysics radicalized this criticism, but more importantly also prevented Hegel from achieving a historically adequate under-standing of modern theories of natural law.

II

The point from which Hegel's criticism of particular theorems of natural law originates and to which it constantly returns is that they posit the 'being of the individual . . . as primary and supreme'. On a 'lower level' of abstraction, the modern 'absoluteness of the subject' appears in the Enlightenment doctrine of eudaemonism; natural law elevates this absoluteness, which achieves self-understanding and 'conceptual' form in the philosophy of Kant and Fichte, to a theoretical level in the systems 'which are called antisocialistic' (Hobbes, Rousseau).[27] In seventeenth-century natural law theory this principle converts the moments of absolute ethical life into two particular 'decisive factors', the state of nature and the legal order, in each of which individuality is defined differently: in the state of nature it is absolute freedom, and in the legal order absolute submission to a power external to the individual and hence itself individual as well as particular. Yet the cancellation of individuality is only an appearance; in truth it is constantly reproduced through the relation of 'submissive unification'. The ethical union (*unio civilis*) remains alien to the united many, a formless and external unity, which natural law theory presents 'under the names of society and state'.[28] Hegel contrasts these empty names with the 'absolute idea of the ethical'.

26 If ethical consciousness, as it expressed itself in current moral and legal philosophy, 'inserts any other individual element as a ground [between] the unity of the universal and the particular of which the former is the ground', then Hegel simply explains it as 'not ethical consciousness'. Cf. 'System der Sittlichkeit', p. 466; also 'Naturrecht', p. 349; *NL*, p. 74.
27 'Naturrecht', pp. 343 f., *NL*, p. 70.
28 *WWB*, Vol. I, pp. 337 f., *NL*, p. 65.

There individuality is not fixed and relatively identical as a relation of submission, in which it is an absolutely posited element; rather, 'individuality as such is nothing, and simply one with absolute ethical majesty – which genuine, living, nonservile oneness is the only true ethical life of the individual'.[29] As everywhere, here too the individual is the negative moment whose existence must be 'melded' into the absolute idea. Hegel seldom formulated the perspective of ancient *polis* ethics more clearly than at this time; the living oneness with the ethical whole, which he contrasts to the 'submission' in the natural law tradition's state theory, presupposes the radical negation of the latter's point of origin; it presupposes the 'nothingness of the individual'. This point recurs in Hegel's criticism of Kantian and Fichtean natural law theory. For him concepts such as freedom, pure will, and humanity are simply 'purer negations',[30] which have the advantage of bringing 'being-for-self and individuality' as principles of the current systems of ethics more clearly into view. The relation of 'submissive union', which in the seventeenth-century natural law theories was in part an inconsistency and in part simply domination,[31] becomes (as Hegel shows with the example of Fichte) a system of compulsion whose universality makes the 'living' unity of particularity and universality totally impossible.[32] To be sure, idealistic philosophy preserves the 'important aspect' of positing the essence of law and duty as identical with the essence of the thinking and willing subject. But idealism does not remain true to the principle of identity. Not only is the validity of the principle broken by restriction to the subjective morality of actions and the difference also posited as absolute in legality, but idealism

29 *WWG*, Vol. 1, p. 338; *NL*, p. 67.
30 *WWG*, Vol. 1, pp. 340 f. This criticism is directed simultaneously against his own position ventured in the sketches of the Bern and Frankfurt periods, which seek, with Rousseau, Kant, and Fichte, to make the 'inalienable human right to legislate for oneself from one's own heart' operative in abstract terms. Cf. *Theologische Jugendschriften* ed. H. Nohl (Tübingens 1907), pp. 212 f. (Eng. tr. T. M. Knox, *Early Theological Writings* (Chicago, 1948), p. 145), and also pp. 42, 53, 71, 139 ff., 173, 188 ff., 365. Cf. *Briefe von und an Hegel*, ed. J. Hoffmeister (4 vols., Hamburg, 1952–60), Vol. 1, pp. 23 f. An initial modification of this position already shows itself in the writings: 'Über die neuesten inneren Verhältnisse Württembergs' (1798) and 'Die Verfassung Deutschlands' (1801–2), which, however, can be omitted in our investigations.
31 See 'Naturrecht', p. 337; *NL*, p. 65.
32 *WWG*, Vol. 1, pp. 362 ff., *NL*, p. 85.

comprehends both as equally valuable and unconditionally in-dependent. The possibility of the union of the subject with the essence of law and duty (= morality) is contrasted to the possibility of disunion; to the system of freedom the system of compulsion is opposed.[33]

Therefore, although Hegel honours its ideas as the 'important aspect' of the Kantian and Fichtean philosophies, morality, for him, only represents the negation of individuality in a purer form. For experiencing the union of consciousness and duty as a pure possibility separated from legality throws the subject back on his individuality. It is not, as Hegel puts it, the 'positive absolute', or 'ethical nature', which comprises the essence of both morality and legality giving them the possibility of union, but rather it is the negative or 'absolute concept' which is unconditionally opposed to ethical nature as we have discussed it. This opposition within the idealistic system of natural law and the fixation of the negative in the principle of morality are now also contrasted with the position of 'absolute ethical life'. Methodologically this is done by appealing to 'intellectual intuition' in which there is, according to Hegel, no distinction between possibility and actuality, concept and being ('nature'). For the intuition of ethical nature, which historically reconstructs the ancient theory of the *polis* in its various aspects, contains like this theory the presence of the actual, a 'this' which is 'living relation and absolute presentness'.[34] In this context Hegel turns to language to justify his method of contrasting classical politics with modern natural law theory. The general pre-supposition made by language – that it is part of the 'nature of absolute ethical life' to be 'a universal or an ethos' – is indicated admirably 'by this Greek word for ethical life like the German one (*Sitte*)', so that even the 'newer systems of ethics, in making independence and individuality into a principle, cannot fail to expose the relation of these words. This inner allusion proves so powerful that these systems, to define their subject-matter, could not misuse these words and so adopted the word morality

33 Cf. *WWG*, Vol. I, pp. 360 f.; *NL*, p. 84.
34 Cf. *WWG*, Vol. I, pp. 357, 359; *NL*, pp. 82–4. One can also observe here how pro-ductive the method adopted from Schelling for historically appropriating ancient ethics and politics has become in Hegel's hands.

(*Moralität*).'[35] The approach to classical natural law theory, which leads inevitably to relating the intellectual intuition of ethical life in general to the concrete ethical 'this', expresses itself above all in Hegel's evaluation of morality. Although as the doctrine of virtue it is the immediate ethical life of the individual, absolute ethical life appears in morality under the form of negation, and in this form remains wholly negative for Hegel. 'Negative morality' includes not just the reflexive morals of modern subjectivity, but also the externally self-manifesting individual virtues adapted to the context of the ethical whole (which Hegel wishes to have understood on the pattern of classical ethics, which is their natural description).[36] This constitutes the formal difference between morals and natural law (= politics understood as the construction of 'ethical nature's' law); but this difference is not to be interpreted as it is by Kant and Fichte, 'as if they are separated, this excluded from that; instead, their content is wholly within natural law'.[37] Just as morality is assigned the domain of what is in itself negative, that being the ethical life of the individual as a mere possibility of the universal, so natural law is assigned the domain of the 'genuinely positive', whose reality Hegel designates as 'real absolute ethical life' or 'ethical nature'. The construction of this 'nature' in its law, which is something posited by a people, defines the task for natural law theory according to Hegel. If, as was the case for the scientific approaches to natural law current in Hegel's day, 'the specific character of natural law' were to be expressed by 'the negative', by the abstractness of morality 'of the pure will and the individual's will', and further by the 'syntheses of these abstractions (such as coercion, the limitation of individual freedom by the concept of universal freedom, etc.)', its concept could itself be only a negative one – 'a natural *wrong* (*Naturunrecht*) ... since on the basis of such negations as realities, ethical nature is thrown into utter corruption and misery'.[38]

35 *WWG*, Vol. 1, p. 396; *NL*, p. 112.
36 Cf. *WWG*, Vol. 1, p. 399; *NL*, pp. 114–15.
37 Cf. 'System der Sittlichkeit', p. 465; also 'Naturrecht', p. 396; *NL*, p. 113.
38 'Naturrecht', p. 397; *NL*, p. 113.

Hegel did not adhere long to this concept of natural law and to the corresponding methodological placement of ethical life in a 'people', whose structure is all too clearly shown by 'intellectual intuition' to mirror the outlines of the Attic *polis*; he modified this view almost immediately after the appearance of the 'natural law essay', and finally towards the end of the Jena period he gave it up entirely. This striking conceptual shift, noticed only occasionally in the Hegel literature, [39] fits in with the general transformation in the foundations of Hegel's thinking which took place between the Jena lectures of 1803–4 and 1805–6.[40] Hegel's liberation from Schellingian terminology and method in these years, which seems to run parallel with a renewed study of Fichte, simultaneously signals the surrender of his previous concept of nature rooted in Aristotle and Spinoza. To the extent that the presuppositions and consequences of this change in Hegel's system and conceptual framework can be worked out in detail, they are to be observed on the one hand in the relationship connecting nature, 'concept' and law, and on the other hand in these terms, relationship to 'individuality' and its significance in the system. The fact that Hegel defined the being of the individual as wholly negative and submerged it in the 'ethical nature' of the whole both in the draft for the 'System der Sittlichkeit' and in the natural law essay cannot finally be traced to the fact that at this period he still predominantly equated the negative with the 'nothing' of – tendentially – pure negation. Hence, the being of the individual, which the new natural law theory assumes as a basis for its deduction of 'society and state', appears in the first systematic sketch under the title *The Negative, or Freedom, or Crime*.[41] Its themes are: physical

39 Cf. F. Darmstädter, 'Das Naturrecht als soziale Macht und die Rechtsphilosophie Hegels', in *Sophia*, v (1937), 215, n. 13, which to be sure notes only that Hegel advocated various interpretations of the state of nature, without inquiring what grounds this diversity might have. That Hegel employed 'the concept "nature" in very different senses' was also noted by Th. Haering whose comments in this connection reflect very clearly the helpless state into which the fact puts him. (Haering, *Hegel*, Vol. II, pp. 392 f.) It is false to say that Hegel's terminology still remains vacillating later on (p. 393).

40 Cf. in this context already Rosenkranz, *Hegels Leben*, pp. 178 ff.; F. Rosenzweig, *Hegel und der Staat* (2 vols., Munich/Berlin, 1920), Vol. I, p. 183.

41 Cf. 'System der Sittlichkeit', pp. 446–60.

destruction, robbery, theft, subjugation, murder, vengeance, battle, and war. This segment of the system stands between two parts without actually making contact with either (1) 'natural morality' (*Absolute Ethical Life in Relation*) and (2) (absolute) *Ethical Life*. To the extent that ethical life is presented simply as 'the positive', the possibility of a transition must be rejected in advance. In the systematic sketches which follow, this same part takes on a completely different function. In the lectures of 1803–4 it is still placed between natural ethical life (the family) and the people, but by now it has lost its own important systematic place.[42] Already one finds here that transition to absolute ethical life which is excluded from the first systematic sketch and the natural law essay as a result of the natural positing of the 'people'. Finally, in the lectures of 1805–6 this part of the system appears reduced to a few pages which surface, moreover, either in completely disparate places or in the margin.[43]

Admittedly, of course, Hegel had already given the first hint of a possible transition from the individual's negative being to the positive being of ethical life in the natural law essay. The negative, which the individual in himself is, can be posited by the individual, and the negation of his particular determinations can be totally negated. Of course, this capacity of abstracting from all limitations is also something negative, but it is such that the individual becomes 'absolute individuality taken up in the concept, negative absolute infinity, pure freedom'. Freedom understood as the 'concept' of the individual exists as the negative absolute moment of the absolute itself, which means that it is contained within absolute ethical life. It appears in the 'class of free beings' which verifies pure freedom in the struggle between life and death. But this negative activity has a prior positive activity for its condition, the 'absolutely ethical element (i.e., membership in a people); the individual proves his unity with the people unmistakably through the danger of death alone'.[44] The restrictions which surface here belong to Hegel's point of view at that period;

42 Cf. *Jenenser Realphilosophie* (hereafter *JR*) (1805–6), ed. J. Hoffmeister, Vol. 1 (Leipzig, 1932), pp. 226–32. The section is without its own title. Cf., here, the penetrating observations by K.-H. Ilting (see above, n. 21), p. 56.
43 Cf. *JR*, Vol. 11, pp. 210–12, 239–41 (marginalia following Hoffmeister, p. 237, n. 3).
44 Cf. 'Naturrecht', pp. 370 ff.; *NL*, p. 93; 'System der Sittlichkeit', pp. 465 ff.

the possibility of transition is reserved for the free while the class of unfree people abides in individuality as a result of the inadequacy of their labour *vis-à-vis* the 'concept'.[45] In addition it happens that the negative activity of the first class creates nothing permanent (positive) from itself; rather, the positive existence of ethical life is already always presupposed.

Hegel still makes this presupposition in the lectures of 1803–4. The passage concerning the completion of the transition from individuality to universality follows the 'System der Sittlichkeit' and the journal essay nearly word for word: 'the individual as a member of a people is an ethical being whose essence is the living substance of universal ethical life; as individual he is an ideal form of a being only as something annulled. The ethics of a people constitute ethical life's existence in its living multi-plicity.'[46] This is still wholly the view of ancient *polis*-ethics with all the methodic and systematic consequences which have been spelled out above. It is clear that as long as the classical influence prevails the relationship to modern natural law theory must remain invariably negative. At this point Hegel noted in the margin: 'no composition, no contract, no tacit or explicit original contract. The individual must not surrender merely a part of his freedom, but rather himself altogether.'[47] Nevertheless, the restriction of the transition to a 'class of free people' disappears. Negative activity is no longer taken to be the battle for the preservation of the ethical whole, but instead the battle of individuals for mutual recognition.[48] For the first time the 'negative', which assumed a purely independent place in the system sketches and was tied

---

45 Cf. 'System der Sittlichkeit', p. 473: 'They are not in the infinite concept, through which it would be something only posited for their consciousness as external but really their own absolute spirit moving them, which would overcome all their fixed determinations. That their ethical nature achieves this insight is an advantage granted them by the first class.'

46 *JR*, Vol. 1, p. 232.

47 *Ibid.*

48 This theme plays a role already in the 'System der Sittlichkeit', without however securing a precise and significant role: on the one side it follows a sphere of recognition (= universalization of individuality) which expresses itself in barter, property, money and commerce; on the other side it precedes family relationships in whose 'indifference the results of the battle for recognition (the master–slave relation) annul themselves. Cf 'System der Sittlichkeit', pp. 440–3, and further pp. 495 ff., where the system of law is interpreted in retrospect as the structure of recognition.

to the contingencies of a particular class in the journal essay's theory of transition, now begins to assume the function which will form one of the most crucial bases for Hegel's thinking about law: the mediation between individuality and universality. The battle for recognition mediates here principally between the 'natural' ethical life of the *family* and the 'absolute' ethical life of the *people*, and in this process the latter is still circumscribed as much as ever by Aristotelian–Spinozistic categories.[49] Although the recognition of individuality, which contains the latter's assimilation into the absolute ethical substance in itself, means the disappearance of the individual as such,[50] the first step is thereby taken towards overcoming the abstract methodological position of ancient *polis* theory and re-evaluating modern natural law theories.

This can easily be seen in the relevant sections of the lectures of 1805–6 in which Hegel systematically, methodologically, and substantively draws the conclusions from this beginning. The Schellingian method and its terminological implications disappear entirely; the categories with which Hegel now works are no longer the 'positive' and 'negative', 'ethical nature' and its law, the opposition between 'intuition' and 'concept', and so on; but rather 'intelligence' and 'will', whose origin is the 'self'. What showed itself in the lectures of 1803–4 in the mediating function assigned to 'recognition' has now become fully evident: in the second half of the Jena period Hegel once again renewed his struggle with Fichte, and after 1804 he returned to him in his lectures on the philosophy of Spirit and natural law.[51] The theme

49 Cf. *JR*, Vol. 1, p. 232: 'The absolute spirit of a people is the absolutely universal element, the ether, which has incorporated all individual consciousnesses into itself, the *absolutely simple*, living, *unique* substance.'

50 *JR*, Vol. 1, 'This *absolute consciousness* [at this level the result of the battle for recognition – M. R.] is thus an annulment of consciousness as individual ... it is universal existing consciousness; it is not the bare form of individuality without *substance*, but instead individuals no longer exist; it is *absolute substance*.'

51 The positive reception of Fichte's 'metaphysics of subjectivity', which shaped the construction and arrangement of particular bits of the Jena lectures, certainly plays an important role in the Jena logic which, according to the editors (H. Ehrenberg and G. Lasson), belongs to the earliest of Hegel's lecture sketches, dated around 1801–2. But its theoretical basis, the grasp of the 'self' as a synthesis of individuality and universality (cf. *Jenenser Logik, Metaphysik und Naturphilosophie*, ed. G. Lasson (Leipzig, 1923), pp. 161, 163 ff., 178 f.), has still not been established in the lectures given between 1801 and

of recognition, which is handled in a way that reveals the direct influence of Fichte,[52] is now introduced expressly into the problem context of modern natural law theory: 'This is the relation that is usually called the *state of nature*: the free, equal, reciprocal being of individuals; and natural law is to explain what rights and duties individuals have towards one another in these relationships and what the necessity of their action is, for their (in their own view) independent consciousness.'[53] Hegel himself answers with the well-known Hobbesian argument 'exeundum e statu naturae' which he had already used once, albeit with a different basic intent in Thesis IX of the Jena inaugural dissertation.[54] The same argument also proves for Kant and Fichte that individuals receive no rights and duties 'by nature' and that instead civil society the 'state', is required for their reality (= validity). What is 'posited' is no longer 'nature', however understood, but rather the 'concept', and it is this latter which is to make its law effective: 'The concept of reciprocally free self-consciousnesses is posited, but only the concept. Because it is a concept, it must realize itself, i.e., it must annul itself, in conceptual form, in favour of its reality.'[55] The self-realizing concept is nothing other than

---

1803, and in part not even in the lectures of 1803–4, a fact which *inter alia* the just discussed first version of Hegel's theory of natural law verifies. A turn occurs first in the lectures of 1805–6 whose tendencies also obviously agree in other respects with the relevant chapter of the *Jenenser Metaphysik* (3: 'Metaphysik der Subjektivität' pp. 161 ff.).

52 Cf. Fichte, *Grundlage des Naturrechts* (1796), *Sämtliche Werke* (8 vols., 1845–6), Vol. III, pp. 44 ff. and 85 ff., with Hegel: *JR*, Vol. I, pp. 226 ff.; *JR*, Vol. II, pp. 194 ff. and 203 ff. The possibility of a link comes, for Hegel, in Fichte's interpretation of 'recognition' as the synthesis of ('real') acts and the 'concept', in which individuals reciprocally 'posit' one another.

53 *JR*, Vol. II, p. 205.

54 Cf. Hegel, *Erste Druckschriften*, ed. G. Lasson (Leipzig, 1928), p. 400: 'status naturae non est injustus, et ob eam causam ex illo exeundum'. To be sure Hobbes and Spinoza argue exactly the reverse: that the *status naturae* is to be abandoned because it is not just. Hegel indicates this in the passage pointed out above in note 53.

55 *Jr*, Vol. II, p. 205. Older Hegel literature has tried to express the shift in Hegel's conception of natural law, which is described here, by the quite inadequate formula 'deromanticization of morality', which one refers principally to the developmental leap which is presumed to have occurred with the *Phenomenology of Spirit*. Cf. R. Haym, *Hegel und seine Zeit* (Berlin, 1857), pp. 207 ff.; W. Metzger, *Gesellschaft, Recht, und Staat in der Ethik des deutschen Idealismus* Heidelberg, 1917), pp. 310 ff.

he movement of recognition; it does not immediately change into ethical life's 'absolute substance', which in the lectures of 1805–6 is still the unique positive element. Instead it passes into 'ethical life in general' and indeed into its immediacy: *Law*.[56] This remarkable transformation in the understanding of ethical life signifies a reversal of the bases of Hegel's previous conception of natural law. The 'concept' from which the movement of recognition arises is not the negative factor of the individual's 'pure freedom' which in the literal sense emits 'nothing' from itself, for this very movement of the concept itself produces that positive element in which individuality achieves permanence, i.e., the law. Law is the *relation* of persons in their conduct towards one another, the universal element of their free being or the determination, the limitation of their empty freedom. I do not need to concoct this relation or limitation and produce it for myself, rather the object is itself this production of law in general, i.e., the relation of recognizing ... that which is recognized is recognized as *immediately* valid by virtue of its being, but just *this being is produced from concepts*.'[57] The movement of the concept interrupts the previous ('immediate') relationship of nature, ethical life, and law, and establishes itself, against nature, in law. The polemical battle which Hegel fights with natural law theory's concept of nature should not cause us to overlook the fact that the debate has now taken up a criterion which is itself indebted to the later, idealistic phase of natural law theory and is exactly opposite to the earlier phase. This criterion is the universal legal capacity, the 'person' as the pure concept (= self) of human being, the discovery of which presupposes a break with every pre-given order of nature and its 'laws'. 'Law includes the *pure person*, *pure recognition*. [The person] does not exist in the state of nature; where he is submerged in existence; only by virtue of the fact that he is human [is he] in his *concept*; but in the state of nature he is not in *his concept*; instead, as a merely natural being, he is in his *existence*. [The] question is immediately self-contradictory – I am considering the human being in his *concept*, that is, not in

56 *JR*, Vol. II, pp. 206 and 212.
57 *JR*, Vol. II, p. 206.

the state of nature.'[58] The *rapprochement* with Fichte shows itself chiefly in the systematic arrangement of the sections of the lectures which interest us here. During 1803 to 1804 the recognitional process was a 'potency' of consciousness which annulled itself in the 'absolute consciousness' of ethical life; but in the lectures of 1805–6 its basis is the spontaneity of the 'self' which posits itself as 'intelligence and will'. This spontaneity is the above-mentioned movement of the concept whose 'positive' form expresses recognition. It is not accidental that in the context of this chapter Hegel identifies the 'self' with the 'concept': 'self, the concept, is itself process. It proceeds through the *other*, brings this into self-movement, and this latter vice versa in its *otherness.* is the objectification of the self, and being-for-itself.'[59] The 'self' which Hegel had already conceived in the Jena *Logic* as the unity of individuality and universality and had connected with the category of recognition,[60] no longer appears here as an empty unity subordinated to the 'living' element of nature; nor does it appear as a mere unification of opposed moments, but rather as their mediation founded by positing activity, as the self-mediation of the concept.[61] With this move the positive significance which Hegel assigned to the traditional title 'natural law' must be abandoned. Consistent with this tendency Hegel had already subordinated nature to spirit in the Jena *Logic*[62] and differentiated 'physical' and 'ethical' nature in the essay on natural law,[63] but he made no use of this distinction with regard to the foundation and concept of natural law. The cause of this is to be found in the one-sided orientation towards classical politic and Spinozistic substance metaphysics. Working from this orientation, Hegel derives the meaning of 'law' and 'ethical nature' from natural law and identifies it with the substantive ethical life of

58 *JR*, Vol. II, p. 205 (a marginal note by Hegel). [The second sentence is translated and corrected by Riedel, who inserts a semicolon after 'in das Dasein' and adds 'ist er W. W.]

59 *JR*, Vol. II, p. 204 (margin note).

60 See *Jenenser Logik*, ed. Lasson, pp. 164 ff., 171.

61 Cf. here J. Schwartz, *Hegels Philosophische Entwicklung* (Frankfurt on Main, 1938), pp 339 f. Schwartz points comparatively to 'System der Sittlichkeit', p. 431, and 'Glaube und Wissen', pp. 56 f., as opposed to *JR*, Vol. II, pp. 190, 195, n. 5.

62 Cf. *Jenenser Logik*, p. 192; 'Naturrecht', p. 395.

63 'Naturrecht', pp. 346 f.

'people'. Hegel initially goes beyond this point of view and develops a definition of the concept of natural law based on the modern theory's 'negative' concept of nature in the lectures of 1805–6 after his renewed engagement with Fichte and (probably) with Rousseau.[64] Its construction does not involve developing the law for an indeterminate 'ethical nature', but rather grows out of the process of recognition in which both the existence of individuality and the law are produced. This process finds its necessity in the 'concept' of the individual; it is, as Hegel says, 'its own and not that of our thinking in opposition to the content. As recognition, it is itself the process, and this process annuls even its own natural state: it is recognition; the natural merely *is*, it is not *spiritual*.'[65] The process of recognition, whose 'concept' constitutes law, results on the side of individuality in a 'will' which is 'cognitive' or 'general' – Rousseau's 'general will' whose immediate reality is the legally competent 'person'.[66] Taking these two categories into the system of ethics signifies a move away from classical political thought and its concept of nature which Hegel abstractly opposed to modern natural law theory from 1802 to 1804. With the recognition of 'law' as the immediacy of ethical life and its assimilation into the concept, the moment of individuality, the point of origin of modern natural law theory, is established. In this way, after the vacillations of the early Jena period, Hegel finds his way back to the view of natural law found in Rousseau, Kant, and Fichte, which he had supported once before during the 1790s.[67] The justification of the individual by means of the

---

64 Cf. *JR*, Vol. II, pp. 213 ff. and 244 ff.; here are found quite explicit references to formulations of the 'social contract' although Rousseau's name does not appear. In the previous sketches the concept of a 'general will' plays nearly no role at all.

65 *JR*, Vol. II, p. 206. The passage must be taken together with p. 242: 'Spirit is the *nature* of the individuals, its immediate substance and their process and necessity.'

66 *JR*, Vol. II, p. 212: 'This cognitive will is then *general*. It is being recognized. Opposed to itself in the form of universality it is being, reality in general, and the individual. The subject is the *person*. The will of the individual is the universal, and the universal is the individual, ethical life in general, but immediately it is law.' Cf., on the other hand, K. Larenz (*Die Rechts- und Staatsphilosophie des deutschen Idealismus* in *Handbuch der Philosophie*, Part 4, (Munich/Berlin, 1934), p. 153), who holds that will as a category emerges first in the *Phenomenology of Spirit*.

67 See *Briefe*, Vol. I, pp. 18 and 23 f.; *Theologische Jugendschriften*, pp. 42, 53, 62, 72, 139 ff., 173, 18ff, 365. Hegel studied Kant's theory of law in 1798, Fichte's *Natural Right*, in 1796. Cf. Rosenkranz, *Hegels Leben*, pp. 48 and 87; W. Metzger, *Gesellschaft, Recht, und Staat in der Ethik des deutschen Idealismus*, pp. 331 f.

'concept' (= self), in which individuality and universality are mediated, is the consequence of the insight which Hegel achieved at the end of the Jena period. According to this insight 'everything' depends on 'grasping and expressing the ultimate truth not as substance but as subject as well'.[68] That is not finally sufficient for comprehending natural law; its truth is (to quote once more from the Preface to the *Phenomenology* where Hegel secures his philosophy's new methodological horizon) the subject which is 'actual' only in so far as it is 'in the process of positing itself, or in mediating with its own self its transitions from one state or position to the opposite'.[69] Natural law theory no longer has for its object 'ethical nature' and its law, which Hegel chiefly identifies with the substantive ethical life of the Greek *polis*, but rather the 'concept' of law, which in its development permeates ethical substance.

IV

Hegel first steps before us as a complete 'moral philosopher' when he gains insight into the movement of the self-positing concept, which explodes the distinctive 'natural' immediacy and the 'nature' of substantial ethical life. The doubled movement suits the original position from which both the aporias of Hegel's initial conception of natural law and their overcoming develop historically. At the end of the Jena period Hegel's criticism of modern natural law theories from the standpoint of classical politics undergoes a transformation when he also criticizes classical politics from the standpoint of natural law theory. This tendency initially appears in the lectures of 1805–6. On the one hand Hegel interprets Rousseau's theory of the general will, originating in the wills of individuals, by recollecting the Aristotelian thought that the whole is naturally prior to its parts, from which it follows that for individual wills the general will is 'primary and the essence'.[70] On the other hand, and not simply as a result of the inclusion of this natural law theory, Hegel contrasts the separateness of

68 See Hegel, *Phänomenologie des Geistes*, ed. G. Lasson and J. Hoffmeister (Hamburg, 1952), p. 19 (Eng. tr. J. B. Baillie, *The Phenomenology of Mind* (hereafter *PM*) (London, 1931), p. 80.)
69 *Phänomenologie*, p. 20; *PM*, p. 80.
70 Cf. *JR*, Vol. II, pp. 244 f.

'the absolute self-knowledge of individuality' as the *higher principle of modern times* to the 'immediate unity of universal and individual' in ancient *polis* morality.[71] The same criterion, based on the concept's double movement, meets us in the lectures on the history of philosophy. Hegel applies it continually to politics and natural law, and also uses it to understand the limits of both. The coincidence is not accidental since, as is well known, Hegel held this course of lectures for the first time during 1805–6 and even made use of the Jena notes later on. In the 'Plato' lecture the 'substantial, universal element' which is basic in the *Republic* is contrasted with that which 'might be law by nature ... [and] is law by and for individuals'.[72] Hegel calls this natural law theory of the moderns a 'trivial abstraction from the real practical essence, the law'; but in contrast he emphasizes the limits of the Platonic idea of the *polis*, its exclusion of individuality, of individual consciousness, of the 'person',[73] all of which first come into play in modern natural law theory: 'The opposite of Plato's principle is the principle of the conscious free will of the individual which in later times is made primary, particularly in Rousseau: that the spontaneous choice of the individual qua individual, the expression of the individual, is necessary.'[74]

Understanding the boundaries of classical politics and modern natural law theory presupposes equally a determinate historical understanding of modern natural law theory itself; and Hegel takes the criterion for his criticism not from just any author but from Rousseau, who serves as his foil. In the lectures on the history of philosophy and philosophy of history it can actually be shown that this type of understanding was at issue for Hegel. To be sure he shared the widespread opinion of the eighteenth and

71 *JR*, Vol. II, p. 251.
72 Hegel, *Vorlesungen über die Geschichte der Philosophie*, in *Werke*, Vol. XIV, pp. 269 ff. (Eng. tr. E. S. Haldane and F. H. Simpson, *Hegel's Lectures on the History of Philosophy* (3 vols., London, 1896).) The term 'ethical nature' is still used here, but is characteristically given a different sense: as 'the free will in its rationality' (p. 262).
73 Cf. *WWG*, Vol. XIV, pp. 290 f.
74 *WWG*, Vol. XIV, p. 295. In the lecture on Aristotle's *Politics* (p. 400) the double direction of Hegel's criticism recurs. Also compare the judgment on Plato's *Republic* (p. 275) with *JR*, Vol. II, p. 251: 'Plato had not presented an ideal, rather he grasped the state of his times intrinsically. But this state has passed ... because it dispenses with the principle of absolute individuality' (marginal note).

nineteenth centuries that the 'Enlightenment' found the basis for natural law theory in Hugo Grotius' *De jure belli ac pacis* (1625). At the same time, however, Hegel points out that in that book Stoic–Ciceronian natural teleology is dominant, a view in which legal consciousness is 'natural' or innate in human beings (*natura insitum*); so that neither Grotius, Pufendorf and Wolff nor the Scottish school of moral philosophy represents a break with the tradition.[75] According to Hegel, the truly 'revolutionary' theory of natural law, which springs from the fundamental connection of 'nature' and law also assumed by Grotius, is owed to Thomas Hobbes; for it was he who initially 'tried to trace the social union, the nature of state power, back to principles which lie in ourselves, which we recognize as our own'.[76] For Hobbes, the theory of law and society stands under the conditions of a natural order (*ordo naturalis*) only to the extent that nature gives the conditions which make it necessary for us to have such a theory. Thus, because of Hobbes, an ambiguity arises in the traditional title 'natural law', an ambiguity which is of the highest importance for Hegel and to which he draws attention in interpreting *De Cive*: 'The expression "nature" contains this ambiguity, that human nature is man's spirituality, or rationality; his natural state, however, is the other aspect: that human beings behave artlessly.'[77] According to Hegel this ambiguity is intensified in Rousseau, Kant, and Fichte, all of whom deepen the break with traditional theories of natural law, initially made by Hobbes. Rousseau takes human 'spirituality, rationality' to mean human freedom, which releases us from nature and serves as an absolute distinguishing mark *vis-à-vis* animals.[78] His principle, that human beings are free and

75 See *Einleitung in die Geschichte der Philosophie*, ed. J. Hoffmeister, 3rd edn (Hamburg, 1959), pp. 159 ff.; *Vorlesungen über die Geschichte der Philosophie*, in *Werke*, Vol. xv, pp. 439 f., 445 f., 502; *Vorlesungen über die Philosophie der Weltgeschichte*, ed. G. Lasson (Leipzig, 1920), pp. 917 ff. Hegel's allusion to the 'natura insita' of ancient natural law theory obviously refers to Cicero, *De Legibus Libri Tres*, ed. J. Vahlen (Berlin, 1883), 1, 6, 18, where natural law (*lex naturalis*) appears as the 'ratio summa insita in natura, quae jubet ea, quae facienda sunt, prohibetque contraria'. Cf. also 1, 12, 33.

76 *WWG*, Vol. xv, p. 442.

77 *WWG*, Vol. xv, p. 443.

78 *WWG*, Vol. xv, p. 527. Hegel cites the well-known passage from *The Social Contract*, Book I, Ch. 4, tr. Charles Frankel (New York, 1947); cf. Chs. 1, 8, 9; Book III, Ch. 9, n.; *Discours sur l'origine de l'inégalite parmi les hommes*, ed. K. Weigand (Hamburg, 1955), pp. 106 f. Cf. also *Vorlesungen über der Philosophie der Weltgeschichte*, pp. 920 ff.

that the state erected on the basis of the 'general will' is the realization of this freedom, must, as Hegel said, be 'judged to be correct'. Rousseau's 'ambiguity' first originates in the fact that he allows the general will to be composed out of the wills of individuals by the natural inclination of their freedom. With this the 'freedom of nature' once again annuls 'freedom as the unconditional absolute' which Rousseau builds into the concept of the general will.[79] Yet for all that, Rousseau has brought to consciousness the fact that freedom is the 'concept of human being'.[80] For Hegel this grounds the emergence of 'the transition to Kantian philosophy', which puts an end to the 'ambiguity' in the concept of natural law by radically separating the legislation of nature from that of freedom, the 'empirical' from the 'free and pure' will.[81] The 'concept' of human being achieves self-understanding in the perspective of transcendental philosophy. The 'simple unity of self-consciousness', or the 'self', is the 'impenetrable, absolutely independent freedom and source of all universality, i.e., thought determinations', freed from all pre-given natural constraints.[82] 'Consciousness of the spiritual' becomes the foundation of natural law theory; it discovers a 'cognitive principle for the state ... which is not any longer some principle of meaning such as a sociability instinct, the need for the security of property and so on, nor piety as with the divine right of kings. Instead it is the principle of *certainty* which is identity with its own selfconsciousness ...'[83]

One must be aware of this historical evaluation of modern natural law theory, divergent in essential points from that in the journal essay, to be able to grasp the metaphysical basis of Hegel's *Philosophy of Right* as well as its unique, ambivalent stance towards the results of natural law theory. The dialectical movement of

---

79 See *WWG*, Vol. xv, p. 328: 'These principles, so abstractly presented, must be judged to be correct; though the ambiguity commences right away. The human being is free, and this is surely its substantial nature. This freedom is not only not surrendered in the state, but in fact realized for the first time there. The freedom of nature, the disposition towards freedom, is not actual freedom; rather the state is the first actualization of freedom.'

80 Cf. *WWG*, Vol. xv, p. 528.

81 *WWG*, Vol. xv, pp. 529, 552 f., 590.

82 *Vorlesungen über die Philosophie der Weltgeschichte*, p. 922

83 *Vorlesungen über die Philosophie der Weltgeschichte*, p. 924.

the 'concept', which forms the horizon of Hegel's thinking about law after 1805–6, is, as is now obvious, not just an empty abstract formula; instead, the content of this movement is the absolute 'freedom' of the will, which has been elevated to the principle of all law following Rousseau, Kant, and Fichte. That this principle of law implies the overthrow of nature as a criterion of natural law theory had been recognized already by Rousseau. He distinguished two types of natural law: (1) 'natural law properly speaking' (*droit naturel proprement dit*) which rests on a natural feeling (the natural law of sympathy) and makes society possible for men in the state of nature; (2) 'reasoned natural law' (*droit naturel raisonné*) which rules in civil society after the foundation of the state.[84] Rousseau denies 'rational' natural law in the sense of a law which reflects the order of nature, a kind of law to whose constitutional validity Grotius and his eighteenth-century disciples appealed. In this he agrees with Kant and Fichte, who nevertheless went a step further. Kant occasionally mentions the same 'ambiguity' in the concept of nature which Hegel discussed in his 'Hobbes' lecture. 'Without civil ordering', Kant notes in his *Reflections on Moral Philosophy*, 'the whole law of nature (*Recht der Natur*) is a mere doctrine of virtue, and has the name of "law" only as a plan for possible external coercive laws . . . Since formerly the term "natural law" (*natürliche Recht*) has been used in this ambiguous way, we must employ some subtlety to avoid ambiguity. We distinguish Natural Law (*Naturrecht*) from natural law (*natürliche Recht*).'[85] Natural Law (*Naturrecht*) is the law of reason immanent in civil order, while natural law (*natürliche Recht*) bases itself on particular determinations of nature and can be either private or public according to its contents. Over against Rousseau and Kant, Fichte not only subdivides the traditional title, but overthrows it altogether. According to Fichte it is indubitably certain that 'in the sense in which the words are frequently understood, no Natural Law' is possible 'except in a common state

---

84 Cf. *Première Version du Contrat Social*, ed. C. E. Vaughan (Manchester, 1918), Vol. I, p. 493.
85 Refl. 7084 (about 1776–7) in *Kants gesammelte Schriften*, ed. Königlich Preussische Akademie der Wissenschaften (22 vols., Berlin/Leipzig, 1900–42), Vol. XIX, p. 245.

and under positive legislation'.[86] In the third phase of his thinking about the philosophy of law, Hegel draws the conceptually and historically inevitable consequences from this distinctively modern dilemma of natural law. The extent of his approximation of the standpoint of Hobbes, Rousseau, Kant, and Fichte nowhere shows itself more clearly than in the meaning which he now attaches to this 'ambiguity' between nature and law. As early as in the *Encyclopedia of the Philosophical Sciences* (1817) he says: 'The expression "natural law", which until now has been the customary title for the philosophical doctrine of law, contains this ambiguity: Is law to be understood as something, as it were, *implanted* by *immediate nature*, or is it to be understood as it determines itself according to the *nature of the case*, that is, *to the concept*? But the former sense was the one customarily intended before now, so that a prior *state of nature* was usually imagined in which natural law is to be valid.'[87] The 'concept' concentrates the meaning of 'nature' wholly in itself, as mediated through the juridical term 'nature of the case'; it means the very same here as at the end of the Jena period: law, in so far as it and all its determinations are grounded in 'free personality' – 'a *self-determination* which is rather the opposite of *determination by nature*'.[88] Of course, after he has come to a final understanding concerning the historical significance of modern natural law theory, Hegel now identifies the abstract self-movement of the concept with the self-determination of the 'person', who is free from all 'natural' determinations, much more explicitly than he did in the Jena period. A concept developed in idealistic natural law theory, i.e., freedom, the infinite 'concept' of humanity, unlimited by anything external, is the sole principle of law.

Hegel once again expounded the connection of concept (= nature), freedom, and law in the Berlin lectures on the

---

86 *Grundlage des Naturrechts*, in *Sämtliche Werke*, Vol. III, p. 148. (Eng. tr. A. E. Kroeger, *The Science of Rights* (Philadelphia, 1870), pp. 55, 92 f.), *Nachgelassene Werke* (3 vols., Bonn, 1834–5, repr. Berlin, 1962), Vol. II, pp. 498 f.

87 *Enzyklopädie* (Heidelberg, 1817), par. 415. Cf. here E. Fleischmann, *La philosophie politique de Hegel* (Paris, 1964), pp. 17 and 113 f.

88 *Enzyklopädie* (1817), par. 415. Cf. also Hegel, *Nürnberger Schriften*, ed. J. Hoffmeister (Leipzig, 1938), pp. 156, 170 f.; above all, p. 284 (*Enzyklopädie*, par. 181): 'Spirit as free, self-conscious being is the self-same self, which in its absolute negative relation is first of all excluding self, individual free being, or person.'

philosophy of law. The first lecture of 1818–19, held even before the appearance of his book, takes up this theme in par. 3, not included in the same form in the printed edition: 'The principle of law is not contained in nature, neither externally nor in the subjective nature of humankind, in so far, that is, as their will is naturally determined: i.e., in the sphere of needs, instincts, and inclinations. The sphere of law is the sphere of freedom, in which, indeed, to the extent that freedom externalizes itself and gives itself existence, nature plays a role but as something dependent.'[89] All the moments of the historical–social ('objective') actuality of human beings, as they are presented by the philosophy of right, beginning with the forms of appearance of abstract right, up to the family, civil society, and the state, are externalizations of freedom. That here, above all, 'natural' relations play a role is unquestionable. The question is whether these forms give rise to the law which rules them. The necessity, which belongs, for example, to the existence of the state in relation to individuals, no longer means for Hegel that it is a law of nature for individuals to have to live in the state. The necessity of the state rests rather on the law which freedom gives to itself. Hegel's comment on par. 3 gives unambiguous evidence of this: 'This paragraph is occasioned by the term "natural law". The unification of freedom and necessity is not brought about by nature but rather by freedom. Natural things remain as they are; they have not freed themselves from law in order to make laws for themselves. Spirit, however, tears itself free from nature and creates for itself its own nature, even its law. Hence nature is not the life of law.' As for Fichte, so for Hegel, the name 'natural law' is 'only customary', and inappropriate to the reality, the 'concept' of law, since 'by "nature"' is understood '(1) essence, concept (2) unconscious nature as the true meaning'; the 'correct name' must be *philosophical doctrine of law*.[90]

89 *Natur- und Staatsrecht* according to Hegel's lectures in the Winter semester 1818–19, ed. G. Homeyer, Ms. Germ. quart. 1155, p. 9. These and the subsequently mentioned transcripts are to be found in the Staatsbibliothek of the Stiftung Preussischer Kulturbesitz, Berlin.

90 Hegel also points out this double meaning of 'nature' in the *Vorlesungen über die Philosophie der Weltgeschichte*, Introduction. Cf. *Die Vernunft in der Geschichte*, ed. J. Hoffmeister, 5th edn (Hamburg, 1955), p. 117: 'If the word "nature" indicates the essence or the concept of a thing, then the state of nature is the law, natural law the state, which ought to belong to human beings in accordance with their concept, the concept of

Thus in the third phase, which must be located between the years 1816 and 1820, the development of Hegel's thinking about law leads back to the domain of that philosophy of freedom which the natural law essay struggled to overcome by constructing a law of 'ethical nature'. Nothing more can be said about the matter since we have now come to the conclusion of this long process of working out the basic concepts of a 'philosophical doctrine of law', a process which at the same time has clarified the relation of these concepts to traditional natural law theory. Hegel too distinguishes nature and freedom, law of nature and law of justice. 'In nature', Hegel asserts, introducing the Berlin philosophy of right lectures during the Winter semester 1822–3, 'is found the highest verification that there is a law in general; in juridical laws the fact matters not because the law demands that it is to correspond to a particular criterion ... If we consider this distinction of two types of law and ask what grounds juridical law, we see that law originates only from spirit, for nature has no rights.'[91] Thus Hegel categorically puts aside the traditional notion that the 'law of nature' can be a model of law for human beings to the extent that they simply recognize and comply with it; the sole law which sustains historical human existence is the law of freedom which is given not by 'nature' but rather by the 'concept' itself.[92] The self-legislation of the concept is for Hegel the thought of humanity's universal capacity for law,[93] which lifts itself up

---

spirit. But this is not to be confused with what spirit is in its natural state.' Further, cf. *Vorlesungen über Philosophie des Rechts*, Winter semester 1824–5, transcript by Griesheim, Ms. Germ. quart. 545, p. 5, 'we must notice that the expression "nature" has immediately an important double meaning which can lead to total error. On the one hand, "nature" means natural beings, as we find ourselves in our various aspects immediately created, the immediate side of our being. In opposition to this determination and as distinct from it, nature also means concept. The nature of a thing means its concept, that which it is from a rational point of view; and this thing can be totally different from what is merely natural.'

91 *Philosophie des Rechts: Nach dem Vortrag des H. Prof. Hegel*, Winter 1822–3, transcript by H. G. Hotho, MS 2, p. 2. Parts of Hotho's transcript of Hegel's introductory lecture are printed in Gans's edition of the *Rechtsphilosophie* as notes to the Preface (*WWG*, Vol. VIII, pp. 8 f.)

92 See Hotho transcript, p. 3, 'The concept of a thing does not come to us from nature.'

93 See *ibid.*, p. 5, 'It is to be honoured as something great, that the human being, because he is human, is regarded as needing to have rights, so that thus his humanity is more important than his status.'

against what exists and breaks through the appearances of naturalness, behind which freedom, the 'thought of law', had so far been
concealed. This thought, which was initially grasped by the
idealistic natural law theory of Rousseau, Kant, and Fichte, makes
existing law the same as the knowledge of it. As he says in the
introductory lecture of 1824–5, it may be that in 'customary
natural law', which is based on nature, natural needs, purposes,
and so forth, the thought of freedom is not consciously excluded,
but 'in fact, this is not sufficient, since both principles are taken
up without appreciation of their particularity'. Freedom cannot
be thought in the form of nature, but rather must be thought in
the form of the 'concept' which mediates freedom with itself as
well as with nature. And if freedom steps forward with the
'concept's' claim which maintains that 'freedom alone is that with
which law and morality are concerned, then the name natural
law is sent spinning'.[94]

In these lectures, Hegel expressly distinguished natural law
theory and philosophy of law; their opening statement contains
a clue to the 'double title' of his book:[95] *Naturrecht und Staatswissenschaft oder Grundlinien der Philosophie des Rechts.* That this title is
no accident is obvious from all I have said. In a very concrete
way it preserves precisely those aspects which have become constitutive for the prehistory of the work. The subtitle *Naturrecht
und Staatswissenschaft im Grundrisse* points to the origin of Hegel's
legal thought, his struggle with classical politics and modern
natural law theory, in the course of which he came to understand
the limits of both and the condition for overcoming them. The
outcome of this understanding is the title *Philosophie des Rechts*,
which stands in front of the whole and unifies natural law and
political science in itself. It should be pointed out that the title
'philosophical study of law'[96] which Hegel introduced and the
content designated by it, i.e., the 'concept' of freedom, arise historically from idealistic theories of natural law, whose heir Hegel
knows himself to be in his philosophy of right.

---

94 *Vorlesungen über Philosophie des Rechts*, transcript by Griesheim, pp. 9 f.
95 See *ibid.*, p. 3.
96 *Grundlinien der Philosophie des Rechts*, par. 3 (Eng. tr. T. M. Knox, *Hegel's Philosophy of
Right* (Oxford, 1942), p. 17).

Part III

Political Economy and
Political Philosophy

5

The Influence of
Modern Economic Theory

If one views Hegel's engagement with classical politics and modern natural law theory in the working context of contemporary thought, then the principal agent in the debate seems to be that tendency within practical philosophy which, appealing to the power of reason to clarify and dissolve traditional objects and principles, struggles against the Platonic–Aristotelian tradition. However, the contrast between politics and natural law theory could not properly be called fundamental if it limited itself to the opposing principles of Rousseau's *Social Contract* and Plato's *Republic*, that is, to the moments of 'individuality' and 'universality'. Rousseau himself had worked out this contrast much more sharply than did Hegel. And yet Rousseau drew false conclusions from the 'true' premises which were at his disposal: his design for the *Social Contract* succumbs to the traditional illusions by thinking of the state as a 'community of citizens' in the manner of Plato's *Republic* and Aristotle's *Politics* as well as by identifying it with 'civil society'. On the contrary, one of the most important results of Hegel's debate with classical politics and modern natural law theory is that on the basis of the double insufficiency of both their principles he draws a conclusion which severs their traditional relationship at just this decisive point. As distinct from natural law theory, which from Hobbes to Kant posits 'individual' and 'general' will, or 'civil society' and 'state' as mutually identical, Hegel, under the influence of the historical experience of the French Revolution, begins with the insight that the opposition between these terms as a differentiating principle must be recognized and made theoretically valid. The contrast between classical politics and modern natural law theory made it clear to him that clinging to the identity of state and civil society is an illusion and a contradiction of the presuppositions historically conditioning each.

Although Hegel did not fully develop the modern concept of 'civil society' as distinct from 'state' until the *Philosophy of Right* (1812), he already articulated the necessity for this 'distinction' in the Jena lectures of 1805–6. Here, the carefully formulated critique aimed at the legal philosophies in both Plato's *Republic* and Rousseau's *Social Contract* is worked out on the basis of Hegel's twofold quarrel with classical politics and modern natural law theory. The counterpart and completion of this critique is found in his debate with modern political economy, whose model of society raises fundamental questions about natural law theory's doctrine of contract. The immediate unity of individual and general wills belongs historically to the ancient *polis*;[1] but its renewal, which concerns Rousseau (as well as the young Hegel in theory and Robespierre in practice,[2] proves incompatible not only with the social conditions unleashed by the revolution but also with the general structural form and elements of life in the modern state. Among the latter, Hegel numbers the 'new science of political economy, which arose during the eighteenth century and took as basic the principle of individuality, although in different terms than did natural law theories.

I

Hegel's assimilation of the most advanced theories of political economy, as found in the classical British thinkers from James Steuart to Adam Smith and (in the *Philosophy of Right* of 1821) David Ricardo, had no parallel in the German idealistic philosophy of his period. Kant totally excluded economic theory (interpreted as domestic economy, agriculture, and state economics) from practical philosophy. He did so because, taken as a whole, it contained only technical/practical rules for producing effects which are possible according to the concept of natural causality

1 See *Jenenser Realphilosophie* (hereafter *JR*), Vol II (1805–6), ed. J. Hoffmeister (Leipzig 1931), pp. 249 f.: 'This is the beautiful happy freedom of the Greeks, which has been and is to be envied so much. "The people" is broken up into the multitude of citizens and remains at the same time the sole individual, the government. It is in reciprocity only with itself. The *same will is the individual* and *the general*. But a higher abstraction is necessary, a greater contrast and culture, a *deeper* spirit.' Cf. also K. Rosenkranz, *Hegels Leben* (Berlin, 1844).

2 See *JR*, Vol. II, pp. 245 ff.

but which, as such, are irrelevant to the concept of society.[3] Admittedly, Kant in his *Rechtslehre* (1797), par. 31, takes over Adam Smith's definition of money as a body whose expression is both the means and measure of labour. But predictably he relates it individualistically to the contractual 'concept of right in the interchange of mine and thine (*commutatio latio sic dicta*)' rather than to the contractual construction of society itself. It is the same with the political economic intuitions of Fichte, who, as a follower of the physiocrats, falls short of Kant. Schelling never paid serious attention to this theme. But Hegel's assimilation of political economy is not an isolated occurrence, however it might appear given the absence of concern for these matters in the philosophical work of his contemporaries. Hegel's involvement with political economy stands historically in close relationship with the German Enlightenment's broad current of acceptance for progressive Western European social theory, a current which went by the somewhat derogatory name 'popular philosophy'. Political economy, as the science of a newly forming civil society, belonged to the preferred objects whose popularization Garve, Schlosser, Abbt, and Iselin intended to bring about. It was through them that Hegel became acquainted with the works of Steuart and Smith, Ferguson and Hume. Indeed, the idea of enlightening the public about its own private purposes was overshadowed by the real political interest Hegel took in the French Revolution and its influence on Germany. As distinct from his eighteenth-century philosophical predecessors, the young Hegel's studies in political economy no longer grew out of the need to enlighten a bourgeois public, which made sure of the identity of its private ends with public purposes by the popularization of science; instead his studies grew from the disruption of both this very need and the possibility of such assurance by the progress of the revolution. During his Bern and Frankfurt periods, Hegel had tried actively to engage himself in this progress by essays and pamphlets, and the original source for his interest in modern political economy is probably to be found there. He recognized that the French Revolution's contradictory realization of the natural law ideal of

3 *Kants gesammelte Schriften*, ed. Königlich Preussische Akademie der Wissenschaften (22 vols., Berlin/Leipzig, 1900–42), Vol. v, p. 172.

a 'best constitution' was not due to the revolution's ideological standards but to social conditions which were inconsistent with them. When Hegel applied himself to the analysis of these conditions, the horizon of his revolutionary experience was extended: next to France stood England, the original home of the Industrial Revolution. This is of paramount significance for the basic historical position of Hegel's philosophy of right. As George Lukács remarked decisively, Hegel not only possessed the 'highest and most precise insight into the essence of the French Revolution and the Napoleonic period of anyone in Germany, but he also was the only German thinker at the time who seriously struggled with the problems of the industrial revolution in England'.[4]

But it is not merely this conjunction which is critical for the development of Hegel's philosophy of right; rather it is the fact that he brought his adoption of political economy, which was motivated by an interest in actual political realities, to bear historically on classical politics and modern natural law theory. Precisely because of this he was compelled to move beyond their limits. Still, this reflective application, which nearly parallels the general shift in Hegel's youthful development from 'what ought to be' to 'what is', at once puts limits to his adoption of political economy itself, limits that Hegel was able to put behind him only gradually and by many advances in his thinking. This chapter traces out these limits to the point at which Hegel succeeds in breaking through from bare acceptance of political economy to the exposition of the modern theories of society and state. In opposition to the common view that the young Hegel already possessed a clear insight into the 'essence of civil society'[5] or saw himself confronted by the 'problems of capitalist society' (Lukács), I maintain that up to the end of the Jena period he had no theory at his disposal which would have permitted him to grasp the materials of his economic and political–historical studies as a whole. At the beginning we have in hand nothing more than the fragments of such a theory. The contradictions and obscurities in Hegel's treatment of the categories of political economy can

4 *Der junge Hegel und die Probleme der kapitalistischen Gesellschaft* (Berlin, 1954), p. 25. (Eng. tr. R. Livingston, *The Young Hegel* (Cambridge, 1966).)
5 See Rosenkranz, *Hegels Leben*, p. 51.

be explained on the basis not only of Germany's social backwardness[6] but also of the structural particularities of his assimilative process, to which the rest of the chapter is devoted.

The process itself can be dated from Hegel's Bern period. In the course of his historical–political studies and sketches, Hegel in his usual scrupulous fashion familiarized himself (by excerpts from such materials as newspapers and parliamentary reports) with England's commercial and social conditions. According to Rosenkranz, the debate over the poor-tax captured his particular interest.[7] Hegel gathered his insights concerning the practical–social significance of need and work, the division of labour and wealth, charity and taxation (public administration, etc.), into a commentary on the German edition (1769) of Sir James Steuart's *Inquiry into the Principles of Political Economy* (1767) which is now unfortunately lost.[8] Next to Steuart, the economic theories of Adam Smith achieve great influence at the beginning of Hegel's Jena period. Hegel became acquainted with Smith's *Inquiry into the Nature and Causes of the Wealth of Nations* (1776) in Christian Garve's translation (1794–6).[9] What is remarkable about Hegel's method of work in this period is that his reconstruction of the ancient theory of the *polis* walks side by side with these contemporary studies. Just as he reached back to Aristotle's *Politics* in his struggle with natural law theory, so he now used elements of classical economics as a foil for handling the political economic problems raised by the English. However, the contrast which arises here between the structure of economics and politics based on Aristotle and these realities (a contrast which Hegel develops in his original systematic conceptions) is incomparably harsher than in the case of the criticism of natural law theory.

The agreement with Aristotle appears most strikingly in Hegel's earliest sketch of a political system, the 'System der Sittlichkeit'

6 See Lukács, *Der junge Hegel*, pp. 127 f. and *Passim*.

7 See *Hegels Leben*, pp. 85 f.

8 See *Hegels Leben*, p. 86, according to Rosenkranz's testimony written between 19 February and 16 May 1799. Cf. here P. Chamley, *Économie Politique et philosophique chez Steuart et Hegel* (Paris, 1963).

9 See *JR*, Vol. 1 where Smith is cited from Vol. 1 of the Garve edition (Breslau, 1794). Basic on the subject of Hegel's engagement with political economy is Lukács, *Der junge Hegel*, pp. 208 ff., 369 ff.; further, K. Höhne, 'Hegel und England', in *Kant Studien*, XXXVI (1931), 201 ff.

(1802). The first part, 'absolute ethical life in relation' or 'natural ethical life', corresponds in critical sections to the economics which Aristotle takes up in Book I of the *Politics*. As in Aristotle, Hegel's analysis of the activities and human associations which arise from natural need and drives (work, use of tools, possession, barter, relation of man–wife, parent–child, master–slave) flows into the 'family' as the highest 'totality' which the naturally grounded relative ethical life is capable of achieving by mastery and domestic economy: 'The difference is the superficial character of mastery. The man is the lord and administrator, not the proprietor, in opposition to the other members of the family. As the administrator he has only the appearance of free power to dispose. Work is divided simply according to the nature of each individual, but their products are communal; each produces a surplus just because of this division of work, but it is not property. Transfer is not trade, but is rather immediately, in and for itself, communal.'[10] The treatment of labour as directed to various aspects of nature (earth, vegetation, animal) connects with Aristotelian themes[11] every bit as much as the analysis of specific economic manifestations (trade, commerce, price, money).[12] All the activities and cooperative enterprises in this 'relative ethical life' are for Hegel preliminary steps on the path to self-sufficient 'absolute' ethical life of a 'people': that is, to a society constructed on the model of the *polis*, in which the possibilities of human action are fully realized.[13]

However, Hegel's partial and quite limited reliance on the categories of classical economics cannot hide the fact that they are no longer an adequate basis for the facts of industrial and social–economic emancipation, whose importance he learned to understand through the study of political economy. While for

10 See *Schriften zur Politik und Rechtsphilosophie* (hereafter *SPR*), ed. G. Lasson (Leipzig, 1913), p. 44.
11 See *Politics* I, 8, 1256a19–b7.
12 See *Politics* I, 9, 1257a5–b30. On the other hand, it is again worth noticing that Hegel gives a modern turn to Aristotle's hint about the 'automatic' tool (*Politics*, I, 4, 1253b33–1254a1), that is, the machine; he derives it directly from the 'mechanical deadening of labour, which makes it possible in the abstracted labour process to employ the 'movement of water, of wind, of smoke, etc.' as labourers (*SPR*, pp. 433 f.).
13 *SPR*, pp. 460 ff.

Aristotle the 'economic' activities stand apart from the 'total system', that is, they are either bound to the 'individuality' of a slave who labours for an equally 'individual' master or are excluded in some other way from the *polis* as a political community (*koinōnia politikē*), for Hegel they have from the beginning a specifically 'social' character because they are socially formative, independent of sovereign political action: 'Since labour becomes universal in just this way, because it does not have to do with the totality of need materially but rather only conceptually, there is posited a universal dependency [on it] for the satisfaction of physical needs.' Thus, in total contradiction to Aristotelian presuppositions, economics appears within the *System der Sittenlehre* as the praxis of the bourgeoisie, under the name *Government* – expressing the public political role which it has assumed for Hegel as against Aristotle.[14]

If one looks for the basis of this necessary appropriation of economic–political activities within Hegel's system of ethical life, the answer is not far to seek. It lies in the assimilation of modern political economy, itself a newly-developed 'system' in which the 'determinations' and 'manifold reality' of products originating from need and labour make themselves independent and create a sphere of universal social dependency for individuals: 'These realities in their pure inward formlessness and simplicity, that is, as feelings, in the practical sphere are feelings which reconstitute themselves out of the difference and the annulment of indifferent self-feeling, pass through a negation of intuitions and restore themselves; physical needs and enjoyments, posited once again in totality, obey a necessity in their infinite complications and form, on the one hand, the system of universal reciprocal dependence concerning physical necessities as well as the labour and acquisition for these, and, on the other, as a science, the system of so-called political economy.' The basic contradiction with which Hegelian thought must come to terms in this phase of its development

14 Here already Hegel speaks of the 'system of needs', later the basis for his analysis of modern civil society in the *Philosophy of Right*. One can see, however, that Hegel still does not posit the system in the plurality of 'needs': *Philosophie des Rechts* (Eng. tr. T. M. Knox, *Hegel's Philosophy of Right* (hereafter *PR*) (Oxford, 1942), third Part, pars. 189–208, but starts instead from the system and totality of individual needs. Cf. also *SPR*, p. 490.

is that it attempts to follow the Platonic–Aristotelian model, making moral–political ('ethical') activity more important than the productive process of labour. At the same time it recognizes the formative social function of economic–poietic activity as prescribed by modern political economy. Thus it comes about that on the one hand Hegel wants to see the ethical whole handle the 'system of reality' in a 'totally negative way' and submit it 'to its dominance'.[15] But on the other hand, since this system of reality has deepened and developed itself internally so much that it 'must disturb free ethical life where this latter mixes with these relations and is not primordially separated from them', he advocates the thesis 'that this system is consciously taken up, recognized in its right, excluded from the noble class, and granted a particular class as its domain'.[16]

Given Hegel's acknowledgment of the system of political economy in his first systematic sketches, a wider contradiction develops which is closely related to the one previously mentioned. Along with the restriction of the economic–political sphere to a specific class goes a historically and philosophically modified construction of 'absolute ethical life', a modification, as Hegel sees it, which is demanded by the modern world in contrast to the classical.[17] But the historical–philosophical modification, which was still unknown in the 'System der Sittlichkeit', produced a series of difficulties of its own, having as much to do with basic constituents which Hegel's construction borrowed from classical political philosophy as with the elements which it adopted from modern political economy. Hegel asserts that the 'class' which corresponds historically to these latter elements 'is characterized by the fact that its sphere is possession generally and the justice possible here

15 SPR, pp. 487 f.
16 SPR, p. 499.
17 Once again the motives for this grounding are given in Schelling's *Jena Vorlesungen über die Methode des Akademischen Studiums* (held in Summer semester 1802, published in 1803): 'The first struggle for every individual who wishes as a free person to comprehend the positive science of law and the state, has to be this: to secure for himself by means of philosophy and history the living intuition of the later world and of the forms of public life necessary in it' (Hegel's *Sämtliche Werke*, Jubiläumsausgabe (hereafter *WWG*), ed. H. Glockner (20 vols., Stuttgart, 1927–30), Vol. v, p. 315). Cf. also the remark concerning the difference between the modern 'civil' state and the classical *polis*, from which Hegel's historical–philosophical presentation begins in the natural law essay (*WWG*, Vol. i, pp. 497 ff.; *NL*, pp. 101 ff.).

in matters of possession, that it also makes up a cohesive system, and that as an immediate consequence of the fact that the relation of possession is taken up into formal unity, each individual, being as such capable of possession is related to all others (the community) as a burgher in the sense of a *bourgeois*'.[18] But Hegel explains this very class, which he appears to associate with the modern middle class,[19] historically and philosophically as a product of the decay of the classical *polis* ethical life. With the 'loss of absolute ethical life', the decline of the *polis* in its distinctive form into the universality of the Roman Empire, the old 'classes' of the free and the unfree became alike, and 'with the loss of freedom, slavery ceased of necessity'.[20] Hegel, influenced by Gibbon's *Decline and Fall*, conceived the living ethical life of the *polis* as congealed into the lifeless formality of Roman law, in which the principle of universality and the equality of humans as 'private persons' achieved a validity quite as abstract as that of the equality of souls before God in the Christian religion. The historical falsity of this account in an essential point (namely that Roman law in its cultivation of the concept of the person in no way annuls the distinction of the classes named by Hegel but rather establishes this very distinction in the title *status libertatis*)[21] would not be all that important were it not that the 'performance of the tragedy of ethical life', which is dramatically staged by Hegel and whose location and time is intentionally undetermined, is tied in precisely to this point. The 'obscurity' or even the 'mysticism' of this tragedy, which the interpreters of Hegel's early writings lament with an otherwise rare unanimity,[22] has its real source in the fact that at this time Hegel is still unclear about the concept and origin of modern 'civil society'. His misinterpretation of Roman law (first corrected in the *Philosophy of Right*)[23] is the external occasion for that peculiar projection of the image of the bourgeoisie to the end of the classical world. This projection

18 *WWG*, Vol. I, p. 499; *NL*, p. 103.
19 Which is also concretized by the fact that he introduces into the discussion the specific-ally modern origin of the aristocratic middle class. Cf. *WWG*, Vol. I, p. 495; *NL*, p. 100.
20 *WWG*, Vol. I, p. 496; *NL*, p. 101.
21 See R. Sohm, *Institutionen des Römischen Rechts*, 4th edn (Leipzig, 1891), pp. 100 f. and 105 ff.
22 See Lukács, *Der junge Hegel*, p. 465, with H. Glockner, *Hegel*, Vol. II, p. 330.
23 See *WWG*, Vol. VII, pp. 40 ff.; *PR*, pp. 17 ff.

allowed Hegel to clarify the conflict between the *burgher* as citizen
and as bourgeois, which arose historically with the political and
social emancipation of modern ('civil') society, in terms of Aeschylus' tragedies praised as valid at all times.[24] The tragedy of ethical
life does not yet express the difference which this conflict posits
between 'civil society' and 'state'.[25] Instead, it expresses the difference between the 'first class' which, as a result of its activity's
bearing on the ethical whole, stands in an unopposed ('indifferent')
relation to it, and the second class, sunk into the determinateness
of production, whose 'indifference' is only relatively bound to
the 'existing contradiction'.[26] This 'performance of the tragedy
of ethical life', which the absolute eternally enacts with itself, is
designed to guarantee the insight that this opposition (viz., the
mutual dependence of the second class and the first and their
joint dependence on the product of labour) is the 'fate' and
'necessity' of the idea of ethical life itself. As much in order to
be conceived as to be given 'form' under the historical conditions
of the intrinsically deepened and strengthened system of political
economy, ethical life must be so constituted that it 'maintains
its own life purified', since it 'consciously concedes' its own independent existence through the 'sacrifice of a part of itself'.[27]
The result of the tragedy of ethical life, the reconciliation of
classical *polis* ethics with the system of political economy as a
'fate' from which it intends to protect itself by 'segregation' and
'resistance', still contains all the contradictions which we have
discussed and which characterize the first phase of Hegel's philosophical understanding of right and the state. The contradictions
produced by the simultaneous acceptance of modern political

24 See *WWG*, Vol. 1, pp. 500 ff.; *NL*, pp. 104 ff.
25 This in opposition to G. Rohrmoser, *Subjektivität und Verdinglichung: Theologie und
Gesellschaft im Denken des jungen Hegel* (Gütersloh, 1961), pp. 86 ff., who allies himself
at this point with G. Lukács's proposals, which in general leave out of account considerations of Hegel's development.
26 See *WWG*, Vol. 1, pp. 500 and 505; *NL*, pp. 104–9. The Hegelian presupposition, that
absolute ethical life is represented by the 'class of the noble and the free', comes even
more clearly into view in the first sketch of a class system from 1801–2. Cf. also *SPR*,
pp. 472 f. To this extent it is incomprehensible that G. Lasson, who verified the
identification which the natural law essay establishes between absolute ethical life and
the first class (*SPR*, Introduction, p. xxxvii), dates the 'System der Sittlichkeit' later for
that very reason and views its construction as richer.
27 *WWG*, Vol. 1, p. 537.

economy and the classical political doctrine of the relation between action and labour develop out of the distinctive 'segregation' of the first and second classes, which Hegel introduces in the structure of his 'System der Sittlichkeit'. It is obvious that he thereby simply reproduces the classical distinction between politics and economics, but – and here lie the difficulties we have found in his initial system and conceptual scheme – he does so on the basis of modern political economy, which had broken through the classical dividing-lines.

Hegel's thinking overcomes these contradictions as it develops. If one moves from the first elaboration in the natural law essay towards the Jena lectures of 1803–4 and 1805–6, one notices immediately that system and realities appear to split completely. The proposed classifications in the style of Plato and Aristotle are abandoned. But what characterizes the sketches of this period is not merely the 'amassing of materials without any organic pattern'.[28] This can be explained at least in part by the fact that in this case we are concerned with lecture notes rather than works destined for publication. What is more noteworthy is the breadth of acceptance which political economy finds at this period of Hegel's conceptual and systematic development in marked distinction to the previous period. The categories which have grown from it are neither limited to a particular realm of objects nor fixed on a 'class'. Instead they penetrate into various parts of the system. There are two points of particular interest. First, Hegel develops a connection between economic categories and the categories of modern natural law theory, a connection which allows the relation between political economy and 'formal' law (which up to now he had equated with Roman civil law) to appear in a different light. Second, he no longer limits 'the system or reciprocal dependence between needs and labour' to a 'class', but rather recognizes that this idea implies a concept of society which makes further adherence to the traditional doctrine of classes impossible. Regrettably, the manuscript of the lectures of 1803–4 gives not evidence for the transformation of this significant part of Hegel's political philosophy; it terminates just at the point at which, after a comparatively broad treatment of political economic

28 As K. Rosenkranz in *Hegels Leben*, p. 194, would have it.

problems, he moves to the concepts of 'property' and 'person'. This might well be an accident, of course, but if one reflects on the arrangement of the lecture fragments immediately preceding, it can easily be seen that Hegel here dissolves one side of the contradiction of his Jena writings while recapitulating the other in an extreme form. On the one hand, he conceives 'absolute ethical life' in his usual way as the 'people' to which individual being has a merely negative relation; as 'totality', individuality is 'something merely possible and not self-referring, which in its make-up is just the sort which is always ready for death and has renounced itself. It is not a totality as an individual, but as a family and in possession and enjoyment, but in such a way that this relation is an ideal one for it and proves to be one of self-sacrifice.'[29] On the other hand, Hegel incorporates the system of political economy into absolute ethical life as its natural basis. It is of course taken as the 'inorganic nature' of ethical life [30] just as in the natural law essay, but at the same time it is a nature which is mediated through the 'people' rather than just through a 'class', the restriction which had previously limited its importance for the whole. Thus, one can still draw an inference on the basis of Hegel's discussion, even if the section of the manuscript concerning the doctrine of 'classes' is missing. The aspect of 'universality' which he discloses in such economic categories as labour, possession, value, and money, is itself a moment in the existence of a people, and in this context it becomes 'immediately an other, as it is in its concept'. Thereby labour, which satisfies individual needs and whose immediate form of development is individual, becomes something universal: the rule of labour or labour for the needs of all.[31] According to Hegel the classical example of this process

29 *JR*, Vol. 1, p. 231.

30 See *JR*, Vol. 1, p. 234. In this connection it is interesting that Hegel connects economic and political activity to the spirit's same 'necessity' of going to 'work' in a people. To be sure, the former's work, as distinct from the 'ethical work' of virtuous action, is 'negative, [spirit's] directness against the appearance of what is other than itself, or its inorganic nature' (p. 234).

31 On the universalization of labour cf. *JR*, Vol. 1, p. 236: 'For labour as such the demand is equally present now: it will *be recognized* and have the form of universality; a *universal method*, a rule of all labour, is what is something for itself, appears as something external or as inorganic nature, and must be *learned*; but this universal is the true essence from labour's point of view'; on the universality of needs cf. *JR*, Vol. 1, pp. 237 f.

is the division of labour described by Adam Smith. This division occurs as the differentiation of the labour process in manufacturing, which as 'individualization of labour' incomparably increased the quantity of produced goods and thereby the interdependence of 'individual labour with the whole infinite mass of needs'. As Hegel now recognizes, the system of political economy establishes in a 'people' a 'system of social solidarity and reciprocal dependence' which requires other means for its 'dominance' than the 'division' and demarcation of classes.[32]

The exposition of this system, which undercuts not only class divisions but also the blueprints for the transition from a state of nature to a state of society in natural law theory, is found in the lectures of 1805–6. There one finds these latter elements replaced by the process of social labour in which the individual externalizes himself and his consciousness into a thing in order to mediate himself with himself *in* this externalization. The movements of recognizing and being recognized are admitted into the movement of economic processes as a general form of social mediation. The greatness of these lecture outlines is that they free the social concept of modern natural law theory from the abstraction which had clung to it right up to Fichte. They achieve this by recalling it to the soil of political economy, or, to express it in a formula, by uniting Adam Smith and Rousseau.

It is not only the relation of the wills and rights of individuals that is constitutive for the composition of a society, but also their relation to things, grounded in need and labour: 'Being recognized is immediate actuality, and in its element the Person is initially being-for-itself in general; he is enjoying and working. Here for the first time *desire has the right to appear* since it is *actual*, i.e., it *itself has universal spiritual being*. It is the labour *of* all and *for* all, and pleasure – the pleasure of all.'[33] Object-constitution or

32 *JR*, Vol. I, p. 239. Cf. on the other side *Wissenschaftliche Behandlungsarten des Naturrechts*, in *WWG*, Vol. I, p. 498; *NL*, pp. 102–3, where the expansion of the economic system is tied to the prior constitution of a class.
33 *JR*, Vol. I, p. 213.

'consciousness' self-objectification'[34] is as essential to the social process of labour as is the labour of the individual. But in society labour and need are always universal – 'abstract labour' and 'abstract need'. The abstraction lies in the 'for-itselfness' of the individuation of the individual, which completes itself within society. Both are the 'abstract elements in its development', for-itselfness and society, which rest on the self-reflective movement of the individual and his labour: 'the content of his labour exceeds *his* need; he works for the needs of many as does everyone. Thus each satisfies the needs of many and the satisfaction of his many particular needs is the work of many others.'[35] Externalization into thinghood in labour and enjoyment means also that the thing itself enters the process of social mediation and in it the moment of being recognized, the 'general will', steps forward.

Hegel demonstrates this point in the economic mode of the existence of things (value, money, barter) and in legal categories like the contract. A 'movement' must take place between the 'multifarious abstract products', so that things produced for abstract needs can become 'concrete' again. At the same time the possibility of this movement is to be found in the abstraction of labour, the mutual comparability of things; social labour is the 'element of universality' in which they have become 'universal' and 'equal'. The universality of produced things is 'their *identity* or *value*. In this they are the same. This value itself taken as a thing is *money*. The return to concreteness, to possession, is *exchange*. The *abstract* thing expresses what it is in exchange, namely, to be this transformation, to turn back from the thing into the self, and indeed in such a way that *its thinghood consists in* being the possession of another ... This *equality in things* as their inward soul is their *value* which has the full agreement of myself and the other – my positive assertion and equally the other's, the unity of my will and the other's will, and my will itself holds good as more actual, more existent; recognition is

34 *JR*, Vol. 1, p. 214: 'The self's *inorganic nature as existing* stands opposed to its *abstract for-itselfness*; the self relates itself negatively to this opposition and cancels it in the unity of both, but in such a way that the self forms the other as its own self, contemplates its own form and in just this way consumes its self ... But this laborious process is itself multiform; it is *"consciousness'-making-itself into a thing."*'
35 *JR*, Vol. 1, pp. 214 f.

existence.'[36] Labour and exchange are the forms of mediation which constitute 'society' as a relation of will and right; in the same way that labour mediates the individual with himself and with nature as 'thinghood', exchange mediates his labour with the labour of all. For Hegel, the forms of mediation are the *existence* ('fact') of recognition, in which individuals contemplate the universality in terms of which they have formed themselves through the medium of thinghood. In agreement with modern political economy, Hegel no longer gives a role to occupancy, natural law's traditional legal title to property, a title which made the construction of a social contract necessary in securing the transition from a state of nature to a civil state. Labour and exchange, rather than occupancy, are the genuine title for the acquisition of property, which always presupposes the 'existence' of recognition as well as the social forms of alienation and mediation: 'The same universality is mediation with *property* (as knowing movement and thus as immediate *having*) brought about through recognition, which is to say, its existence is spiritual being. Here the contingent character of *occupancy is annulled*; I *have* everything through *labour* and *exchange* in recognition ... The sources, origin of property, these are here the ground of labour, of my *doing* itself – immediate selfhood and recognition.'[37]

With this Hegel has grasped labour as the form of emancipation for modern society in which the individual is 'formed' to the freedom of legal personality. Labour's 'social' character remains

---

36 JR, Vol. 1, pp. 215 f. Concerning this point Hegel notes in the margin: 'In his abstract *labour* he views his own universality, his form, or the fact that it exists *for another*. Thus he wishes to share this positing with others, or these others ought themselves to be *seen in it*: a second movement, which contains the developed moments of the first. "I" is an activity in relation to another I (indeed as recognized by the latter) as one who relates himself to my possessions but who will have them only *with my consent* just as I [concern] myself with his possessions only with his consent. – The *equality* of both individuals as *recognized–value*, meaning of the thing. The thing has the meaning of *relation to another*' (pp. 215 f.).

37 JR, Vol. 1, p. 217. Cf. *ibid.*, the summary of this section, in relation to which it is to be noticed above all that Hegel grasps not only exchange and contract but also labour as forms of externalization: 'I have desired in trade, posited my thing as value, i.e., *inward* movement, inward action, *as labour which is submerged in being*; in both cases it is the same *externalization*. (In labour I transform myself *immediately* into a thing, to a form, which is [a] *being*.) In this way I externalize for myself my own existence, make it into *something alien to me and keep* myself in this state ... Thus I contemplate here my being recognized as existence, and my will is this value' (p. 217).

hidden both from classical politics (as a consequence of the fact that it ranks moral action above production) and from modern natural law theory (as a consequence of its orientation to relations of will and contract). The 'social' fact of the contract is a consequence of this original recognition which the individual wins for himself through labour and exchange. The certainty that connections and achievements of individuals have been contractually secured makes the contingent social relationships which rest on labour and exchange both calculable and rational: 'My word *must be good* not on the moralistic grounds that I must be inwardly true to myself, not alter my opinions, convictions, and so forth.' It must rather be good because the will has its existence only as 'recognized' or 'social': 'I not only contradict myself but rather the fact that my will is recognized. One cannot trust my word, i.e., my will is merely mine, mere opinion.'[38] The contract is worked out by free and equal individuals whose wills are not closed up in the isolation of *opinion* but rather are calculable as *general will*. To be sure, 'concept' and 'existence' are differentiated in the contract, which Hegel also labels as an 'ideal exchange', an exchange of clarifications (rather than things); the contract can be broken because the individual will holds good as such, and not just in so far as it is universal. Only the accomplished fact is 'existence', or the 'existing general will'.[39]

Even in the contract the general will is 'concealed beneath the determinate things'[40] so that individuals are drawn together in the act of externalization. In Hegel's view the general will must emerge from its concealment, for contracts indeed regulate relations between individuals within the social whole but not the movement which is immanent in this whole. And here, in the knowledge of the laws of this movement, Hegel completely transcends the limits of natural law theory. After the section on 'recognition' which adheres at least formally to the theory of the transition from the state of nature to the civil state, but still prior to the discussion of 'ethical life' (politics, which here has the mean-

38 See *JR*, Vol. 1, pp. 219 f. Cf. also H. Marcuse, *Vernunft und Revolution* (Neuwied, 1962) pp. 81 f. (Eng. tr., *Reason and Revolution* (New York, 1955).)

39 *JR*, Vol. 1, pp. 218 f.

40 See *JR*, Vol. 1, p. 220.

ing of constitution and public administration), a further section

ing of constitution and public administration), a further section
appears: on 'the power possessing law', which recapitulates the
material already discussed from the new standpoint of submission
to law. In it one can observe the extent to which the wider
inclusion of political economy within political philosophy has
systematic consequences as well.[41] While in the previous section
Hegel presented the 'element of universality' as the 'social' aspect
of the economic–legal categories which for their part remain fixed
to the contingency of individual acts, here he calls it explicitly
by name: it is *Society itself* which now finds its place under the title
'power possessing law'. 'The universal is ... a necessity to the
individual labourer. He has his unconscious existence in the universal; society is his nature on whose elemental blind movement
he depends to sustain or destroy him spiritually and physically.'[42]
'Society', set free politically and consigned to the economic laws
of its movement, appears in two ways. (1) In the form of affirmation
of the contingency and right of the self-existing individual,
through whom society reproduces itself as a whole and shows itself
superior to the substantial ethical life of the traditional political
society. An expression of this affirmation is the law of which Hegel
says that it 'includes within itself the self of the individual',[43] or
the *person*. (2) But the same society is given over to the 'elementary
necessity, contingency of the individual' in such a way that when
left to itself, this society produces a series of antagonisms against

41 In the lectures of 1803–4 this does not come to light nearly so obviously. To be sure,
here as well as in the discussion of 'absolute ethical life', Hegel recapitulates the 'natural
powers' such as language, tool, family, family property, etc., but he undertakes no
changes in regard to the systematic place of the ethical life of the 'people'. Corresponding
to this is the fact that the process of recognizing, which concludes the first part of the
system, does not have a proper sphere of 'recognition' as a result, but instead moves on
immediately to the presentation of ethical life. In 1805–6 'recognition' is the first step of
(a) 'actual spirit', which in connection with (b) contract (c) crime and punishment, and
(d) power-possessing law, forms that second part of the system which inserts itself as an
independent domain between the first (the developmental history of the theoretical and
practical self) and third parts of the system (Constitution–political and administrative
science). Cf. in this regard F. Rosenzweig, *Hegel und der Staat* (Munich/Berlin, 1920),
Vol. 1, pp. 178 ff., who, however, judges the systematic structure of the lectures of
1803–4 (which still adheres wholly to the early Jena essays) in a factually insufficient
manner.
42 *JR*, Vol 1, p. 231.
43 *JR*, Vol. 1, p. 225. Cf. pp. 226 f. for the characterization of the particular moments of
the law.

which it and the existence of the individual threaten to shatter. People's labour, the possibility of sustaining their existence, is 'subordinated to the whole's contingency in its full complexity. Thus a mass is damned to the totally dulling, unhealthy, and unsafe unskilled labour in factory, manufacturing and the mine; and branches of industry which sustain a large class of people dry up overnight because of fashion or undercutting through discoveries in another country; and this mass is abandoned to a poverty which it cannot avoid. The contrast between great wealth and great poverty appears – a poverty in which it is impossible to save anything.'[44]

In response to this contradiction which rends 'ethical life, the absolute bond of the people', the 'System der Sittlichkeit' sees the preservation of the whole still guaranteed by the 'immediate constitution of the class in itself'.[45] The lectures of 1803–4, which no longer reduce the contradiction to the peculiarities of a class but rather conceive it as a moment of the 'huge system of solidarity and reciprocal dependence' posited in the 'people itself', give us no further information on this subject since they terminate the presentation of the system.[46] It is different with the lectures of 1805–6, which, under the modern name of Society, externally separate the system as 'State' from the 'constitution' of the people. These lectures not only give more space to the analysis of social antagonisms,[47] but even develop the dialectic of their 'necessity' both more purely and more clearly than could previously be done. The elementary necessity of the social whole, which infiltrates the consciousness of the individuals in question, is tied up with the equally basic form of contingency, through whose movement the whole sustains itself and the individuals. The same law which on the one hand affirms this contingency of individuals must on

44 *JR*, Vol. I, p. 232.
45 See *SPR*, p. 492. Indeed, the antagonism arises within the 'system of needs', but since Hegel then conceived this as linked with his class doctrine, it appears inside the 'commercial class', in which it 'again divides into many particular classes of commerce and these into classes of varying wealth and pleasure' (p. 491). Concerning the 'external limitations imposed by the government, see *SPR*, pp. 493 f. Compared with the class structure these are sketched relatively briefly and in essence concern only the system of taxation.
46 See *JR*, Vol. I, pp. 239 f.
47 See *JR*, Vol. II, pp. 231–3.

the other hand deny it again. It must do this, that is, when the blind process of society separates contingency from itself and surrenders its own existence to ruin. Antagonistic society cannot free itself from this power; in order to relax its grip, society requires a *deus ex machina* which binds necessity and chance together in a law. This law which settles the social antagonisms and once again mediates the movement of the whole with itself and with the movement of the individual is for Hegel *The State*: 'This necessity, which is the complete contingency of individual existence, is however also the latter's *sustaining substance*. The power of the state enters in and must take care that each sphere is preserved, or step into the middle, search for outlets, new channels of commerce in other lands, and so on ... Freedom of vocation [remains necessary]; intervention *must* appear to be improbable to the maximum degree – because it is the domain of caprice.'[48] Thus, even before Hegel's presentation of the economic forms of 'societal' development makes the transition to the state (3: *Constitution*), it encounters the latter in the concept of the 'power possessing law'. Although society expressly so-called is already distinguished from the 'law' of the individual in the law of the *family* ('the persistence of his immediate existence')[49] and the sphere of *Person* and *Property* which follows the latter's dissolution, at this stage of his thinking Hegel has only one term for the existence of the individual *between* family and state, and that is '*state*'.[50]

Thus, concept and presented reality are still separated. At the same time, however, the concept ('state') more and more assumes the historical physiognomy of the material which the lectures so richly display. If in the last section the state was the 'state as wealth', so now under the heading 'Constitution' it becomes the state as 'universal might' and 'absolute power'.[51] It is as if while

---

48 *JR*, Vol. II, p. 233.
49 Cf. *JR*, Vol. II, p. 227: 'A. The law [as] the persistence of its *immediate existence*. The individual is immediately as a natural whole within it; he exists as family. He is valid as this natural whole, not as person; he must first become this' (cf. pp. 228 ff.).
50 *JR*, Vol. II, p. 231: 'B. This law of the immediate existence of the individual is, as a law, its will, or it sustains the latter as such in the disappearance of contingent being. [Through the] death of the parents it becomes positive; it appears as the existence which it was before – State.' Cf. here Rosenzweig, *Hegel und der Staat*, Vol. I, pp. 180 f.
51 See *JR*, Vol. II, pp. 242 and 244 f.

working out this section Hegel had in hand his essay on the German constitution from the years 1799 to 1802, the first part of which presents a 'concept of the state' quite comparable to that of these lectures.[52] Without doubt this connection which links Hegel's 'state' with the modern concept of the political (the rules of self-assertion and exercised power developed from Machiavelli to Hobbes) coheres closely with the progressive introduction of political economy into political philosophy observed earlier. The modern concept of society, which constitutes itself within the traditional conceptual and systematic structure of political and natural law theory, renders impossible both the fixed adherence to traditional class doctrine and the one-sided orientation of the concept of 'state' towards the 'substantive ethical life' of the ancients. Thus, in these lectures Hegel finally abandons the *polis* concept of his younger days. He grasps the secret connection which links this ideal and the doctrine of the social contract: 'one represents the establishment of the general will as if all citizens come together, deliberate among themselves, take a vote and thus the majority constitutes the general will'.[53] He rejects natural law theory because it assumes that the general will must first create itself from individual wills, while at the same time assuming that it is found in them already, even before their entry into a 'state'. For Hegel, this contract model is incompatible with the historical and social basis of the 'state' (by which one must always understand the 'modern' state, whether absolutistic or post-revolutionary). This is expressed with supreme clarity in the lectures. General will is not the *cause* but rather the *outcome* of the state, which owes its origin to external power. 'The general will is the state's implicit being, i.e., it is its external power which compels it. Thus, all states are founded by the sublime power of great men . . .'[54] With this Hegel turns towards the 'state' of his own time, which means

---

52 See *SPR*, p. 17 ff. with *JR*, Vol II, pp. 246 ff. The agreement comes about above all in regard to the criterion of sovereignty and the rules of self-assertion, on which point Hegel cites Machiavelli's *Prince* in both writings. Rudolph Haym rightly asserted (*Hegel und seine Zeit* (Berlin, 1957), p. 167) that the concept of the state in the constitution essay universally contradicts the concept 'construed' in the early philosophical sketches. However, Haym omits mention of the fact that this is no longer true of the lectures of 1805–6.

53 *JR*, Vol. II, p. 245.

54 *JR*, Vol. II, p. 246.

for him the modern European state shaken by the French Revolution and reformed in its foundations. The revolution realized the social contract which views the general will in terms of the will of all as 'the principle of the *true, free state*'.[55] It did not, however, actualize the ideal of the *polis* but rather its image, intrinsically altered under the economic and social conditions of modern political life. The immediate unity between universal and individual wills, from which contract theory sets out, distinguishes itself according to historical reality into 'the extreme of the *universal which is itself individuality* as government, [it is] not an abstraction of the state but *individuality* which has the universal as such for its purpose; and the other extreme of the same unity which has the individual as its purpose. But individualities are like the same thing. The same person cares for himself and his family, labours, and concludes contracts, while also working for the universal and having this as a *purpose*. On this side he is called *bourgeois*, and on the other *citizen*. The *universal* will is obeyed as the majority of all wills, and it is *constituted by the concrete expression and agreement of individuals.*'[56]

This 'two fold way' in which the unity binding individuality and universality exists historically points to the blueprint for the *Philosophy of Right* (1821), which divides the study of civil society (human being as *bourgeois*) from that of the state (human being as *citizen*). To be sure, at this time (1805–6) Hegel is not yet clear in his own mind about the problem posed by the French Revolution: differentiating between the person as *citoyen* and as *bourgeois*. Still, the passage cited earlier advances directly to the discussion of ancient democracy so that one cannot really tell what the two antithetical French terms which underlie the revolutionary realization of democracy have to do with the 'beautiful happy freedom of the Greeks'. However, the lectures give unambiguous evidence on one point, and that is the principle of the modern state's superiority to ancient democracy. Clearly the principle of the modern state is its ability to sustain the contradiction between *bourgeois*

---

55 See *JR*, Vol. II, p. 245.

56 *JR*, Vol. II, p. 249. Hegel remarks in the margin here, 'Townsman (*Spiessbürger*) and German citizen (*Reichsbürger*), the one formally as much a bourgeois (*Spiessbürger*) as the other'.

and *citoyen* precisely because it produces the contradiction and pushes it to the limit both in thought and reality: 'The deeper quarrel is thus that each person *turns back completely into himself*, knows his *simple self* as the essential thing, and arrives at the capricious resolution to take itself as absolute even though separated from the existing universal.' In Hegel's conception the principle of the modern state consists in the fact that the individual leaves the universal alone and vice versa; since they leave one another alone in this way, both spheres increase their independence. The general will no longer constitutes itself through the wills of individuals but is instead free from them, 'free from the knowledge of all'.[57] That Hegel deduces hereditary monarchy from this as the form of the state appropriate to the modern world is, viewed from the perspective of legal and social philosophy, less decisive than the fact that *with this principle he removes the basis both for deriving the concept of the state from a contract and for accepting the concept of an intrinsically political ('civil') society.* Here for the first time the 'state', separate from society, wins a place corresponding to its modern concept, a place which can ground the philosophy of right's later structure. It is free in both directions: free in relation to the will of individuals who have lost their claim to 'civil' independence, and free in relation to the disposition of the monarch, who is only the 'empty node' of an 'organized' whole which lives in its institutions and knows how to bear the antagonisms ('extremes') which it forms in itself.[58]

57 See *JR*, Vol. II, pp. 249 f.
58 See *JR*, Vol. II, p. 251: 'Things are now differently run and lived in states whose constitutions are the same – and this gradually changes with time ... each domain: city, guild [is operative] in the administration of its particular concerns. [A] people is bad when it is the government – as bad as it is unreasonable. The whole, however, is the mid-point, the free spirit which stands back from these completely fixed extremes as from the disposition of the rules; it is the empty *node*.' Cf. p. 252. A similar thought occurs already in the writing *Über die Verfassung Deutschlands* (1801–2) in *SPR*, p. 27

6

'State' and 'Civil Society': Linguistic Context and Historical Origin

If one compares the statements made by Hegel's contemporaries between 1820 and 1850 concerning the presentation of civil society in the third section of Hegel's *Philosophy of Right* – much admired even then – with the statements of modern interpreters, the question of this concept's historical place does not seem to be an issue for either group. For one of Hegel's immediate students, such as Edward Gans, who edited the second edition of this work in 1833 for the great *Hegel-Ausgabe* prepared by the 'group of the deceased's friends', it was self-evident that here 'nothing which could have relevance to the state was omitted' since 'even the science of political economy' had 'found its appropriate place and treatment in civil society'.[1] The same judgment is reiterated by Chr. Hermann Weisse, Arnold Ruge, Constantin Rössler, and Bruno Bauer; and as concerns the substance of the matter, the reduction of the problem to political economy, the earliest works in 'natural law theory' and 'political science' emanating from Hegel's philosophy of right, Konrad Moritz Besser's *System des Naturrechts* (1830) and J. Fr. Gottfried Eiselen's *Handbuch des Systems der Staatswissenschaften* (1828), both operate within the framework set up by Gans in their characterization of civil society. Johann Eduard Erdmann does not conceive the place of civil society all that differently in his *Vorlesungen über den Staat* (1851). For him, its 'essence' consists in 'prudent accounting, the rational calculus, industry, and so on', and in 'credit'. This, its distinguishing characteristic, is pre-eminently displayed in the 'manufacturer'

---

1 Preface to Hegel, *Grundlinien der Philosophie des Rechts*, in *Werke*, ed. P. Marheineke *et al.* (18 vols., Berlin, 1832–45) (hereafter *Werke*), Vol. VIII (1833), p. viii. We will refer to this edition throughout this chapter (Eng. tr. T. M. Knox, *Hegel's Philosophy of Right* (hereafter *PR*) (Oxford, 1942).)

who is the 'burgher *par excellence*'.[2] Thereby Erdmann moved civi
society into closer relation with the middle class; Hegel's use o
the word would, in that case, run parallel with the seventeenth
and eighteenth-century European movement of liberation for the
middle class.

Marx and many others of his time, men like Wilhelm Heinrich
Riehl, Lorenz Stein, J. C. Bluntschli, and Hermann Wagener
understood the concept of 'civil society' in precisely these terms
As Marx argues in the *Preface to the Critique of Political Economy*
Hegel has 'brought together' the 'totality' of 'material relations
of life' according to the 'precedent of the eighteenth century
English and French, under the name of "Civil society"'.[3] The
reference to the eighteenth-century English and French explicitly
tags the concept as modern. Even before Marx people referred
to the individualistic notions of modern natural law theory in
order to put Hegel's civil society into historical perspective, a
did, for example, Romeo Maurenbrecher, one of the most im
portant scholars of German constitutional law before 1850.
Similarly, for Lassalle, too, Hobbes's 'bellum omnium contra
omnes', as one of the versions of this natural law theory, is merely
'that which one calls, by way of comparison to its distinction
from the state, the sphere of civil society, submitted to free com
petition'. And not least of all was Ferdinand Tönnies who, setting
out in *Gesellschaft und Gemeinschaft* (1887) with conceptual distinc
tions taken up in opposition to modern natural law theory, related
'civil society' in the Hegelian sense to the modern society o
contract, trade, and labour.[5]

Among modern interpreters, Franz Rosenzweig in his book
Hegel und der Staat (1920) raises the question not so much about
the historical as about the biographical and genetic origin of the
word. His results, pointing out Hegel's early excerpts from
Sulzer's *Kurzer Begriff aller Wissenschaften* (1759) as well as hi

2 *Philosophische Vorlesungen über den Staat* (Halle, 1851), pp. 28–9. as in *Vorlesungen übe
akademisches Leben und Studium* (Leipzig, 1858), pp. 97–8.
3 *Zur Kritik der politischen Ökonomie*, Preface, quoted from the Berlin edition (1951), p. 12
4 *Grundsätze des heutigen deutschen Staatsrecht*, 2nd, unchanged edn (1843), pp. 22 ff.
5 Lassalle, *Herr Bastiat-Schulze Delitzsch* (1864) in *Gesammelte Reden und Schriften*, ed
Edward Bernstein (12 vols., Berlin, 1919–20), Vol. v, p. 69 and Ferdinand Tönnies
Gemeinschaft und Gesellschaft, 2nd edn (Leipzig, 1912), p. 25.

familiarity with Ferguson's *Essay on the History of Civil Society* (1767), simply are not enough to be convincing. The civil society of Hegel's philosophy of right is first viewed in a more comprehensive perspective by Karl Löwith, because he connects its differentiation from the state (corresponding to the concrete mode of its exposition with reference to par. 260 of the *Philosophy of Right*) to the dichotomy between the classical age and Christendom, Rousseau's *Social Contract* and Plato's *Republic*. At the same time, Herbert Marcuse, in his book *Reason and Revolution: Hegel and the Rise of Social Theory* (1941), is able to work out the theory of society immanent within Hegel's philosophy of right and its influence on modern sociology, although, of course, this leads to an inevitable attenuation of the historical dimension within which both Hegel himself and his era move. It is this attenuation above all which leads in George Lukács's book *Der junge Hegel und die Probleme der kapitalistischen Gesellschaft* (written in 1938 but not published until 1948) to a permanent disparity between the interpreter and his object which only competent individual studies can dissolve. Nothing illustrates this more clearly than Lukács's introduction of the expression 'civil society' into Hegel's analysis, although it does not occur even once in the texts which he is interpreting. Finally, the same point could be illustrated in Joachim Ritter's study *Hegel und die Französische Revolution* (1957) which, energetically motivated by the actuality of the question, presents Hegel's civil society as the first conceptual presentation of modern working society.[6]

But the question which arises here is whether the authentic historical content of Hegel's concepts in general can be grasped by this sort of interpretation *post festum*. If one interprets Hegel's 'civil society' within the tendency towards modern sociology, must one not also ask in what relation it stands to the older use of the same word which one finds repeatedly in Kant and Christian

6 See F. Rosenzweig, *Hegel und der Staat* (Munich/Berlin, 1920), Vol. II, p. 118; Karl Löwith, *Von Hegel zu Nietzsche* (Garden City, NY, 1941), Part 2, Chs. 1. 2; (Eng. tr. *Der junge Hegel* (Berlin, 1954), above all, pp. 152 ff., 227 ff., 280 ff., 368 ff., and 435 ff. (Eng. tr. R. Livingstone, *The Young Hegel* (Cambridge, 1966)); J. Ritter, *Hegel und die Französische Revolution* (Cologne, 1957), above all, pp. 35 f. and 38 ff. – compare also the corresponding interpretations of 'civil society' by E. Weil, *Hegel et l'État* (Paris, 1950), pp. 71 ff., and M. Rossi, *Marx e la dialettica hegeliana*, Vol I: *Hegel e lo Stato* (1960), Book III, pp. 543 ff.

Wolff? Still further: beyond Kant and Wolff, how does the concept relate to such concepts as the Aristotelian *koinōnia politiké* or Cicero's *societas civilis* in medieval school philosophy and in modern natural law theory? For to the extent that the possibility of historical understanding consists in placing the moving actuality of what is at issue (in our case the phenomenon of modern society) into the past's comprehension while at the same time bracketing the latter's proper horizons and making modifications in them, it would also be legitimate to measure Hegel's 'civil society' directly against the tradition of this concept in European political philosophy.

I

It will always remain a remarkable phenomenon in the history of the concept of 'civil society' that at nearly the same time – around 1820 – the word appeared not only as a substantive innovation in Hegel's *Philosophy of Right* but also as the key political concept in Carl Ludwig Haller's *Restauration der Staatswissenschaft*. For this professed theoretician of the Restoration, 'civil society' is a revolutionary concept of Enlightenment philosophy, which had been taken over from Roman republican idiom complete with its classical dress. The artificial adoption of this classical political concept actually caused the great revolution of the eighteenth century and its overthrow of all natural social relationships: eliminating mastery and dependence between men, subordinating them to the state, destroying worldly and spiritual 'powers', autonomous communities and corporations. Thus, the Preface to the Bern patrician's six-volume work on the Restoration reports, 'The mother and root of all error' in the revolutionary period is, above all, 'the unholy idea of a Roman *societas civilis* which was transferred into all other social relationships'.[7] Since people were called free and equal members *of one* 'civil society', the 'social alliance' had dissolved, as Haller never tired of repeating. According to him, modern natural law theory since Grotius and Hobbes initially recognized a 'so-called *civil* society' as distinct from 'natural society'. He saw the seed of this distinction primarily

7 See *Restauration der Staatswissenschaft* (1816–20), Preface to Vol. I, p. xxviii.

in the Latinate idiom of the learned classes of modern Europe.[8]

Hegel also took a critical posture towards modern natural law theory in defining 'state' and 'civil society' in par. 182 of the *Philosophy of Right*, where he objects that it has not clearly distinguished the two concepts: 'If the state is represented as a unity of different persons, as a unity which is only a partnership, then what is really meant is only civil society. Many modern constitutional lawyers have been able to bring within their purview no theory of the state but this.' Opposing this confusion and double mistaking of state and civil society, Hegel defines the latter factually as the 'difference' between state and family: 'civil society is the difference which intervenes between family and state; because as difference it presupposes the state; to subsist itself it must have the state before its eyes as something self-subsistent'.[9] Here, too, in the established distinction between civil society and state, or more especially between family and civil society, 'the social alliance', to use Haller's term, has been dissolved; but unlike the fanatical theorist of the Restoration, Hegel interprets this process positively as the emancipation of the state from society and of society from the state, which for the first time brings both terms into their true relationship. For clearly the critical objection to modern natural law theory means that the state is not the state if it always merges with civil society, and the latter is not 'society' when it is 'political' society, or the state.

Nevertheless, Hegel's view of civil society and its alleged confusion with the state remains within Haller's perspective; both limit the origin and historical significance of the concept to modern natural law theory, especially that of the eighteenth century, without grasping its old European tradition and its actual point of origin, in ancient political philosophy, above all in Aristotle's *Politics* and its appropriation in the medieval and modern periods. To be sure, without Hegel being aware of it, his objection is,

---

8 See *Restauration*, Vol. I, pp. 89–90: 'Since Latin has republican modes of speech and nomenclature almost exclusively, or at least when it is an issue of governments these are most frequently used, the same expressions are applied to totally different things and relationships. Just as, therefore, the citizens of Rome formed among themselves a community, a citizenry, a true *societas civilis*, so also must all other human connections and relationships be called *societates civiles* or civil unions.'

9 *Werke*, Vol VIII, par. 182, Addition, pp. 246 f.; *PR*, p. 266.

at its root, an objection against this very tradition of classical political philosophy which was still at work shaping modern natural law theory and which defined the state (*polis*, *civitas*) as identical with civil society (*koinōnia politiké*, *societas civilis*). For in its theoretical understanding of the politically ordered human world, the state neither contains society in itself nor pre-supposes its existence; rather it *is* 'society', but 'civil' or 'political society'. In its older and more original meaning, the word 'society' (*Gesellschaft*) means nothing else than association, union – *koinōnia* in Greek and *societas* or *communitas* in Latin usage. To this extent state and society (which our contemporary consciousness conditioned by the nineteenth century understandably separates and juxtaposes) were politically tied together by a single concept in old European political philosophy as late as the middle of the eighteenth century, and were drawn together into a social whole, which, at the beginning of Aristotle's *Politics*, made the constitution of the ancient *polis* explicit. This was achieved by the basic classical political concept of the *koinōnia politiké* or the *societas civilis*, the old civil society, which receives its public political structure from the substance of society as itself 'civil' or political. In this context we quote from the beginning of the first book of the *Politics* (*Politics* I, 1, 1252a1–7) in the rendering of the earliest German translation of Aristotle by J. G. Schlosser, which still freely uses the word 'society' in its older sense appropriate to *koinōnia*, even though it intended explicitly to re-establish the influential force of the *Politics* after the experience of the revolutionary period.[10] 'Es ist offenbar dass ein jeder Staat aus einer Gesellschaft besteht. Eine jede Gesellschaft hat aber, wenn sie sich verbindet, die Absicht, einen gewissen Vorteil zu erreichen. Denn alle Menschen handeln bloss, um das zu erreichen, was ihnen nützlich scheint. Es ist also auch kein Zweifel, dass die Gesell-

10 Schlosser published his translation with a *preface instead of an introduction*, which begins with the characteristic sentence: 'During the era in which everyone believes himself called to affirm and deny propositions concerning the forms of the state and revolutions, the rights of citizens and duties of rulers, it seemed to me to be not unprofitable to make known in German that which is still left over of the book on politics which Aristotle wrote a couple of thousand years ago.' (Aristotle, *Politik und Fragment der Ökonomie*, translated from the Greek with notes and textual commentary prepared by J. G. Schlosser, (1798), Part 1, p. iii.)

schaften alle in dieser Absicht zusammentreten, und dass die wichtigste und vortrefflichste, nämlich der Staat, oder die bürgerliche Gesellschaft, auch auf den höchsten und vortrefflichsten Vorteil hinzielt.' ('It is obvious that every state consists of a society. But each society, when it establishes itself, aims at achieving some gain. For all people act simply to achieve what seems useful to them. But there is also no doubt that societies all share this purpose and that the most important and best society, namely the state, or civil society, also aims at the highest and best gain.')[11] The state or civil society, *hé polis kai hé koinōnia hé politiké, civitas sive societas civilis sive res publica* – these are the classical formulae of traditional European political philosophy before the modern distinction between state and society, as they remained in effect from Aristotle to Albertus Magnus, Thomas Aquinas, and Melanchthon, even from Bodin to Hobbes, Spinoza, Locke, and Kant. 'From among the number of things', says Albertus Magnus in his commentary on Aristotle, 'which make up human nature, those which are natural for man are the state and civic or political conversation.'[12] Bodin determines the *res publica* as *societas civilis* in the same way: 'for public affairs (*res publica*) are the same as civil society (*societas civilis*) which is able to stand by itself without guilds and corporations, but not without the family'.[13] Melancthon and Spinoza deviate formally from the definition of *civitas* only in the fact that they identify it with *societas civium*: 'This society, firmly established by law and with a power of self-preservation, is called a "state" (*civitas*), and those who are protected by its right are

11 *Ibid.*, p. 1. Compare here also the translation of the *Politics* by Christian Garve which appears shortly after Schlosser's (*Die Politik des Aristoteles*, tr. Ch. Garve, published with notes and essays by G. Fuelleborn (Breslau, 1799)) and which also applies the phrase 'civil society' or 'civil union'. Only under the influence of the modern economically shaped concept of society, and in particular of Tönnies's distinction between *Gesellschaft* and *Gemeinschaft*, do the most recent translations of the *Politics* (Aristotle's *Politics*, newly translated, with an introduction and explanatory notes, prepared by E. Rolfes (1912), as also the new translation by O. Gigon, Aristotle's *Politik und Staat der Athener* (1955), pp. 1 and 55) render *koinōnia* with *Gemeinschaft*, which looks particularly strange when *koinōnia politiké* is paraphrased as 'staatliche Gemeinschaft'. The influencing force of the old traditional concept and its exemplary character, as it remained binding for Schlosser and Garve, has been lost in this neutral rendering.

12 *Commentarii in Octo Libros Politicorum Aristotelis*, Book 1 Ch. 1, in *Opera Omnia*, ed. August Borgnet (38 vols., Paris, 1890–9), Vol. VIII (1891), p. 6.

13 *De Republica*, 4th edn (1601), Book III, Ch. 7, pp. 511–12.

called "citizens" (*cives*).'[14] And Methanchthon says much the same in his commentary on Aristotle's *Politics*: 'The state is a society of citizens founded on law for mutual benefit and for the greatest security. Citizens are those who are able in this society to seek civic office or judicial power.'[15] The traditional identification of state and civil society also occurs, at least in conception, in Hobbes's 'civil union' which ends the state of nature in the submission of citizens to the state, for regarding this he says, 'The union thus constituted is called *state* or *civil* society.'[16] Finally, in this connection one might also refer to John Locke's *Two Treatises of Government* (1689) and the first part of Kant's *Metaphysik der Sitten* (1797). Locke entitles the seventh chapter of his book 'Of Political or Civil Society' and Kant, in par. 45, once again defines the state as '*civitas*', which he identifies in par. 46 with 'civic society', explained as *societas civilis*: 'The members of such a society (*societas civilis*), i.e., of a state, who are assembled for legislation are called citizens (*cives*).' These 'citizens' (*Staatsbürger*) in the Kantian sense (the word was taken by his contemporaries as a neologism and met with initial rejection) are in fact the legally competent and politically empowered citizens of the old civil society all over again, the *politai* of the *polis*, the *cives* of the *civitas*. Distinguished by the specific civic quality of *civility*, of 'knowledge of civic affairs and prudence' (Cicero, *De Orat.* I. 14.60), the citizens take part in public life, legislation, and administration. For until the eighteenth century only those men were 'citizens' who lived in '*status civilis sive politicus*', and civil society was based on this status as well, which cannot be the theme of a 'social' mode of analysis but rather only of politics in the comprehensive sense. 'That part of philosophy', says Christian Wolff, 'in which man is viewed as living in a republic or civil status, is called *politics*. And so *politics* is the

14 Spinoza, *Ethics*, ed. James Gutmann (New York/London, 1949), Part 4, Prop. xxxvii, n. 2, p. 217.
15 Melanchthon, *Commentarii in Politica Aristotelis* (1530) in *Ph. Melanchthonis opera quae super sunt omnia* (28 vols., Brunswick, 1834–60), Vol. xvi (1850), ed. Bretschneider/Bindseil, column 435.
16 Hobbes, *De Cive* Paris, 1642), Ch. 5, par. 9. (Eng. tr. S. P. Lamprecht, *De Cive or The Citizen* (New York, 1949).)

science of directing free activity in a civil society or republic.'[17]

Thus one can say that 'civil society' in the old European sense is a traditional political concept, indeed the fundamental central category of a political world, in which 'state' and 'society' are not yet distinguished. Instead, they there form the internally homogeneous system of domination of civil–political society, which rests on the 'economic' sphere, that is, on domestic-servant labour, slavery or serfdom and the wage system, to all of which it contrasts itself. For in this classical tradition in politics, not all inhabitants of the community distinguish themselves by 'civility'. Neither the unfree of every kind, who must carry out the necessary elementary nurturing labours underlying the public–political civil sphere in the private circle of the home, nor the artisan, equally active 'economically' but bound to the domestic workshop, nor women, belong to *societas civilis sive res publica*; since they are a part of the *oikos*, 'domestic society', they lack the political standing which confers civility. The basic principle of Aristotelian politics, which serves equally as the premise of his economics, 'that there is no *polis* for slaves' (*Politics* III, 9, 1280a32) still clearly holds for the servants, day-labourers, and artisans *qua* hired servants, as Kant describes them in his time at the end of the eighteenth century. Their life runs its course outside the literally civil society which as such defines and contrasts itself by reference to them. And this constitutes the second basic structural element of old civil society, after its relationship to politics: its separation downwards from economics and the household – the classical political dichotomy of *societas civilis* and *societas domestica* as it is still to be found in Christian Thomasius, Wolff, and Kant. 'The society of men', says Thomasius, 'is in itself, however, neither civil nor domestic. It is the ground of both because civil society here means nothing but a union of many domestic societies and the persons dwelling in them in so far as they stand under common regulations.'[18]

17 *Philosophia Rationalis sive Logica* (Frankfurt/Leipzig, 1728), 'Discursus praeliminaris', Ch. 3, par. 65.
18 *Kurtzer Entwurf der Politischen Klugheit* (1725), pp. 204–5. This contrast between civil and domestic society holds for Kant as well; indeed, the old identity of civil society and state is preserved for that very reason – despite his revolutionary political principles

II

If one abstracts from the variety and variability of historical–political life in its detail and also its divergent description in the great political works from Aristotle to Kant, then one must admit that the modern relation of state and society remains without its own proper 'concept' in this specific old European scholarly tradition leading up to Hegel. This is not merely a fortuitous result of the traditional concept of 'civil society'. The continuity of this concept, the long history of its tradition and its prototypic significance for the science of politics, all of which as it seems were no longer present in Hegel's mind, were not able to hinder him from using it in the future and even expressing by it his break with this very tradition and the old political world whose complement it was, thereby arriving at a new understanding of civil society. Only against the background of the great European break with tradition around 1800 can one begin to explain why Hegel, the representative of historical thinking in European metaphysics, remained within the horizon of Carl Ludwig von Haller and his historical protest against civil society and its 'confusion' with the state. From the nature of the case one can also say, vice versa, that the redefinition of the concept presupposes the completed break with the old European political tradition, which was initiated by the revolution at the end of the eighteenth century and in which stood the strained and antagonistic thinking of the Restoration, as can be seen in von Haller. Only if one reads the introduction of Hegel's concept in the *Philosophy of Right* in this context and, as is attempted here, in opposition to its usual in-

---

directed at the freedom of the citizen – because he still recognizes the old European 'law of domestic society' (*Metaphysik der Sitten* (Königsberg, 1797), Part 1 pars. 24 ff. in *Kants gesammelte Schriften*, ed. Königlich Preussische Akademie der Wissenschaften (22 vols., Berlin/Leipzig, 1900–42) hereafter Akademieausgabe), Vol. VI, pp. 276 ff.), the 'judicially personal law' connected with this (par. 22, pp. 276 ff.) from which on the other side his entire difficulty arises of determining the 'class of a man' who 'is his own master (sui juris)'. 'Über den Gemeinspruch: Das mag in der Theorie richtig sein, taugt aber nicht für die Praxis' (1973), Part 2, Akademieausgabe, Vol. VIII, p. 295. (Eng. tr. H. B. Nisbet, 'On the Common Saying: "This May be True in Theory But it Does Not Apply in Practice"' in *Kant's Political Writings* (Cambridge, 1970).)

terpretation by Marx and Lorenz Stein[19] (which means above all on the basis of the political tradition and the pre-revolutionary world) can its true significance and historical actuality for the nineteenth century be measured.

While the great tradition of political metaphysics from Aristotle to Kant names the state 'civil society' because for them social life is already political – in the legal competence of the citizen, or *cives* as Kant, keeping to the Latin, explained it – and because the *status politicus* of the human world understood in these terms contains within itself the genuine 'economic' and 'social' element in the stratification of ruling and domestic classes, Hegel in contrast separates the political sphere of the state from the realm of 'society' which has become 'civil'. In this way the expression 'civil' gains a primarily 'social' content as opposed to its original meaning and is no longer taken to be synonymous with 'political', as it was in the eighteenth century. It now names only the 'social' position of the self-supporting citizen within the state which has become absolute politically, and which from its side grants society its own centre of gravity and sets it free as 'civil'. If, as has occurred since Marx, Lassalle, and Tönnies, one locates the origin of Hegel's concept in modern natural law theory, one transfers this historical process into the natural law model of the *status naturalis* and *status civilis* without doing justice to the essence of modern natural law theory and the tradition which continues to work within it. *Societas civilis* in Hobbes, for example (*De Cive* Ch. 12, V 9), is not the *bellum omnium contra omnes*, the barter society in which individuals contract with and against one another, as Adam Smith and the physiocrats originally represented it; instead it remains a political ordering concept opposed to the *status naturalis*. In Germany, as late as August Ludwig von

19 Characteristic for this is above all Paul Vogel, *Hegels Gesellschaftsbegriff und seine geschichtliche Forthildung durch L. Stein, Marx, Engles und Lassalle* (Berlin, 1925). In opposition to this compare the – also philosophically erelvant – expositions on the problematics of the modern social concept of the historian Otto Brunner, in *Neue Wege der Sozialgeschichte* (Göttingen, 1956) (above all pp. 7 ff., 30 f., and 207) and Werner Conze, 'Staat und Gesellschaft in der früh revolutionären Epoche Deutschlands' in *Historische Zeitschrift*, CLXXXVI (1958), 1 ff., now in expanded form also in the anthology *Staat und Gesellschaft im deutschen Vormärz* (1962), pp. 207 ff., to which I gratefully refer.

Schlözer,[20] Aristotle's notion of the independent patriarch who rules freely in his domestic situation, and therefore becomes a member of civil society, preserves itself in the *status naturalis*. It so happens that for the first time this is contrasted with the 'state' in Schlözer's work, independent of natural law models, on the grounds of the historical difference, already described, between state and society, a difference which runs parallel with the centralization of political activity in the state (administration, constitution, and military affairs) and the relegation of 'civil affairs' to society. It is this difference, named as such by Hegel himself, which shapes the inner structure and historical content of the section on 'civil society' in the *Philosophy of Right* of 1821. Here the concept of citizen, emancipated from its political–legal meaning, and the equally emancipated concept of society, are joined together. Their political substance, which received its classical expression in the ancient *societas civilis*, is dissolved into the social functions which were assigned to both 'citizen' and 'society' in the European break with tradition at the end of the eighteenth century which was precipitated by the Industrial Revolution. It is only then that the citizen as bourgeois becomes the central problem of political philosophy. This occurs simultaneously with the evolution of modern society as it progressively dissolves the substance of the old household while it largely takes over the function of 'economics'. And as the household was previously the basic social element in civil society, so now the changed image of civil society forms the social foundation of the modern state.

The historical process briefly sketched here reveals itself in detail in the semantic shifts undergone by political concepts. After 1800, the structure of 'civil society' appears to rest on a new centre which overlays the old units of meaning. Thus the difference between Hegel's concepts and those of the eighteenth century, and their inner affinity with the nineteenth century, become clear at once, if one pays attention to the distinction in natural law theory between man as man and man as citizen, which is codified

---

20 *Allgemeines Staats Recht* (1974), where the members of civil society are defined as 'full blooded, thus free patriarchs' (Part 1: *Metapolitik*, par. 17, pp. 64, 65). Schlözer defines its structure with the traditional formula: '*Societas civilis* or *civitas*' as distinct from 'state' as '*societas civilis cum imperio*' (note to par. 44). In this contrast, which only hints at the Hegelian 'difference', he conceives the distinction between 'state and civil society'.

in the human and civil rights of the North American and French Revolutions. As man, he is, from the perspective of natural law theory, a member of the *societas generis humani*, species-being and individuality at the same time, and subordinated to the laws of *ethics* unrestricted in their universality. But as citizen, he belongs to civil society, to the state and its laws, obeying the demanding rules of politics.[21] By contrast, in 'civil society', according to the *Philosophy of Right*, the man *qua* man of natural law is the representative of the species melted down in its natural indigence into what Hegel refers to sarcastically in his commentary on par. 190 as the 'composite idea which we call man', and as such remains allied with the 'standpoint of needs'.[22] And this composite, which par. 190 defines as the abstract universal system of needs in relation to the natural distinction between human beings and animals, succumbs now to the object of civil society, i.e., to the 'burgher' – as 'bourgeois', as Hegel comments in French with inverted commas. As a mere (i.e., natural) man, the human being is a being with needs, and as a being with needs he is a private person, i.e., citizen as bourgeois. Human being and citizen are no longer opposed as they were in the eighteenth century, but rather in modern civil society the bourgeois contains the human being.

In this altered structure of historical concepts, one more connection still lies hidden: the link connecting the European revolution to the old quarrel between antiquity and modernity, which can only be mentioned here as a hint. One of the characteristic marks of the waning eighteenth century was that, as a result of the fact that it took up the political concepts of the ancients, it became aware of its distance from antiquity, from the old civic freedom of the Greeks and Romans. For the first time in the history of the European political tradition this assimilation lacked

21 Cf. in this connection, *inter alia*, Wolff, *Philosophia Rationalis sive Logica*, 'Discursus praeliminaris', Ch. 3, pars. 64–6, also Kant, *Metaphysik der Sitten* (1797), Part 1, *Einleitung in die Rechtslehre*, and Rousseau, *Émile* (Amsterdam [Paris], 1762), Book III, in *Oeuvres complètes*, Vol. III (1823), p. 371.

22 *Werke*, Vol. VIII, p. 256; *PR*, p. 127. Cf. the following restrictions which we today must read with reference both to the Marxist universalization of the system of needs and to their fixation of human being in the movement between production and consumption: 'Thus this is the first time, and indeed properly the only time, to speak of man in this sense' (*ibid.*).

'application'[23] to the historical realities of the time, such as the modern independent state, the 'subjects', inhabitants of the state, and modern society. Certainly this change is evident in the problematic of the concept of 'citizen' in the eighteenth century, but also, as we shall see, in the problem which modern 'society' sets for political thought. Rousseau's advice may be taken as particularly symptomatic for the sudden failure of application of old concepts. He suggested that words like 'citizen' (*citoyen*) or 'fatherland' (*patrie*) be totally stricken from the language.[24] In the less radical German thinkers of this period, who did not know the distinction between *bourgeois* and *citoyen*, one was satisfied with *ad hoc* definitions: the concept of citizen was defined in terms of a 'universal' and a 'particular' sense. To the former belongs the citizen as 'member of the state (*civis*)', so that, consistent with the traditional pattern, 'even the monarch' appears as 'the first citizen of his nation'.[25] In the 'particular' sense, one understands the member of a municipality, the citizen of a region, and, therewith, the class of citizens as distinct from the nobility and the peasantry. The decisive thing here is that the modern political state reduces the 'universal sense' in the concept of citizen to a minimum because this state widely uproots the social basis of the *civis*, the self-government of the governed in the *societas civilis*. Hegel had already understood this process by around 1800 as scarcely any of his contemporaries was able to do; for it is only after him that *citoyen* and *bourgeois* stand side by side, the citizen of the state (a status extended to all subjects) next to the private citizen. Since then, the modern difference between administration concerned with the 'universal', or the state on the one hand and

23 This concept is used here in the sense which Hans-Georg Gadamer in his 1960 book *Wahrheit und Methode* (Eng. tr. G. Borden and J. Commung, *Truth and Method* (New York, 1975)) pointed out as a traditional essential moment in hermeneutics.
24 See *Émile*, Book 1, p. 15.
25 Cf. in this connection the Göttingen legal thinker Scheidemantel who was influential in his day (*Teutsches Staats-und Lehnrecht* (1782), Part 1, par. 2). Achenwall also says something similar in that the sovereign does not stand wholly outside civil society, but is 'himself comprehended within it as the most eminent citizen (*civis eminens*) of the republic', *Staats Verfassung der europäischen Reiche* (1792), p. 2. But the real problem for both is the relation between citizens and subordinates, and hence the political concept of citizen, for 'One finds subordinates who are not citizens, e.g., aliens or servants; others are both subordinates and citizens. On the other hand there are citizens who are not subordinates, e.g., the monarch' (*Teutsches Staats und Lehnrecht*, Part 1, p. 439).

the 'extreme' which takes the 'individual as its purpose', the burgher, on the other, becomes clear in contrast to the 'old ethical life' and its political substance: 'The same individual cares for himself and his family, works, makes contracts, and so on, and equally he works also for the universal and has it as a purpose. On the first side he is called *bourgeois*, on the other, *citoyen*.'[26] The young Hegel saw this process at work already in the decline of the Greek city states and wished to base the legal establishment of the bourgeois in Roman law; but there can be no doubt about the fact that he also sharpened questions of his own time on the phenomena of late antiquity.

In his later Berlin lectures, proceeding much more historically and substantially in political terms, Hegel makes a comparison near the end of his analysis of Aristotle's *Politics* between the modern state and the only social phenomenon of modern times which is adequate to it: the factory. Here he speaks about the 'abstract right of our modern states, which isolates the individual and as such leaves him alone' and in which a necessary inter-relationship develops, though in such a way that 'in no one is there either consciousness of or activity for the whole; each acts on the whole without knowing how, he is only concerned with protecting his individuality'. In this context Hegel points out the obvious image of the factory where, as in state and society, the whole of active life has broken up and become internally differenti-ated: 'It is a divided activity of which each has only a piece; as in a factory no one makes a whole, possessing only one part and not the other skills, while only a few make the total assembly.' Free peoples, as antiquity produced them, had consciousness and activity only in the whole, but in the modern period as individuals in their own right they are not free – '*civil* freedom is just the renunciation of the universal, the principle of isolation. But civil freedom (in German we do not have two words for *citoyen* and

---

26 Hegel, *Jenenser Vorlesungen* (1805–6) in *Jenenser Realphilosophie* (hereafter *JR*), Vol. II (1805–6), ed. J. Hoffmeister (Leipzig, 1931), p. 249. Transferring the words to specific German relationships, Hegel notes in the margin: 'Townsman and national subject, the one formally as much a townsman as the other.'

bourgeois) is a necessary moment, which the old states did not recognize.'[27]

III

Insight into the historical necessity of this moment and its positive valuation come only for the later Hegel; for doubtless it was only around 1820 with the section on civil society in the *Rechtsphilosophie* that he grasped the fundamental change at the heart of the social and political constitution of Europe, and he accomplished this as a result of the fact that he made it fruitful systematically rather than merely recognizing it as he had done since the beginning of his economical and political studies in Bern, Frankfurt, and Jena. It is easy to see at first glance at the essays, excerpts, and lectures from the Jena period that facts and theoretical insights regarding the modern social situation which he adopted from the study of English and French works stand by themselves without relationship to the productive adaptation of ancient cultural traditions. Thus, as has already been mentioned, the bourgeois is compared with the Roman *imperium*; and the economic spheres of society, need, labour, and possession taken from Steuart, Smith, and Ricardo are given the label 'relative ethical life' in contrast to the 'absolute' ethical life of Greek *politeuein* so that they appear simultaneously as the background for ancient tragedy and comedy, and the analyses of the labour system in general either stand awkwardly under titles like 'people' and 'administration' or ensue independently of one another in the context of the 'practical' action of living beings in nature.[28] Without being able to locate them conceptually or at least to connect them systematically, the young Hegel places the hard facts of modernity, labour and the division of labour, the machine, money and commodities, wealth and poverty, unaltered next to the living cultural tradition of the

27 *Vorlesungen über die Geschichte der Philosophie*, ed. Karl Ludwig Michelet, Vol. ii, in *Werke*, Vol. xiv, p. 400. (Eng. tr. E. S. Haldane and F. H. Simpson, *Hegel's Lectures on the History of Philosophy*, (3 vols., London, 1896).)

28 See here *Kritisches Journal der Philosophie*, ii, no. 2 (1802), 79, *Schriften zur Politik und Rechtsphilosophie* (hereafter *SPR*), ed. G. Lasson (Leipzig, 1913), pp. 418 ff. and 464 ff., but above all *Jenenser Vorlesungen* of 1803–4 in *JR*, Vol. i (1803–4), ed. J. Hoffmeister (Leipzig, 1932), pp. 220 ff. and 236 ff. and 1805–6, in *JR*, Vol. ii, pp. 197 ff. and 231 ff.

ancients, which affects them so overwhelmingly. The material contents of a world out of joint seemed to him in the Jena period to deny any grounded systematics of the 'objective spirit' as he later called the historical sphere of the human world. And on the other hand, when he initially tried to work out the systematics of this material in bringing together antiquity and modernity – for the first version of the *Encyclopedia* from 1817 – his antiquarian style of forming concepts constantly hinders the appropriate presentation of the modern relationships, as is quite obvious when we look at the second edition from 1827. Par. 433 of the Heidelberg *Encyclopedia*, which is devoted solely to this theme, speaks simply of 'universal work' and its specification into 'classes'. To be sure, the family does appear as a 'class of individuality'; however, that sphere whose work is the 'needs of particular existence and whose next aim is particular subjectivity', but whose achievement pre-supposes the labour of all others and thus engages with them, is not what is called later 'civil society' but rather 'class', or as he vaguely and schematically puts it, the 'class of particularity'.[29] Thus one might also say of the sphere of 'society' that Hegel himself came to know his own historical position precisely through the radical disparity between the conceptual structure of the modern economic system and society and that of Greek *polis* life. Around 1820 the inapplicability of the traditional classical con-cepts, rooted in the realm of ancient politics, to the social constel-lation of the revolutionary era became the springboard for the growth of the Hegelian concept of 'civil society' as the sphere of the difference between state and family. Prior to 1820 he employed neither the term as such nor its principal conceptual meaning. Hence, Franz Rosenzweig's allusion to his student excerpts from Sulzer's *Kurtzer Begriff aller Wissenschaft* and

29 *Enzyklopädie der Philosophischen Wissenschaften* (1817), par. 433. One may compare here the comprehensive alterations of the *Enzyklopädie* (1827) (pars. 513 ff.) after the ap-pearance of the *Philosophy of Right*. Here the term 'ethical life' among others was put in a historical context by being connected with the development of family, civil society, and state in the modern period (par. 552). However, already by the end of the Jena period in the *Phenomenology* (1807) we find the first historical schematization of antiquity and modernity, especially since Roman law stands next to the Attic community (in the paragraph 'The True Spirit, Morality'), and the dualism of state authority and wealth appears as a specific phenomenon of the seventeenth and eighteenth centuries (in the paragraph 'Alienated Spirit: Culture').

Ferguson's *History of Civil Society* is erroneous because both these
sources concern the old traditional concept, even if in a faded
form. The passage to which Rosenzweig clearly refers serves
Sulzer for the consideration of civil society in the old sense, as
the constitution of a 'civil state', to use his words. For Sulzer
what grows out of the 'universal concept of a civil society' is
just the 'particular concept of official and judicial power, of submission, of punishment and reward, and so forth'.[30] Ferguson
likewise still takes the concept to be identical with 'political
society' (Part 3, Sec. 6), but under this title he also presents the
'arts and sciences' next to a broad discussion of political relations –
especially in Sparta, Athens, and Rome.

Even if, as is very doubtful, this clarified the external origin
of Hegel's concept, the question would nevertheless remain why
the term occurred only in the student excerpts and the early
theological–political fragments[31] and not in subsequent writings.
In them he renders *societas civilis sive civitas* with the term *Staatsgesell-
schaft*, thereby agreeing with the weakening or dissolution of the
traditional formula as it had occurred since around 1780 among
inter alia Christian Jacob Kraus, Friedrich Gentz, Wilhelm von
Humboldt, and Hufeland.[32] This latter term reveals very clearly
that Hegel *no longer* has at his service the old concept of civil
society and does *not yet* have his distinctively new one. This so-
called state-society subdivides, according to the *Nürnberger Propädeutik*, into the family as 'natural society' and the state as the
'society of people under legal relations'. Thus there is not yet
to be found between the two what was later called 'civil society',
since 'the natural society of the family grows into a universal

30 *Kurzer Begriff Aller Wissenschaften* (1759) p. 189–90.
31 See *Theologische Jugendschriften*, ed. H. Nohl (Tübingen, 1907), pp. 41 f., 44, and 191,
where 'civil society' is synonymous with 'state' following the idiom of the end of the
eighteenth century. To this extent the objection raised against my thesis by Rolf K.
Hocévar (*Stände und Repräsentation beim jungen Hegel* (Münchener Studien zur Politik)
(1968), Vol. VIII, p. 9, n. 23, and p. 201, n. 79) is not tenable. Particularly illuminating
for the traditional idiom is the proposition (*Ibid.* p. 191) that it lies 'in the nature of
civil society ... that in it the rights of individuals have become rights of the state'.
Hegel's prototype here is Moses Mendelssohn, *Jerusalem* (1783) in the edition from
Leipzig (1869), pp. 132 f., 146.
32 On this point see my article, 'Bürgerliche Gesellschaft', in *Lexikon der politisch–sozialen
Begriffe der Neuzeit*, ed. O. Brunner, W. Conze, R. Kosselleck, Vol. II (1970).

state-society which is every bit as much a union grounded in nature as one entered by free will'.[33]

Now, to be sure, the Nüremberg Gymnasium preparations, which stand between the Jena lectures and the Heidelberg *Encyclopedia*, are only of very limited importance for Hegel's conceptual world. They are only symptomatic to the extent that in them, too, no trace is to be found of 'civil society'. Only after 1817, that is, after Hegel gives up his antiquarian style of political conceptualizing, does the factual realization of the Jena period (that, with modern society and the 'bourgeois', a phenomenon of a different kind from the political tradition of the ancients confronts the classical world) become the principal historical insight into the inner structure of modern constitution. What Hegel perceived in the sphere of the 'individual worker' in 1805–6 and restricted solely to this sphere – 'classically' if you will – was this: 'He [the labouring individual – M.R.] has his unconscious existence in the universal; society is his nature. He depends on its blind elemental movements and it sustains or destroys him physically and spiritually.'[34] This presents itself conceptually in 1820 as 'civil society' and its characteristic elementary necessity. In it appears the 'civil freedom' of the bourgeois (his separate existence dependent on the 'system') about which Hegel spoke in his lectures on the history of philosophy. Seen thus it is no accident that Hegel drew 'civil' and 'society' together into one of the basic concepts of political philosophy, a concept which, when viewed externally, corresponds to the tradition of Aristotle's *koinōnia politikē*, Bodin's, Melanchthon's, or Wolff's *societas civilis*, and Kant's 'bürgerliche Gesellschaft', but which actually presupposes for its appearance a complete break with this tradition. To this extent one might well say that before Hegel the concept of civil society in its modern sense did not exist. Indeed, it did not exist even in his own works prior to 1802. With it he was first able to solve the previously mentioned problem of 'application' in a manner that was difficult to follow, but was also both necessary and fruitful. Hegel thereby undertook by far the most important alteration in the structure

33 *Nürnberger Propädeutik*, in *Werke*, Vol. XVIII (1840), ed. Karl Rosenkranz, pp. 47 ff. and 199.
34 *JR*, Vol. II, p. 231.

of political philosophy since Bodin established the concept of sovereignty and Rousseau postulated the general will, an alteration which shortly after his time was to become the genuine problem of modernity.

IV

What Hegel made the times aware of with the phrase 'civil society' was nothing less than the result of the modern revolution: the emergence of a depoliticized society through the centralization of politics in the princely or revolutionary state and the shift of society's focal point towards economics, a change which this society experienced simultaneously with the Industrial Revolution and which found its expression in 'political' or 'national–economy'. It was initially in this process within European society that society's 'political' and 'civil' conditions were separated, conditions which up to now in classical politics had been one and the same – the 'civil or political society' in Aquinas and even in Locke. Hegel too was thoroughly aware of this old identification of the civil and political. He even referred at one place in the *Philosophy of Right* to the union of these words in their primordial meaning. In par. 303, addressing the modern idea of an apolitical civil–class society and its divergence from the old political classes, he says: 'So-called theories of this kind involve the idea that the classes of civil society and the Estates, which are the classes given a political significance, stand wide apart from each other. But the German language, by calling them both *Stände*, has still maintained the unity which in any case they actually possessed in former times.'[35] That Hegel here turns against the liberal–revolutionary idea of a contrast between state and society cannot change the fact that he recognizes and brings to expression the connection of the modern revolution with 'civil society' with more conceptual clarity than even the liberal movement in its action against the

35 See *Werke*, Vol. VIII, par. 303, p. 398 (*PR*, p. 198). Naturally this passage was noted by Marx in his critical commentary on Hegel's *Philosophy of Right* and he added directly – 'and, one should conclude, they now no longer possess'. (*Kritik des Hegelschen Staatsrecht* (1843) in Marx and Engels, *Historisch-kritische Gesamtausgabe*, ed. D. Riazanov (Berlin, 1929–32), Part 4, Vol. I, p. 487.) (Eng. tr. J. O'Malley, *Critique of Hegel's Philosophy of Right* (Cambridge, 1970).)

state. The very first paragraph with which its exposition begins, par. 182 of the *Philosophy of Right*, formulates the current detraditionalization of the old civil society unambiguously on the basis of the facts: the isolated individual, the private citizen of the early nineteenth century society which, emancipated from its political condition, thus becomes 'civil', in the intended sense: 'the concrete person, who is himself the object of his particular aims, is, as a totality of wants and a mixture of caprice and physical necessity, *one* principle of civil society. But the particular person is essentially so *related* to other particular persons, that each establishes himself and finds satisfaction by means of the others and at the same time purely and simply by means of the form of universality, the second principle here.'[36] With this sentence, the utility principle of the already emancipated Western European society and the economic model based on it by Mandeville and Smith, the 'personal interest' of Diderot and Helvétius, the 'self-interest' of Bentham and Franklin, all find expression in a German philosophical form. Here, as there, the result is the same: the emergence of an independent network of relations rooted in interests and holding between individuals. The two principles of civil society, 'the actual attainment of selfish ends', and the condition of its reality, the 'universality' of self-seeking, lay the foundation, as Hegel says literally in the next paragraph, for 'a system of complete interdependence', and in just such a way that 'the livelihood, happiness, and legal status of one man is interwoven with the livelihood, happiness, and rights of all. On this system, individual happiness, etc., depend and only in this connected system are they actualized and secured.'[37] In order to be able to understand the designation of society as 'civil' from this point of view, one must read this paragraph (183) with reference to par. 187, whose first sentence reads: 'Individuals in their capacity as burghers in this state are *private persons* whose end is their own interest.' But the

36 *Werke*, Vol. VIII, p. 246; *PR*, pp. 122–3. On the following exposition see my essay, 'Tradition und Revolution in Hegels Philosophie des Rechts', in *Zeitschrift für philosophische Forschung*, Vol. XVI, Part II (1962). This essay appears as Chapter 7 of this volume.

37 *Werke*, Vol. VIII, p. 247; *PR*, p. 123. In the second and third editions of the *Enzyklopädie* Hegel calls civil society simply 'the system of atomistic' (cf. *Werke*, Vol. VII, 2nd edn, ed. L. Boumann (1845), p. 395).

sought-for object of the individual interests of these private citizens rests on the inner connectedness of the objects of all interests, so that this object of individual interests can be attained only when persons define their willing and doing in terms of the 'universal', in which form the nexus of interests, or 'society', confronts them, and they for their part 'make themselves', as Hegel says, '*links* in this chain of social connections'.[38]

What develops with this system of universal dependence and its interlocking links is the constantly self-reproducing network of relations between the 'private person' (par. 187) and 'society' in the modern sense, a network which is distinct from the state and grows on the soil of need and labour. Its inner organization in terms of the economic 'system of needs' (pars. 189–208), the civil 'administration of justice' (pars. 209–29), and the political–moral integration into the state by 'police and corporation' (pars. 230–56) is developed in detail by Hegel in an outline of the society of his time, between 1815 and 1830, a society which was still everywhere bound to a class system, but was also liberated from the political state. This society appeared to be 'civil' because at its roots it had already flowed into a civilly ordered system of interests of the 'citizen as private person'; and it was actually political only to the extent that it functioned in a relatively stable systematic pattern owing to class and corporate cohesion and to its connection with the 'police'.

Therefore, one must take this presentation of civil society (which is not based particularly on Prussia as is usually thought, but rather on the general period after 1815 which was 'turning back' from the revolution)[39] as a whole and as what it is historically. It is, we could well say, the great attempt to construct 'society' neither as a system of need based on labour and enjoyment, nor as a natural element of the old European social constitution, resting in old political arrangements, in lordship and dependence; instead it is the attempt to mediate the 'social' nature of the European human world, liberated since the revolution, with its 'political',

38 *Werke*, Vol. VIII, p. 251; *PR*, p. 124. Compare with this the designation of this connection as a 'social' one, which 'is the universal capacity, from which all receive their satisfaction' in par. 524 of the Berlin *Enzyklopädie* (*Werke*, Vol. VII, 2nd edn, p. 395).

39 Edward Gans uses this expression in the Introduction to his Berlin lectures *Naturrecht und Universalrechtsgeschichte* (Winter semester 1832–3).

legal, and moral orders, and to raise the latter to its new concept *in* this mediation. Hegel's 'civil society' thus undoubtedly contains the 'society' of the later nineteenth century, the object of sociology and political economy, the 'system of atomistic', as he himself called it, but it does so only on the lowest level; to be sure, the 'system of needs' begins the social process, but this is already regulated and organized by the 'administration of justice'. For, as Hegel says in par. 229, 'In civil society the idea is lost in particularity and has fallen asunder with the separation of inward and outward. In the administration of justice, however, civil society returns to its concept, to the unity of the implicit universal with the subjective particular.'[40] Society would not be 'civil' if it were not ordered and maintained legally, morally, and politically. The 'concept' of which Hegel speaks here, while referring to the administration of justice, is thus at the same time the concept of civil society itself. For Hegel, too, it still preserves – above the new economic and civil elements which have become constitutive for society – the old structures of the moral and political, even if they are reduced and restricted to the 'police' and the 'corporation'. For, on the other hand, the substantial necessity of society, whose 'control' (par. 236) and 'moral improvement' (par. 253, Addition) these latter assume, has institutionalized and rationalized the substance of the classical human world: 'ethical powers' (par. 145) in the corporation and the 'constitution of the state' (par. 269) in the police. However, it also bears witness to the pervasive, historical substantiality of Hegel's thinking that he has incorporated just these two ordering elements, police and corporation, in his presentation of civil society.

For us the joint introduction of these two concepts is obscure rather than appropriate: 'corporation' has an anachronistic, and 'police', an extremely concrete sound. Also, the inner affinity and historical connection of the two terms with the changed form of civil society, as it stands before us in the *Philosophy of Right*, are still not all that clear in what Hegel uses them to describe. To explicate this connection, which is directly constitutive of Hegel's concept, we must rather go behind his description in this case as well as to the tradition of old politics which remained strong

40 See *WWG*, VIII, p. 293; *PR*, p. 145.

up to the eighteenth century and ask both what appears in this tradition as 'police' and 'corporation', and more particularly to what extent Hegel himself was aware of their structure.

In the first place, it is necessary to note that the concept of police as employed in the *Philosophy of Right* has very little to do with our usual one. Originally stemming from the institutionalization and bureaucratization of the modern state in the seventeenth and eighteenth centuries, it includes the state's general management of society, which had become increasingly differentiated internally. But to that extent it represents a conceptual consequence of the division of the old *societas civilis sive civitatis* into the realms of 'state' and 'society'. More exactly, it denotes the mediation of depoliticized society and political state through the medium of administration. The 'police' is the old politics itself converted into state administration, a politics which formerly expressed the political constitution of civil society as well as the art of managing it.[41] The young Hegel was quite well aware of these relationships when, in the Jena lectures of 1805–6, he related the modern 'police' to the origin of politics, the *politeia* of classical Greek philosophy: 'The *police* here amounts to this – *politeia*, public life and rule, action of the whole itself but now degraded to the whole's action to provide public security of every type, protecting business against fraud.'[42] The police is also the form in which the difference between state and society appears and is permanently mediated: the only 'political' structure which still seems possible in relation to the autonomous form of civil society – *Administration* – 'oversight and care of the public authority' as it is called in par. 235 of the *Philosophy of Right*.[43] The police, as the 'protecting

---

41 The second half of the eighteenth century is the great period of 'police-science'. Young Robert von Mohl began his investigations of constitutional law with a voluminous presentation of it as late as 1830. Among works of that period cf. *inter alia* J. H. G. von Justi, *Grundsätze der Polizeywissenschaft* (1756–9), J. von Sonnenfels, *Grundsätze der Polizey* (1765), J. F. von Pfeiffer, *Natürliche, aus dem Endzweck der Gesellschaft entstehende allgemeine Polizey* (1779), K. G. Rossig, *Lehrbuch der Polizeywissenschaft* (1786), J. H. Jung, *Lehrbuch der Staatspolizeywissenschaften* (1788), J. F. E. Lotz, *Über den Begriff der Polizey* (1807). Cf. in this connection H. Maier, *Die ältere deutsche Staats-und Verwaltungslehre* (*Polizeywissenschaft*) (Neuwied/Berlin), 1966.

42 See *Jenenser Vorlesungen* of 1805–6 in *JR*, Vol. II, p. 259.

43 *Werke*, Vol. VIII, p. 296; *PR*, p. 147. Cf. the definition of police in par. 249 which corresponds to our explanation: 'While the public authority (*die polizeiliche Vorsorge*)

power of the universal', or, if you will, of the 'concept' of civil society, fight against civil society's 'unimpeded activity', the tendency to 'expanding population and industry', the 'amassing of wealth' (par. 243), and the fall 'of a large mass of people ... beneath a certain subsistence level' (par. 244). Here, for Hegel, the masses appear on the horizon – above all of England (par. 245 n.) – in the 'creation of the rabble', which for him threatens to explode the form of society as 'civil', i.e., as morally ordered and politically founded. If once it was barbaric primitives, as well as the servants, day labourers, and artisans attached to a house, who stood outside the old *societas civilis*, so now it is the rabble, which, for Hegel, however, in contrast with the philosophical tradition of politics, no longer marks the positive boundary in relation to which this tradition justified itself historically. On the contrary, the existence of the rabble requires that the 'unimpeded activity' of society be limited by state administration, i.e., the 'police', and be integrated with civil society – which thus is not yet rigid class society, 'civil' or 'bourgeois society' as the early socialists were to say around 1840.

The corporation, the second constitutive element, stands in relation both to the emancipation of civil society and to the reduction of politics to 'police'. If the police is the 'degenerate' form of classical politics, then the corporation is reminiscent of the old *oikos* unity, the 'domestic society'. With the transformation of civil society from the inside out, the 'economic' and moral-substantial order of the household loses its basis. Hence Hegel no longer discussed, as did Kant, the 'law of domestic society', but spoke rather only about the 'Family' – in the 'form assumed by the concept ... in its immediate phase' as marriage, in its 'external embodiment' in family property and capital, and in the 'education of children and the dissolution of the family' – (pars.

---

must also undertake the higher directive function of providing for the interests which lead beyond the borders of society (see par. 246), its primary purpose is to actualize and maintain the universal contained within the particularity of civil society, and its control takes the form of an external system and organization for the protection and security of particular ends and interests *en masse*, inasmuch as these interests subsist only in the universal (*PR*, p. 152). Basing his claim in this case as well on Hegelian presuppositions, Lorenz von Stein wrote, after 1850, his significant theory and apology for the state-dominated society, the *Verwaltungslehre* (pp. 1869 ff.).

160 ff.) It is this new concept of the family, and no longer the one bound to the economic unit of the household, which is articulated by Hegel in the *Philosophy of Right* with full awareness of the historical change which civil society prepared for 'economics'. Because, in distinction from the classical tradition of politics for which civil society rested on domestic society, the family is something in Hegel's view which 'in civil society ... [is] ... subordinate and only lays the foundations: its effective range is no longer so comprehensive. Civil society is rather the tremendous power which draws men into itself and claims from them that they work for it, owe everything to it, and do everything by its means.'[44] The member of domestic society is, in modern times, 'torn' from it, and becomes a 'son of civil society' which, in place of the 'paternal soil ... from which the individual formerly derived his livelihood', substitutes its own and subjects the very existence of the whole family to dependence on itself, on 'contingency'.[45]

Hegel now sees that the moving principle of civil society, its 'comprehensive effective range' in the sphere of economics, is realized above all in the 'business' or citizen class. While to a large extent the land protects the old economic formation, the 'substantiality' of family life, in the town 'an individual is without rank or dignity; his isolation reduces his business to mere self-seeking, and his livelihood and satisfaction become insecure'.[46] According to Hegel, the corporation is this sole secure, because enduring, element within the process and 'mode of labour of civil society'. It is an 'association' of individuals who are in themselves isolated in their work. This security also lacks the fixed status

44 See *Werke*, Vol. VIII, par. 238, Addition, p. 299; *PR*, p. 276.
45 See *Werke*, Vol. VIII, par. 238, p. 298: 'Originally the family is the substantive whole whose function it is to provide for the individual on his particular side by giving him either the means and the skill necessary to enable him to earn his living out of the resources of society, or else subsistence and maintenance in the event of his suffering a disability. But civil society tears the individual from his family ties, estranges the members of the family from one another and recognizes them as self-subsistent persons' (*PR*, p. 148).
46 See *Werke*, Vol. VIII, pars. 250 and 253, as also the division of society according to city and country – 'The town is the seat of the civil life of business. There reflection arises, turns in upon itself and pursues its atomizing task ... the country ... the seat of an ethical life resting on nature ...' – in connection with the deduction of the state in par. 256 (*PR*, pp. 152–5).

of a class, since here, in the civil society's mode of labour, it is not possible for anyone to live appropriately to his class, for the simple reason that 'no class really exists'.[47] Instead the corporation conforms to the common elements of the old household: as it says in par. 252, the corporation appears as a 'second family' opposed to the contingencies and particularities of social processes, 'white civil society can only be an indeterminate sort of family because it comprises everyone and so is farther removed from individuals and their special exigencies'. In this role is to be found the 'moral basis' of its existence, which appears justified to Hegel despite complaints about 'the luxury of the business classes and their passion for extravagance – which have as their concomitant the creation of a rabble of paupers' and about 'the increasing mechanization of labour'.

It is obvious that, to use Hegel's words, this 'role' (*Stellung*) of corporation and police in relation to civil society corresponds to its proper place in the modern world, a place which has changed since the eighteenth century. For, as I attempted to show at the outset, classical civil society had an intrinsic relationship to the realms of economics and politics from which it received its shape. Based originally on domestic society and its particular economics, and contrasting itself with this, it developed on the grounds of politics, the public political arena, into which only the economically independent citizen of society ventured. By contrast, modern civil society, which Hegel was the first to thematize as a principle and elevate to conceptual self-consciousness, reduced to accidents the ordering structures of economics and politics which were substantial for the pre-revolutionary world of old Europe. It did so because it itself had become the substance of private and public life. Surrendering its political organization to the state, society retains from traditional politics the police as an administrative and regulative function for its particular elementary processes; then society dissolves domestic ties, the 'standing feature' of the older economics, by the development of industrial trades, and it tries to reconnect individuals who are isolated in the divided labour of the cities into a common enterprise. In this way the society which the revolution liberated recovers in the functions of

47 *Werke*, Vol. VIII, par. 253, p. 309; *PR*, p. 153.

police and corporation moral–political elements of the tradition on which it is still able to found itself as 'civil'. They are, as we can say following Hegel, 'the two fixed points around which the unorganized atoms of civil society revolve'.[48] Hegel interrupts civil society's tendency towards modern commercial society, as the latter is prefigured in the 'system of needs', by the limits which the tradition of politics places on its constitution. For society as a system of needs would already be a disorganized civil society which, however, goes beyond its concept, as Hegel understood it and presented it in the *Philosophy of Right*.

Because Hegel conceptually articulated the decisive historical–political process of modern times, the separation of society from state and the reciprocal influence of tradition and revolution in society, he is able to conceive the modern form of civil society and at the same time limit its substantial power by the older structures – although only 'accidentally' and for his own time. One might well say it is initially here that the 'civil society' of the *Philosophy of Right* arises historically and has its true conceptual home, in a 'middle' which is as much mediating as advancing beyond and breaking out of the mediation.

48 *Werke*, Vol. VIII, par. 255, p. 310; *PR*, p. 154. The sentence is interpreted by Hegel himself only in relation to the morality of the family – the sacredness of marriage – and corporation – the dignity of the individual in it – but it is equally basic to section C of civil society.

PART IV

Between Tradition and Revolution

7

The Hegelian Transformation of Modern Political Philosophy and the Significance of History

In May of 1833, a year and a half after Hegel's death, Edward Gans wrote the Preface to the second edition of the *Philosophy of Right* for the great edition of Hegel's works compiled by the 'association of friends of the deceased'. He ended his enthusiastic Preface – for him the whole work was fashioned from 'a single substance, freedom' – with an 'ominous hint' about the book's 'future fate'. As a part of Hegel's system it would, according to Gans, have to stand or fall with it. Perhaps, after a time, *with* the whole system it would pass into the imagination and general consciousness of the time, so that its 'technical language' might melt away and its 'depths' become common property. But then, he continues, the philosophy, which in this book and in general comprehended its own time in conceptual terms, would no longer be philosophically relevant to the times, but rather would be in them as a historical trace; while a new philosophical development would be preparing itself to fit the 'changed reality': 'Then its time is philosophically over and it belongs to history. A new progressive development in philosophy, proceeding from the same basic principles, comes into prominence, a changed understanding of the equally changed reality.'[1] These words of Gans have been prophetic in more than one respect. They anticipate the battles of the Hegelians in the late 1830s and 1840s about the system's proper legacy, at a time when Gans was the sole rebel among them, though he was still devout; they anticipate – of course recalling the July Revolution of 1830 and Hegel's reserved attitude towards it – the altered situation of the period after 1840; and finally they articulate the particular fate of Hegel's *Philosophy of Right*: that, uniquely, its time was already philosophically past shortly after its appearance, but its historical influence was only just beginning. The 'future fate', which Gans

1 Preface to Hegel's *Werke* (18 vols., Berlin, 1832–45) (hereafter *Werke*), Vol. I, p. xvii.

meant to mention only on the occasion of 'this book', soon came true for the Hegelian system as a whole. Still the distinctive manner of coming to terms with the philosophy of right in old-, young-, and neo-Hegelianism is striking; in fact, the book already belonged to history in 1833, even though it still 'made' history in later times, particularly with Lorenz von Stein and Marx.

Unlike the *Phenomenology of Spirit*, the *Logic*, *Aesthetics*, *History of Philosophy*, and *Philosophy of History*, which had grand historical consequences in the nineteenth and twentieth centuries, the *Philosophy of Right* shared the same fate as the *Philosophy of Nature*. Both books met powerful resistance even among Hegel's contemporaries and conflicted with the development of historical political science and positive natural science respectively. The popular prejudice against the *Philosophy of Right* (namely, that it accommodated to the Prussian state and the restoration of the 1920s) may perhaps have contributed much to the distinctive vacuousness of its critics and commentators from Stahl to Erdmann, Haym, Ruge, Rosenkranz, Fischer, and so on. This charge, by the way, holds also for the philosophical efforts of neo-Hegelianism around 1930, as can be seen pre-eminently in Larenz, Dulckeit, Busse, and even the later Binder.[2] Here once again can be found verification of the remarkable accuracy of Gans's Preface which already in its own time had to point out the 'unusual disparity' which 'lies between the substantial worth of this book and its acceptance and circulation'.[3] It is generally recognized that political developments after 1840 further damaged the reception of the *Philosophy of Right*. Its influence on the times did not come through accurate and judicious commentaries but through critiques of its doctrines. Its time was philosophically over by 1840, since the time that followed was not philosophical at all, but political, economic, and historical.

2 For neo-Hegelian commentary on the *Philosophy of Right*, cf. the early essay by J. Kohler in *Archiv für Rechts-und Wirtschaftsphilosophie*, v (1912); the anthology Binder-Busse-Larenz, *Einführung in Hegels Rechtsphilosophie* (1931); J. Binder, *Grundlegung zur Rechtsphilosophie* (1935); and the works of K. Larenz and G. Dulckeit. The basis of neo-Hegelian philosophy of right was 'concrete community (*Gemeinschaft*) itself', which one believed could be found in Hegel as the 'community of people in the state' (cf. G. Dulckeit, *Rechtsbegriff und Rechtsgestalt* (1936), p. 17). The history of the effect of Hegel's philosophy of right in the nineteenth and twentieth centuries still remains to be written.
3 Preface to Hegel, *Werke*, Vol. VIII, p. v.

Lorenz von Stein became Hegel's great advocate in the domain of right and the state in the nineteenth century; but behind the similar terminology in his *Socialismus und Communismus des heutigen Frankreich* (1842) and in his doctrine of state and society, how extensively has the social and historical reality which they present been changed! Ferdinand Lassalle declares himself to be a true descendant of Hegel and Gans; by virtue of his philosophical talent and juridical training he alone among students of Hegel after 1860 would have been able to write a *Politics* on the basis of the philosophy of right. Characteristically, however, in his first and also last venture in this field, the *System der erworbenen Recht* (1861), he preferred to concentrate on a particular juristic problem and pay tribute to the empiricism and historicism of his time. Marx felt himself to be neither Hegel's advocate nor his heir – in the true sense of the word – but rather his critical conqueror; nevertheless he was really the only person in his time who took the *Philosophy of Right* of 1821 for what it actually was: the 'only German history which is *al pari* with the *official* modern times'.[4] The critique of Hegel's constitutional law written by the young Marx in 1843 *vis-à-vis* pars. 261–313 is the work by which Marx radically separated himself from the tradition of political metaphysics altered by the revolution. In places even historically profound, it has remained the only commentary on Hegel's philosophy of right in nineteenth-century Hegel studies which stands on the same level as Hegel's own discussions.

It is clear that this explicative critique, which also regrettably remained incomplete, does not raise the issue of the work's position within the political philosophical tradition and cannot do so given its own historical–political aim. Since Marx's commentary considers Hegel's philosophy of right to possess solely historical interest, and is hence consistent with Gans's prophecy, his critique presupposes at the start that Hegel's time has passed philosophically, and the result of the critique consists, as is known, in freeing philosophy from law in favour of economics. At the

---

4 *Zur Kritik der Hegelschen Rechtsphilosophie*, Introduction, in Marx and Engels, *Historisch-kritische Gesamtausgabe* (hereafter *MEGA*), ed. D. Riazanov (Berlin, 1929–32), Part 1, Vol. 1, Half Vol. 1 (1927), p. 612. (Eng. tr. in T. B. Bottomore, *Karl Marx: Early Writings* (New York, 1963), p. 50.)

same time, however, this professed non-philosophy remains very deeply indebted to the last great metaphysics of right; for it was here rather than in the book of the world that Marx learned to see and grasp the 'contradiction' which is characteristic of the modern period: the contradiction between state and society, the civil and private person, political and social life, middle ages and modernity. The following interpretive endeavour also sees Hegel's 'depth' in the fact that he, as Marx's commentary has it, 'begins above all with the *contradiction* of the determinations (as they are found in our society) and accents it'.[5] In this analysis, as philosophical as it is historical, of the problems and form of the *Philosophy of Right*, and especially of the third part, it will be shown that the 'contradiction' extends right into the formal structure. The work as a whole presents the scheme of a non-Aristotelian 'politics' which has grown up on the basis of the revolution and whose outlines try to identify and circumscribe the basis of the modern period – its state, society, family, and individuals – without allowing the relationship with the classical tradition to be destroyed.

I

At first view it is remarkable that Hegel gave his work a double title: *Elements of the Philosophy of Right*; *Natural Law and Political Science in Outline*. The second title is not merely a subtitle, as one might suppose, but, because of the addition 'im Grundrisse' ('in Outline'), it is a parallel designation to 'Elements' ('Grundlinien') of Right. Nevertheless, the formal emphasis on *Philosophy of Right* has a deeper meaning. The two phrases 'natural law' and 'political science' in the subtitle designate two disciplines of pre-Hegelian metaphysical thinking, of which the one belonging to modern Europe was developed principally in the seventeenth and eighteenth centuries, while the other is found in the old European tradition under the name 'politics' and had a fixed place in school philosophy down to the time of Wolff. Admittedly, the essence of the old politics lay in the fact that there was for it no distinction between natural law theory and political science; because for

5 *MEGA*, Part 1, Vol. 1, Half Vol. 1 (1927), p. 465.

European thought up to the seventeenth, and in Germany right up to the eighteenth century, politics was the comprehensive science of legally ordered human society, the *societas*, or *communitas civilis sive politica*, which had its blueprint in Aristotle's presentation of the *polis* as a *koinōnia politiké*.[6] Since the *polis*, or *civitas* as a *koinōnia politiké* or *societas civilis*, comprehends the whole life of the free citizens, i.e., those who are qualified on the grounds of their political status under freedom and law, the unpolitical and extra-civic appears as the 'barbaric', and the word *civilis* receives its positive meaning as the contrary to *naturalis*. It was only in the sixteenth and seventeenth centuries with Machiavelli, Bodin, and Hobbes, that political science could, simultaneously with the emancipation of the modern state from the politically restricted *societas civilis*, finally emancipate itself from the old politics, so that the eighteenth century could discover the opposition between natural law and political science. Since then, the meaning of *civilis* and *naturalis* reversed themselves completely. Considered in terms of history and politics rather than its philosophical content, natural law theory represents an attempt either narrowly to restrict the modern states' infringements ('illegal' in the old sense) upon society which originally is itself legally ordered, or to overcome state-politics, crystallized into a mere power function, with a revolutionary new concept of freedom and law. The antithesis between natural law and political science, or, as one might rather say in Germany, between morality and politics, leads intellectually to the modern European revolution and constantly accompanies its progress. Hegel's *Philosophy of Right* presupposes this antithesis and is, against the historical background of the revolution which it resembles on this issue, a philosophical–political attempt at overcoming it. And this very fact is plain to see in the curious circumstance of Hegel's putting two titles at the beginning of the work.

The mention of natural law and political science in the second title takes precedence, as we saw, over the first title, which gave the work its proper name, *Elements of the Philosophy of Right*. As a presentation of the modern state, Hegel's political science aims to

6 Cf. here O. Brunner, *Neue Wege der Sozialgeschichte* (1956), pp. 30 and 207, as also the following chapter on civil society.

be a philosophy of right in an emphatic sense. Politics, the science of human social life in the state, becomes the philosophy of right (law) for him, because he tries to annul the revolutionary antithesis between a natural law which precedes the state and a law which state power presents to individuals by grounding both on natural-rational right as such: the freedom of human beings *qua* human. But this natural and rational right of freedom has, for Hegel, historical content, which cannot be specified more precisely here it consists – since the entry of Christianity into world history – in the equality of souls before God and – since the end of the eighteenth century – in the equality and freedom of individuals before the revolutionary state. Because Hegel understands the historical meaning of the revolution and includes its historical content – the freedom and legal capacity of all men – in his political thought, the law in its connection with freedom becomes the central issue in political philosophy. With this result of the revolution, the pre-revolutionary antithesis between natural law and political science loses its significance. From now on, the foundation of politics can only be law or right, but not that of the legally capable citizen in the classical civil society. Instead it is the legal capacity of the 'notion' in humanity which wants its freedom.

Since Hegel tries to mediate the contradiction between natural law and political science positively in a political philosophy grounded on law (*Recht*), he must consequently refer back to the pre-revolutionary political tradition, since the 'contradiction' has no role there. It was, as even Wolff had translated the phrase, the doctrine of 'human social life, especially the community' and nothing else.[7] As fitting as it is for the presupposition of Hegel's philosophy of right to rest in the concept of law made universal and the claim to freedom – both are components which point to its connection with modern natural law theory – it finds its basis a (and in) the doctrine of the state. For Hegel, as for Aristotle, the *polis* is the 'true basis', according to reality the 'first', and according to reason the 'purpose', of all unifications of people in

---

7 The full title of Christian Wolff's German edition of the *Politics* is *Vernünftige Gedanken von dem gesellschaftlichen Leben der Menschen und insonderheit dem gemeinen Wesen zu Beförderung der Glückseligkeit des menschlichen Geschlechts den Liebhabern der Wahrheit mitgetheilt von Christian Wolff* (1st edn, Halle, 1721).

society.[8] In fact, the *Philosophy of Right* is in the eminent sense state science, and its interpretation from Erdmann and Haym, Lassalle and Rosenzweig, right down to the neo-Hegelianism of Larenz and Dulckeit, has always focused on just this point. It is not accidental that this title reminds us of politics' classical tradition of giving a description of the political order of a people or of a society at large, a tradition which Hegel consciously resurrects. The 'philosophy concerning the state' loved by his contemporaries, which had the aim of presenting a unique political 'theory' as if 'no state or constitution had ever yet existed in the world or even existed at the present time, but rather as if nowadays – and this "nowadays" lasts forever – we had to start all over again from the beginning',[9] was rejected by Hegel as by the classical European tradition of political philosophy. Like the latter he commenced with actual ethical life, the *res publica*, and its order. At the same time, traditional consciousness was shattered by the revolutionary political theory of the time, as was evident in the unusually defensive polemics found not only in school philosophy but even in Kant's political writings. Particularly characteristic in this regard is the specific post-revolutionary inquiry into the 'relation of philosophy to reality'. The state's reality and its actual forms of law and dominance were not exploded by the Utopian 'erection of a beyond', as it says in the Preface to the *Philosophy of Right*, but they also did not find a simple statement of their relations, in the sense of traditional *scientia*, or *historia politica sive civilis*. Rather, the 'positive' relation to reality sustained by Hegel's political thinking means the 'investigation of the rational' through 'grasping the present and actual'. Thus his thinking is itself a 'relation' of reality to the concept and, against Hegel if one wishes, a philosophy 'over' (*über*) state and history. What seems to be a mere repetition of the tradition is in truth the tradition itself broken by the revolution and changed in its meaning. Hegel's state science grew up on the ground of modern natural law theory, and the mediation of politics with law is, as will become clear, a middle

8 *Grundlinien der Philosophie des Rechts* (hereafter *GPR*), ed. E. Gans in *Werke*, Vol. VIII (1833), pp. 312 ff. (Eng. tr. T. M. Knox, *Hegel's Philosophy of Right* (hereafter *PR* (Oxford, 1942). I shall follow Knox in the translation of Hegel and give page references to the Gans edition.)
9 *GPR*, p. 7; *PR*, p. 4.

term which is as mediative as it is developing, or escaping from mediation. Still, with this we have passed far beyond an analysis of the meaning of right, natural law, and state science in connection with the double title of Hegel's work and are moving within the structural problematic of legal philosophy and its place in the political–philosophical tradition.

II

One may assume that in 1820 Hegel viewed a presentation separated from the circle of the *Encyclopedia* as necessary not only to meet the need of providing his audience with a guidebook for the lectures 'on the philosophy of right which I deliver in the course of my professional duties'. If one compares the concise section on 'Objective Spirit' in the 1817 Heidelberg edition with the 1821 *Philosophy of Right*, it is clear that more is involved than an 'enlarged and especially a more systematic exposition of the same fundamental concepts', as he says at the beginning of the Berlin Preface.[10] Also, the intention to clarify the 'abstract parts of the text' with additions and 'to take a more comprehensive glance at current ideas widely disseminated at the present time' would not suffice as an occasion for allowing *Elements of the Philosophy of Right* to appear in print. More decisive might be the fact that since 1817 the development of the system led Hegel beyond the *Logic* to a Science of Right. As he also says in the Preface: 'I have fully expounded the nature of speculative knowing in the *Science of Logic*.'[11] The *Philosophy of Right* forms the counterpart to this - since it develops the nature of 'practical' knowing. Here too, as Hegel says, it is a question of 'science', even if this can never be made equally clear in its logical form with respect to the 'concrete and implicitly so manifold properties of the object'. Of the works which Hegel himself published in his lifetime, the *Philosophy of Right* (1821) in fact stands next to the *Logic* (1812–16) in importance. If one considers the *Phenomenology of Spirit* (1807) as a propaedeutic to the system which gathers into a totality of knowing in the *Encyclopedia of the Philosophical Sciences* (1817), then

10 *GPR*, p. 3; *PR*, p. 1.
11 *GPR*, p. 4; *PR*, p. 2.

the obvious parallelism of the systematic articulation of logic and philosophy of right is reminiscent of the traditional division of philosophy into theoretical and practical parts, as customary in European metaphysics and as systematically articulated in the eighteenth century by Wolff and his students on the basis of the traditional Aristotelian doctrine. Here, too, practical philosophy stood next to logic, and the human soul's two-sided power, its division into cognitive and appetitive faculties (*facultas cognoscitiva atque appetitiva*), was designated as the foundation (*fundamentum*) of both. The division into natural law, politics, and ethics was based on the definition of practical philosophy – 'that part of true philosophy which teaches the use of the appetitive faculty in seeking good and avoiding evil, is called *practical philosophy*. Practical philosophy is thus the science of directing the appetitive faculty in seeking good or avoiding evil'.[12]

Characteristically, Hegel appeals directly to this tradition nowhere in his work, unless one were to consider a statement from the Berlin period about the 'completeness of the course in philosophy' at universities to be as serious and important as an explicit factual–systematic presentation. Here he says *inter alia* that in an 'approximate' sense 'completeness can be attained by means of the customary division into lectures on *theoretical* and *practical* philosophy. So, in one semester I read on logic and metaphysics and in the other on natural law and states/science or philosophy of right understood as containing ethics or the doctrine of duties.'[13] His conviction that ancient metaphysics had ended, as expressed most precisely in the Preface to the *Logic* (1st edn), explains Hegel's dim consciousness of the tradition regarding the classical divisions of philosophy; for the quoted sentences are themselves nothing more than 'approximate' reminiscences. It is not accidental that this particular consciousness of 'the complete transformation, which philosophical thought has undergone in Germany during the last twenty-five years and the loftier outlook upon thought which self-conscious mind has attained in this

12 Christian Wolff, *Philosophia Rationalis sive Logica* (hereafter *PRSL*) (Frankfurt/Leipzig, 1740), 'Discursus praeliminaris de philosophia in genere', Ch. 3, par. 62.
13 *Archiv der Philosophischen Fakultät der Universität Berlin*, Lit. K, No. 2, Vol. 1, reported in *Nürnberger Schriften*, ed. J. Hoffmeister (Leipzig, 1938), p. xxiv.

period' became in this very case the occasion for once more altering the systematics of the *System der Wissenschaft* planned in 1807, and for giving up the dichotomy between the phenomenology of mind on the one hand and logic, natural philosophy, and philosophy of mind on the other. Henceforth Hegel's system of philosophy divides into what he called the 'two actual sciences', the philosophy of nature and the philosophy of mind, while the logic as 'pure science' formed their first part.[14]

It is not possible to say more in this context about the problematics of this division. What is essential to our theme is just that, as known, the philosophy of right stands together with the philosophy of history under the title 'Objective Spirit' in the second section of the *Philosophy of Spirit*. The contents of objective spirit are the activities (*pragmata*) of the human world: law and state, commerce and society, politics and history. So, the doctrine of objective spirit thematizes those human actions which have their foundation as well as their purposes intersubjectively in family, society, and state. Such actions, which do not transcend themselves in their meaning and are inseparably linked to the human world whose 'objective spirit' they are, formed in the European tradition the object of practical philosophy which included primarily political philosophy and ethics, and so was a metaphysic of morals in the broadest sense. Corresponding to the constitution of its object (i.e., the socially and politically ordered human world), school philosophy continued well into the eighteenth century to distinguish three scientific disciplines within the realm of *philosophia practica*: ethics, economics, and politics; and indeed, it did this exactly according to the distinctive structure of the practical object and the precise status of people. For this, as Christian Wolff put it, can be viewed in two perspectives – 'either the extent to which one is a man, or the extent to which one is a citizen; or, what is the same thing, either to the extent to which one lives in the society of human kind or a state of nature, or to *the extent to which one lives in civil society*. In two respects, therefore, practical philosophy is distinguished into two parts.'[15] These two

---

14 Cf. *Wissenschaft der Logik*, Part 1, ed. G. Lasson (Hamburg, 1934), Preface, pp. 7–8. (Eng. tr. A. V. Miller, *Hegel's Science of Logic* (London, 1969), pp. 28–9.)

15 (*PRSL*), 'Discursus praeliminaris', Ch. 3, par. 63.

parts are ethics and politics. The moral condition of the human species is the object of *ethics*; hence it investigates moral being (*entia moralia*) in general and the situation of human beings as human. 'That part of philosophy in which man is considered as living in a natural state or in the society of human kind is called *ethics*. For this reason we define *ethics* as the science of directing free action either in a natural state or to the extent that man is his own law, subject to no other's power.' The legal constitution of civil society (*societas civilis*) is the object of *politics*, and thus the latter is concerned not with the moral nature of the species, but rather with the political nature of the *res publica*, or state, determined by laws. It thematizes man not as human, but as citizen. So it removes him from the universality and indeterminateness of his actions in the sphere of ethics and locates him under the particularity of civil law in the state. 'That part of philosophy in which man is considered as living in a republic, or civil state, is called *politics*. Thus *politics* is the science of directing free actions in civil society or a republic.'[16]

Apart from these two basic disciplines of practical philosophy (politics as the doctrine of the citizen and his rights and duties within civil society, and ethics as the doctrine of human being in the whole of humankind's society) there is economics, the science which considers the human being as member of the household. Like Aristotle in *Politics* Book 1, Wolff speaks of 'little societies' (*societates minores*) which formed the foundation of the household (*fundamentum oeconomicae*): 'Prior to the republic or civil society, *there were little societies*, for which indeed there was a place in the state of nature or outside the republic. Instances of these are conjugal, paternal or maternal societies, which usually stem from a single clan.'[17]

In its several centuries of active influence this trichotomy of practical philosophy was more than a congealed scholasticism. It was the expression of the pre-revolutionary condition of European society and a mirror of its political, economic, and legal status. This tradition collapsed with the emancipation of modern society from the state in the revolutions of the seventeenth and eighteenth

16 *PRSL*, pars. 64 and 65.
17 *PRSL*, par. 66.

centuries: initially in England (even Hobbes was anti-Aristotelian in politics, while Locke, Ferguson, and Hume were already firmly grounded in the new 'society'), then in France. Ethics separated itself from politics, and as 'moral philosophy' even became its foe; moreover, economics broke through its previous boundaries and became the 'state' – or 'political' – economy of the eighteenth century – 'one of the sciences which has arisen out of the conditions of the modern world', as Hegel said.[18] The revolution within economics played the decisive role in emancipating modern society from the state and from the corresponding change in practical philosophy's (especially traditional politics') content, as will be shown in detail in the case of Hegel. It is in Germany alone, as against England and France, that the metaphysical tradition of practical philosophy preserved itself distinctively during the eighteenth century. In the work of Wolff and his school, this tradition again reveals the structure of pre-revolutionary society: the allocation of economics and politics to the disparate realms of domestic and civil society (*societas domestica* and *societas civilis*), the unity of the state (*civitas sive res publica*) and civil society (*societas civilis*), the binding of ethical life to valid law, and thus of ethics to politics.[19]

It is no accident that the very distinction between natural law and politics, which was so fundamental for the West European thinkers of this period, played no decisive role for German school philosophy in the eighteenth century – except for the great legal theorists, Pufendorf and Thomasius. This school philosophy never escaped the framework of traditional practical philosophy. Modern natural law theory's function in Western Europe of screening off the rights of 'society' from those of the government and emancipating the former from the latter stands opposed to the Wolffian limitation of natural law theory to a general theory of practical philosophy. The definition of natural law consists in its determination as the science of good and bad action and of people's

18 *GPR*, par. 189, p. 255; *PR*, 126.
19 Cf. Here the notes of the young Wilhelm von Humboldt on the *Teile der praktische Philosophie* which was presented by the popular philosopher Engel (1785–6) following the handbook of Wolff's school. (*Gesammelte Schriften*, ed. Königlich Preussische Akademie der Wissenschaften (17 vols., Berlin, 1903–36), Part 1, Vol. VII, second half (1908), pp. 363 ff.)

inner knowledge of good and evil in advance of desire. 'Natural law', Wolff concludes, 'obviously appears to be the theory of practical philosophy: of ethics, politics, and economics. For this reason, as it is not difficult to distinguish theory and practice, natural law in itself is able to transmit ethics, economics, and politics.'[20] For Wolff natural law theory is only formally distinguished from practical philosophy; its contents can be 'transmitted' in the ethical, economic, and political arrangements of society.

III

If one compares, on the one hand, traditional European practical philosophy's systematic design as Wolff constructs it for the last time in his voluminous books with their heavy dependence on Aristotle and scholastic philosophy and, on the other hand, the external outline of Hegel's political metaphysics, one will be surprised to discover on closer examination that practical philosophy's fundamentals are repeatedly hinted at in the Hegelian 'outlines', even though its total structure was fragmented by the burgeoning political and industrial revolutions in the second half of the eighteenth century. *The Philosophy of Right*'s dialectical founding in the self-development of the concept, which in the practical domain Hegel takes to be human will in its freedom (freedom is the 'concept' of will), leads him to make a trichotomy of this domain into 'Abstract right', 'Morality', and 'The Ethical Life'. 'Abstract Right' and 'Morality' contain the doctrine of human pre-political existence. In the former, one can even recognize a natural law theory now extended to cover the civil law of the modern middle class with its extreme freedom of property and profit; and in the latter one can recognize the *ethics*, sunk in the subjective self-feeling, which took shape in the philosophical revolution of the late eighteenth century. Here, in abstract right as well as in morality, man as man, emancipated from political status arrangements, realizes and expresses himself: partly in relation to externality, to the outer world and the world of contemporaries, in the forms of property (pars. 41–71), contract (pars. 72–80), and

---

20 *PRSL*, 'Discursus praeliminaris', Ch. 3, par. 68, Addition.

wrong (pars. 82–104); and partly in relation to inwardness in the modes of purpose and responsibility (pars. 105–18), intention and welfare (pars. 119–28), good and conscience (pars. 129–41). It is not possible here to undertake a detailed comparison, especially in connection with the metaphysical grounding of civil law, between Hegel's 'abstract right' and natural law theory, which even in the eighteenth century treated matters essentially of civil law.[21] Let us say only that for Hegel, both natural law theory and ethics are abstractions from the ethical–political constitution of the human world: natural-*qua*-civil law, designated expressly as 'abstract right', is the right of abstract personality; ethics *qua* morality, turned subjective in the eighteenth century, is the morals of equally abstract subjectivity. Man as man first fulfils himself 'practically' in man as citizen, as ethical–political existence within family, society, and state.

While abstract right and morality deal with comparatively modern subjects which were unknown to traditional political philosophy – think only of the realization of the person in the external world (pars. 41 ff.), of the grounding of the claim to property in labour and use (pars. 56 and 59 ff.), indeed of the identification of property and legal personality (par. 51) and of the subjectivity of the person, the 'inward comportment of the will to itself' as the 'concept of morality' (par. 112) – 'ethical life' reverts expressly to the standpoint of the old European tradition of ethics. In Hegel, ethical life means the unity of individuals with the 'ethical powers' (par. 145) and 'necessary relations' (par. 148) of a particular people and state, the *ethos* of the ancient citizen, which included ethics as much as politics and aimed at preserving the old unity of right, ethics, and state. 'The ethical life of the individual', as Hegel formulated it in his first essay devoted to the theme of practical philosophy, *Über die wissenschaftlichen Behandlungsarten des Naturrechts* (1802), '[and] conversely the essence of the ethical life of the individual is *the* real and therefore universal absolute ethical

---

21 Cf. here, above all, the detailed Introduction to GPR, in which Hegel develops the 'concept' of the modern legal person and its universal claim to freedom on the basis of a metaphysical theory of the will (pars. 1–32). For Hegel (par. 40) the foundation of the concepts of law and property is not 'a man . . . reckoned . . . as possessing a certain status' as 'citizen' as distinct from slaves, bondsmen, or sojourners, but rather 'personality itself'.

life; the ethical life of the individual is one pulse of the whole system and is itself the whole system. We notice here too a linguistic allusion, elsewhere repudiated, which is fully justified by what has been said – namely, that it is of the nature of absolute ethical life to be a universal, or an *ethos*; this Greek word for ethical life, like the German one, [*Sitte*] expresses this nature admirably, while the newer systems of ethics, in making independence and individuality into a principle, cannot fail to expose the relationship of these words.' This inner linguistic hint is shown to be so essential that the eighteenth century systems 'could not misuse these words' to designate '*their* subject-matter', the isolated individual, 'and so adopted the word "morality", which, indeed, originally meant the same thing, but, because it is rather only an invented word, does not quite as directly resist its inferior meaning'.[22]

One finds the 'antiquarian' style of Hegel's state concept constantly mentioned in the literature; and there cannot be any doubt how significant the ancient *polis* idea became for his rejecting the revolutionary liberation of individuals from bondage to the 'ethical principalities' and for the identification of state organization and consciousness of freedom, ethical life and right. In its form, the third division of the *Philosophy of Right* is thus identical with the third part of the old practical philosophy: 'ethical life' represents the unity of ethics and politics, which was so essential for the traditional doctrine of the ethical–legal constitution of the state, the doctrine of civil society (*civitas sive societas civilis*). Not in vain did Hegel refer in his own 'political philosophy' to the identity of the 'ethical doctrine of duty', as it is 'objective' not 'moralistic', with the 'development of the circle of ethical necessity which follows in this third part', that is, the 'civil' relationships in the state.[23]

In view of this re-petition of an old tradition, it is even more amazing that precisely this recapitulation of the classical concept of ethical life incorporates the contents of the modern political and

22 See *Kritisches Journal der Philosophie*, II, third part (1803), 1–2; *NL*, p. 112.
23 *GPR*, par. 148 – An 'immanent and logical "doctrine of duties"', i.e., ethics in the old sense, 'can be nothing except the serial exposition of the relationships which are necessitated by the idea of freedom and are therefore actual in their entirety, to wit, in the state' (pp. 213–14); *PR*, p. 107.

industrial revolution. For the paradox of the Hegelian *Philosophy of Right* consists just in this, that the book indexes under this very title ('The State') the basic tendencies of the revolutionary age and proposes the most incisive changes in the systematics of political philosophy since Bodin's concept of sovereignty and Rousseau's general will. It is here that Hegel's early comprehensive studies of politics and political economy become fruitful for the first time. In the lectures and essays of the Jena period one finds, as it seems at first glance, insights into the revolutionarily altered constitution of Europe's industrial and political world, insights derived from Hegel's studies of English and French works, standing, basically unconnected, next to the classical cultural tradition. The bourgeoisie is transplanted to the Roman Empire, the economic sphere of society (need, labour, and possession) is labelled 'relative ethical life' – in opposition to the 'absolute' of Greek *politeuein* – ancient tragedy is performed in modern 'relative ethical life.' Analyses of the 'modes of work of civil society', as the philosophy of right knows them, either follow within the framework of individuals' practical interactions with nature or stand inflexibly under such titles as 'people', 'government', 'state', and so forth.[24] The old structure of practical philosophy could no longer support the political, social and economic changes of the waning eighteenth century, as can be seen pre-eminently in the two outlines of the Jena lectures of 1803–4 and 1805–6; the material richness of a world which has burst its bounds overturns the grounded systematic structure. And when, on the other hand, Hegel initially attempted a strong systematization of the 'objective' content of spirit – in the Heidelberg *Encyclopedia* of 1817 – his antiquating manner constantly hinders an appropriate presentation of modern relationships.[25] In the *Philosophy of Right* of 1821 he is able for the

24 See here *Kritisches Journal der Philosophie*, II, second part (1802), 79, in *Schriften zur Politik und Rechtsphilosophie*, ed. G. Lasson (Leipzig, 1913), pp. 418 ff. and 464 ff.; but above all the *Jenenser Vorlesungen* of 1803–4 (*Jenenser Realphilosophie* (hereafter *JR*), Vol. I, ed. J. Hoffmeister (Leipzig, 1932), pp. 230 ff. and 236 ff.) and 1805–6 (*JR*, Vol. II, pp. 213 ff. and 231 ff.).

25 Paragraph 433 of the Heidelberg *Enzyklopädie*, the only one devoted to this theme, speaks simply of the 'universal work' and its particularization into 'classes', whereby the family appears as the 'class of individuality'; the 'particular' class 'whose work is the needs of particular existence and whose proximate purpose is particular subjectivity, but whose fulfilment presupposes the work of all other classes and which therefore meshes

first time to incorporate the results of the revolution within the framework of practical political philosophy, at the cost, however, of exploding its inherited systematics.

At first it seems as if Hegel returned to the old European tradition by conceiving ethical life, i.e., the ethical–political constitution of the human world, its '*actual* spirit', in the known trichotomy of family, civil society, and state. For family (*oikia*) and state (*polis*) compromised the precise basic elements especially thematized by pre-revolutionary political philosophy, which in this matter relied on Aristotle (*Politics* I, 1–2; *EN* VIII, 14, 1162a17 f.; *EE* VII, 10, 1242a23 ff.); in doing so, state (*polis*, or *civitas sive res publica*) is equated with society and named 'civil' society (*koinōnia politikē* or *societas civilis*) – as distinct from the 'domestic' society of the family (*societas domestica*).[26] In fact the similarity in external structure is surprising. Indeed, the historical primitiveness of Hegel's thinking in the *Philosophy of Right* cannot be demonstrated more convincingly anywhere than in the formal incorporation of these three concepts in the last and most important portion of that text. On the other side, the break with the tradition cannot in truth be grasped any more sharply and clearly than by the fact that these same concepts are given a very different meaning and the same words a new content. For in Hegel's *Philosophy of Right* the family is far removed structurally from the older domestic alliance; civil society is radically distinct from traditional European *societas civilis*; and even the Hegelian state can no longer be identified with the tradition's *civitas* model, since it has distinguished itself from the 'compact system of civil society'.[27] The greatness of the systematics of the third section of the *Philosophy of Right* is located precisely in this, that the historical rootedness of these concepts is

with them' is not yet 'civil society' but just 'class'. One can compare this with the comprehensive alterations which Hegel made in this section (pars. 513 ff.) of the 2nd edition of the *Enzyklopädie* (1827) after the appearance of the *Philosophy of Right*. Here, *inter alia*, the term 'ethical life' is historicized, so that it is related to the development of family, civil society, and state in the modern period (par. 552).

26 In opposition to the modern distinction between 'social' and 'political', or 'civil' and 'state', the basic distinction in ancient political philosophy was between *oeconomicus* or *domesticus*, and *civilis*, so that civil society too appeared as public and political.

27 This expression is in the Introductory Lecture of *Philosophie der Geschichte*; cf. *Die Vernunft in der Geschichte*, ed. J. Hoffmeister, 5th edn (Hamburg, 1955), p. 209.

transformed and shattered by the historical substantiality of Hegel's thinking, which incorporates the tendencies of the modern revolutions. At this point the cooperation and conflict of revolution and tradition in Hegel's outline of ethical life needs to be articulated in detail, with special reference to the structure of the three concepts, two of which, state and civil society, are to become in their opposition the genuine centre of gravity of modern political philosophy.

IV

Hegel begins his detailed presentation with a brief anticipatory outline in par. 157. 'Actual mind', the real essence of ethical life in the human world is

(A) ethical mind in its natural or immediate phase – the *Family*. This substantiality loses its unity, passes over into division, and into the phase of relation, i.e., into (B) *civil society* – an association of members as self-subsistent individuals in a universality which, because of their self-subsistence, is only abstract. Their association is brought about by their needs, by the legal system – the means to security of person and property – and by an external organization for attaining their particular and common interests. This external state (C) is brought back to and welded into unity in the *Constitution of the State* which is the end and actuality of both the substantial universal order and the public life devoted thereto.

What is striking in this characterization is the relatively extensive space already given over to 'civil society'. While family and state represent ethical life in the old sense, its substantiality, civil society is the 'destruction of its unity'. Thus, Hegel introduces the concept in such a way that its separation from the moral tradition is clear at once, and the 'contradiction' in this indicated state of affairs leads him to a more detailed specification of the contents – as well as to a novel designation.

The introduction of 'civil society' (in the modern sense of the word) into political philosophy was already recognized as a significant contribution by the earliest Hegel scholars, Eduard Gans, Christian Hermann Weisse, H. F. W. Hinrichs, and Leopold von Henning. No doubt it was with this concept in 1820 that Hegel 'comprehended' the fundamental alterations at the heart of

Europe's social–political order, and did not simply state them, as he had from the beginning of his political studies. While the legal–philosophical tradition from Aristotle to Kant named the state 'civil society', because a human society as such was already ordered politically (in the legal capacity of free citizens (*cives*) and in class privileges) as well as socially (in the economic–substantial position of the household), Hegel distinguished the political sphere of the state from the 'civil' domain of society. Thereby the term 'civil' gained an exclusively 'social' sense and was no longer used, as it had been in the eighteenth century, as synonymous with 'political': it named the purely 'social' status of the modern citizen, privatized in the absolute state, of the citizen 'as bourgeois' in the exact words of the explanation given in the *Addition* to par. 190. The concept of citizen, emancipated from its political–legal meaning, joins with the concept of society, likewise emancipated; their political substance is dissolved into the social function, which both concepts acquire through the revolution. Viewed in this light, it is no accident that Hegel unites 'civil' and 'society' into *one* political category, which had not previously existed and is not even to be found in his own writings before 1820. Rosenzweig's reference to the student excerpts from Sulzer's *Kurzer Begriff aller Wissenschaften* (1759) and Ferguson's *Essay on the History of Civil Society* (1767), which Hegel had known, is therefore wrong, because both cases are concerned with the old traditional concept, even if in a faded form.[28] Nowhere in his writings did Hegel make use of the traditional formula of political philosophy: *civitas sive societas civilis sive res publica latius sic dicta*, which is found from Thomas Aquinas and Albertus Magnus, to Bodin, Hobbes, Locke and Kant, and which expresses the constitution of pre-revolutionary civil society.[29] Indeed, he did not even understand its sense – as can be seen from a passage in the *Philosophy of Right* which seems to refer to this equation – from the new position of civil society: 'If the

28 Rosenzweig, *Hegel und der Staat* (Munich/Berlin, 1920), Vol. II, p. 118. The passage to which Rosenzweig refers consists, in Sulzer's case, of considerations about civil society in the old sense, of the social constitution of a 'civil state' as he says (*Kurzer Begriff*, pp. 189–90). Ferguson's *History of Civil Society* likewise applies the concept as identical with 'political society' (Part 3, sec. 6), but under this title he gives, next to the broad discussion of political relations (especially in Sparta, Athens, and Rome), an account of the 'arts and sciences'.

29 Cf. Chapter 6 in this volume.

state is represented as a unity of different persons, as a unity which is only a partnership, then what is really meant is only civil society. Many modern constitutional lawyers have been able to bring within their purview no theory of the state but this.'[30]

If, on the one hand, Hegel's break with tradition is here again expressed in obviously classical terms, on the other hand, he remains completely aware of the identity of what was previously called civil society with the political state, as is shown in a particularly interesting fashion on the basis of both language and the society of his time which, in its contours, remains bound to classes. 'So-called "theories" of this kind involve the idea that the classes [*Stände*] of civil society and the estates [*Stände*], which are the "classes" given a political significance, stand wide apart from each other. But the German language, by calling them both *Stände*, has still preserved the unity which in any case they actually possessed in former times.'[31] Nevertheless, the first paragraph of the division 'Civil Society' in the *Philosophy of Right* already unequivocally formulates the thorough detraditionalization of the old concept on the basis of the private citizen in a society emancipated from its political basis, which thereby becomes 'civil' in the sense mentioned: 'The concrete person, who is himself the object of his particular aims, is, as a totality of wants and a mixture of caprice and physical necessity, one principle of civil society. But the particular person is essentially so related to other particular persons that each establishes himself and finds satisfaction by means of the others, and at the same time purely and simply by means of the form of universality, the second principle here.'[32] The utility-principle found in emancipated Western European society and its economic model, Diderot's and Helvétius' 'intérêt personnelle', Bentham's and Franklin's 'self-interest', appear here in a German philosophical form. The result is the same as in that case:

30 *GPR*, par. 182, Addition; *PR*, pp. 266–7.
31 *GPR*, par. 303; *PR*, p. 198.
32 *GPR*, par. 182; *PR*, pp. 122–3. The best presentations of civil society are still found in Franz Rosenzweig (*Hegel und der Staat*, Vol. II, pp. 118 ff.) and Karl Löwith (*Von Hegel zu Nietzsche* (Garden City, NY, 1941), Part 2, Chs. 1, 2) (Eng. tr. D. Green, *From Hegel to Nietzsche* (New York, 1967)). Further, one can check R. Kroner's essay in the *Archiv für angewandte Soziologie*, IV (1931), as well as the speculative account of civil society as modern 'work society' in Joachim Ritter's *Hegel und die Französische Revolution* (1st edn, Cologne, 1957).

the formation of an independent, interest-based, relational network between individuals. 'In the course of the actual attainment of selfish ends', Hegel says in par. 183, 'there is formed a system of complete interdependence, wherein the livelihood, happiness, and legal status of one man is interwoven with the livelihood, happiness and rights of all. On this system, individual happiness, etc. depend, and only in this connected system are they actualized and secured.' Individuals who, 'as burghers in this state are *private persons* whose end is their own interest', form themselves, on the basis of the 'necessity' proper to 'civil society' (par. 186), into 'links in the chain' of its powerful nexus.

This necessity characteristic of modern society appears (1) at its lowest level in 'The System of Needs' (pars. 189–208), as *nature* (a. the kind of need and satisfaction), work (b. the kind of work), and possession (c. capital). These elements in turn produce a distinctive necessity in the form of 'sociability': the endless multiplication of needs and the means of their satisfaction (pars. 190–5); the division of labour, by which 'the dependence of men on one another and their reciprocal relation' becomes 'total necessity' (par. 198), with the machine looming on the horizon if labour can become 'mechanical' and 'man is able to step aside' (par. 198); the subdivision of the socially produced 'universal capital' into particular holdings and its result, the given 'inequality of men', which according to Hegel 'in civil society ... is so far from [cancelling itself] that it [is produced] out of mind' (par. 200), just like the distinction of the 'entire complex' of society into classes (pars. 201 ff.). This necessity also rules (2) in the supervening layer of civil society, in which it appears to revert to its old constitutive element, or Law, in the 'administration of justice' (pars. 209–29). But the law in this administration of justice is essentially civil law, 'civil' law in its application to 'the material of civil society (i.e., to the endlessly growing complexity and subdivision of social ties and the different species of property and contract within the society)' (par. 213). The necessity for this sphere consists (a) in the 'posited character' of law (pars. 212 ff.); (b) in the quantitative nature of its content, of the indeterminately many and doggedly particular cases, which heighten its positivity, that is, its being something posited (par. 214); and (c) in the endlessly variable quality of relationship between private persons which it must contain and hold within itself. The third phase, 'the police and corporation' (pars. 230–56), is the first that is able to convert the necessity which rules the individuals in civil society, like the cold ancient fates, into something ethical. To be sure, the 'police' (here too one detects a vestigial concept from ancient society's political conceptions) remain limited to the 'sphere of contingencies' and the adjustment of 'a necessity of which they themselves know nothing' (pars. 231 ff. and 236 ff.). But in the corporation of civil modes of life 'ethical principles circle back and appear in civil society as a factor immanent in it' (pars. 253 ff.).

As 'the universal authority by which security is ensured' (par. 231) the police fight a constant battle against the particularity of society, in this respect almost more necessarily than does posited law. Just before analysing the sphere of the political state, Hegel (pars. 243–8) built the tendencies of the Industrial Revolution into the concept of civil society, after adapting them to the natural economic basis of modern society in 'The System of Needs'. From here on it is a matter of 'industry' as 'the labour organization of civil society' (par. 251). This is no longer composed of 'many households'[33] as was the case with Wolff and in the political tradition; rather, when it is conceived in its 'unimpeded activity', it is composed of totally novel elements: wealth and poverty, industry and proletarian masses, rising population, and colonial expansion. It produces (1) within itself 'expanding ... population and industry'; (2) 'the fall' of 'a large mass of people ... below a certain subsistence level', the so-called 'rabble'; (3) a 'dialectic' which appears in the fact that 'despite an excess of wealth civil society is not rich enough, i.e., its own resources are insufficient to check excessive poverty and the creation of a penurious rabble'.[34] Hegel sees two escapes open to civil society from this dialectic: one is immanent, since civil society's contradictions impel it beyond itself to colonization (par. 248). This 'solution' solves nothing, but only defers the problem. The other 'transcendent' solution, as one might call it, is the incorporation of civil society by the state, with which the third section of the *Philosophy of Right* is concerned (pars.

33 *Vernünftigen Gedanken vom gesellschaftlichen Leben*, par. 214.
34 *GPR*, par. 245; *PR*, p. 150.

257 ff.). However, this solution does not terminate the dialectic; but only jumps over it, as the events of 1840 were to show. If the process of expansion has reached the limits of disposable space, the path of colonization fails in the face of the power of society's internal contradictions, and if the state hesitates in front of time's possibilities as a Utopia, it comes to grief on its own reality.

If ever, it is in this short section of the *Philosophy of Right* (pars. 243–8) and at one place in his lectures on the history of philosophy that Hegel concretizes civil society as a temporal concept. At the end of his lecture on Aristotle's *Politics* he mentions the 'abstract right of our modern states, that isolates the individual and leaves him alone', and which nevertheless establishes a necessary connection, even if it does so in such a way that 'no one's consciousness or activity is directed to the whole; each works for the whole without knowing how, for him it is only a matter of protecting his individuality'.[35] Here Hegel employs the obvious image of the factory to clarify the divided structure of individual, state, and society in the modern world: 'It is a subdivided activity, of which each one has only a fragment; just as in a factory nobody makes a whole but only a part, without possessing the other skills, while only a few do the assembling.' Free people had consciousness and activity only in the whole; moderns are as individuals implicitly unfree – '*civil* freedom is exactly the renunciation of the universal, the principle of isolation' (Hegel's italics).

The temporal relationship obvious here is established even more definitely in paragraphs 305 to 308 – in the third part of 'Ethical Life', the chapter on the state. On the one hand, these paragraphs grasp the social powers of perseverance and flux in civil society, thirty years before Riehl – the duality of the 'class elements', the nobility founded on a fixed natural basis and the bourgeoisie working its way up in the technological industries, which constitute the 'fluctuating element in civil society' (par. 308). On the other hand they base the bicameral legislative system of that time, the hereditary house of lords and the elected house of representatives, in the emergence of the social classes within the

35 *Vorlesungen über die Geschichte der Philosophie*, ed. Karl Ludwig Michelet, Vol. II, in *Werke*, Vol. XIV, p. 400. (Eng. tr. E. S. Haldane and F. H. Simpson, *Hegel's Lectures on the History of Philosophy* (3 vols., London, 1896).)

state: 'In the Estates, as an element with legislative power, the unofficial class acquires its political significance and efficacy; it appears, therefore, in the Estates neither as a mere indiscriminate multitude nor as an aggregate dispersed into atoms, but as a class subdivided into two, one subclass [the agricultural class] being based on a tie of substance between its members, and the other [the business class] on particular needs and the work whereby these are met.'[36] It is interesting here how Hegel turns the concept of, as it were, a politically modified civil class society against the possible dissolution of society into a 'mere indiscriminate multitude', and against an 'aggregate dispersed into its atoms' as much as against the political formalization of the state. Because, according to its class contours, it is still political, civil society ought to maintain a position in the middle *between* the emancipation of isolated individuals and the organization of the state. To this extent it is, for Hegel, not simply a supplement to political science occasioned by British political economy; instead it stands exactly on the spot where the depoliticization of ancient civil society and the emancipation of the state from its influence coincide. Therefore, in par. 308 he says of 'the second section of the estates', the 'fluctuating element' of civil society: 'in making the appointment, society is not dispersed into atomic units, collected to perform only a single and temporary act, and kept together for a moment and no longer. On the contrary, it makes the appointment as a society, articulated into associations, communities, and Corporations, which although constituted already for other purposes, acquire in this way a connexion with politics.'[37] The historical substance and, in a certain sense, paradoxical ambiguity of this Hegelian notion shows itself most fundamentally in the fact that its function is to negate the division between civil and political life which began during the French Revolution, while at the same time it incorporates the economic revolution arising in England. This complex, twofold temporal relatedness of Hegel's notion of civil society, the reference not just retrospectively and prospectively, but also towards France and England as the two strands of the modern revolution,

36 *GPR*, par. 303; *PR*, p. 198.
37 *GPR*, par. 308; *PR*, p. 200.

is what constitutes its historical actuality and founds its political efficacy for succeeding generations.

v

Even if we cannot follow Joachim Ritter's recently proposed interpretation of Hegel[38] in all respects, the simple fact that civil society crops up repeatedly in the structure of the *Philosophy of Right* – as the concrete basis of *abstract right* (pars. 209 ff.), as a wide field of action (in the sphere of poverty) in *subjective morality* (par. 242), as the 'manifest ethical world' lost in its one-sidedness, indeed as the 'loss' of ethical life (pars. 182, 184, and 229), as the individual's 'parent' and the substantive basis of the family (par. 238), and finally as the 'presupposition' of the *state* (par. 182) – this fact certifies the correctness of his thesis that since 1820 this concept 'has moved into the centre of his philosophy and political theory'.[39] Concretely it has become central particularly in the three-fold division of 'Ethical Life', where it represents a middle term between family and state, something previously absent everywhere in the European tradition of political philosophy. Since it is not appropriate in this context to enter more closely on this issue, I shall simply mention how at the start of the eighteenth century Christian Thomasius was able to define civil society: 'But human society in itself', as he says in his *Kurtzer Entwurf der politischen Klugheit* (1725), 'is either civil or domestic. The latter is the ground of the former, because in this context civil society means nothing but a union of many domestic societies and the persons who dwell in them, to the extent that they stand under a common authority.'[40] This definition is totally within the old tradition, and even a late eighteenth century historical–legal work which stands as close to its contemporary social reality as does the *Allgemeine Landrecht für die Preussischen Staaten* (1794) does not move very far from this, when it says in paragraph 2 of the first part: 'Civil society consists of numerous small societies and classes, bound together by nature, Law, or both together.'[41]

38 *Hegel und die Französische Revolution* (1957), new edition, Frankfurt on Main, 1965.
39 *Hegel und die Französische Revolution*, pp. 57 f.
40 Pp. 204 f.
41 Part 1, sec. 1, par. 2.

The sole, though certainly significant, divergence from the tradition might be the supplementing of 'societies' – the *societates minores* of Wolff – by classes. The fact that civil society still appears in the *Allgemeine Landrecht* as political society, as state, is based in the – at least theoretical – preservation of the traditional position for the household, the *societas domestica*, from which *societas civilis* emerges with its structure of political public life. For the very next paragraph of the *Landrecht* asserts: 'The bond between spouses, equally that between parent and child, actually constitutes domestic society. Yet servants too are counted as part of the household.'[42] At this point the author of the *Landrecht* is in agreement with the Kantian *Rechtslehre*, the first part of the *Metaphysic of Morals* (1797), which was written during the same decade and in which *societas civilis* is retained while a special section is dedicated to the *Recht der Häuslichen Gesellschaft*.[43] However, as soon as the development of 'state economics' breaks through the limits of this 'domestic society', as is the case with Hegel, who learned from Steuart and Smith, 'society' takes on the function assigned to *oeconomia*. Conversely, the new understanding of *societas civilis* as 'civil society', whose substantial necessity with the onset of the Industrial Revolution dominates individuals and their 'littler societies', signals the destruction of *societas domestica*.

This interaction can be seen quite precisely in Hegel's concept of the family. The *family*, as the first level of 'Ethical Life', is not a 'society' with a differential status among its members; it does not consist of 'little societies' between husband and wife, parents and children, and certainly not lord and servant; rather, it is nothing else than a legal 'person' which has its external reality 'in its property', but not in the household.[44] Unlike Kant, for Hegel the 'economic' concept of the old European family has disappeared

---

42 Par. 3.
43 *Rechtslehre*, par. 22, in *Kants gesammelte Schriften*, ed. Königlich Preussische Akademie der Wissenschaften (22 vols, Berlin/Leipzig, 1900–42), Vol. VI, p. 276. Characteristics of 'domestic concerns' for Kant is 'personal right of the concrete kind', i.e., 'the possession of an external object as *a thing* and its use as a person' (p. 276). On this cf. Hegel's criticism of this 'objective mode of personal rights' in par. 40 of the *Philosophy of Right*.
44 GPR, par. 169: 'The family, as person, has its real external existence in property; and it is only when this property takes the form of capital that it becomes the embodiment of the substantial personality of the family'; PR, p. 116.

and is replaced by the late eighteenth-century 'sentimental' concept of the family.[45] 'The family', he says in par. 158, 'as the immediate substantiality of mind, is specifically characterized by love, which is mind's feeling of its own unity. Hence in a family, one's frame of mind is to have self-consciousness of one's individuality within this unity as the absolute essence of oneself, with the result that one is in it not as an independent person, but as a member.'

'Necessity' as the fundamental character of civil society, which as we saw intertwines with the family's structure and gathers it into a substantial economic–legal whole, has dissolved the family as the basic economic unit; the individual, although still a 'member' of a family, no longer participates primarily in its substance, but rather stands over against the process of civil society as an 'independent' person. For, according to par. 238, only 'originally' is the family the 'substantial whole' whose function is 'to provide for the individual on this particular side by giving him either the means and the skill necessary to enable him to earn his living out of the resources of society, or else subsistence and maintenance in the event of his suffering a disability'. But in truth it is, as Hegel says, 'something subordinate in civil society which only lays the foundations; its effective range is no longer so comprehensive. Civil society is rather the tremendous power which draws men into itself and claims from men that they work for it, owe everything to it, and do everything by its means.'[46] In this passage the necessity of civil society appears as its intrinsic nature: as the 'tremendous power' over the ethical substance of the family and the subsistence of individuals, which 'estranges' them from one another and recognizes them only as 'selfsubsistent persons': 'civil society tears the individual from his family ties, estranges the members of the family from one another, and recognizes them as self-subsistent persons. Further, for the paternal soil and the external inorganic resources of nature from which the individual formerly derived his livelihood, it substitutes its own soil and subjects the permanent existence of even the entire family to dependence on itself and to contingency. Thus, the individual becomes a son of civil society

---

45 This expression is used by O. Brunner in his essay 'Das "Ganze Haus" und die alteuropäische "Oekonomik"' in *Neue Wege der Sozialgeschichte* (1956), p. 44.
46 *GPR*, par. 238, Addition; *PR*, p. 276.

which has as many claims upon him as he has rights against it.'[47] Hegel never expresses the dissolution of the smaller societies within the union of households and the connection between this dissolution and the concept of civil society more clearly than in this passage.

Now, just as Hegel's notion of civil society requires the revised structure of 'domestic' society in the old sense, it also refers on the other side to the equally changed role of the 'political' *state*. Here, politics is no longer *scientia civilis*, the description of civil society in its political structure; rather it is 'political science' abstracted from all this. State and society, which in the older European tradition are joined in the relational concept civil society, 'posit' themselves for Hegel initially in 'relation', and in such a way that they are also specifically differentiated: 'Civil society is the difference which intervenes between the family and the state, even if its formation follows later in time than that of the state, because as difference, it presupposes the state; to subsist itself, it must have the state before its eyes as something self-subsistent.'[48] Hegel introduces into the traditional form of the classical *polis*-idea of the state as divine, self-contained, fulfilling its aims, and self-sufficient, the modern reality of state constitutions, which essentially fix the internal dualism of state and society. For this state is, as Hegel says explicitly, a 'more modern state' whose characteristic is the fact that 'the universal be bound up with the complete freedom of its particular members and with private well being, that thus the interests of the family and civil society must concentrate themselves on the state, although the universal end cannot be advanced without the personal knowledge and will of its particular members, whose own rights must be maintained'.[49]

That for Hegel the state does not merely 'pose' (*setzt*) civil society but rather *pre*-supposes (*voraus-setzt*) its existence for the reality of its own special constitution, is shown with impressive force by an empirical analysis of the political situation in North America, which is found in the Berlin lectures on the philosophy of history. In this context, Hegel concludes that North America

47 *GPR*, par. 238; *PR*, p. 148.
48 *GPR*, par. 182, Addition; *PR*, p. 266.
49 *GPR*, par. 260, Addition; *PR*, p. 280.

could not yet be viewed as a proper state because it still lacked a civil society. Its development was hampered in this case by the annexation of territory in the West – an 'enduring exodus' of population that hindered urban centralization: 'Only when the simple multiplication of agriculture is limited, as in Europe, will the residents move into urban businesses and trade, form a compact system of civil society, and arrive at the need of an organic state, rather than spreading out into the fields.'[50] In this passage civil society assumes the features of the 'concept of a third class', as the late nineteenth century would say in the words of J. C. Bluntschli.

But Hegel's break with tradition is not revealed only in the fact that the object of politics has changed over to the difference between state and society. It becomes manifest much more significantly through the relationship of this modern 'state' to history. For its presupposition is not just grounded in the dynamics of civil society, but rather extends equally outward to the current of history. At the apex of its fulfilment, the state idea appears 'as a genus and as an absolute power over individual states – the mind which gives itself its actuality in the process of *World History*'.[51] The state is no longer the political status concept of the tradition, no longer a changeless natural model of *civitas sive societas civilis* with which traditional political thinking began and at which it stopped; rather, something stands superior to it as a new court of justice: history, in which 'the ethical whole itself, the autonomy of the state' – *again*, as one must amend Hegel here – 'is exposed to contingency'.[52] Eduard Gans expressed the mood of his generation and the notion of the nineteenth century in general when he observed about this conclusion of Hegel's *Philosophy of Right* that in it 'the deepest value of the present book authentically' resided. For him this ending is a 'tremendous drama'; from the heights of the state one sees individual states 'toss about in history's world sea', and he indicates, pointing ahead of his generation, that 'the short outline of its development' which Hegel gives at the end of

50 Introduction to the *Philosophy of History* cited from *Reason in History*.
51 *GPR*, par. 259; *PR*, p. 160.
52 *GPR*, par. 340; *PR*, p. 215.

the work would be 'only a hint of the more significant interest which would be given this foundation'.[53]

VI

If one comprehensively reviews the conceptual structure of the Hegelian philosophy of right and its formative principles, one would be able to observe that, as outcome and heir of the revolution, these two elements, civil society and state, are embedded in one another. Both equally transform the inner constitution of family and state, as they were presented in a tradition of political reflection which had remained operative since antiquity. As the family stands 'between' the individuals belonging to it as members, and civil society at large, so the state is operative between civil society and history. It is this very leap into the architectonic of the system of classical practical philosophy which creates for Hegel the artistic, dialectical structure of right. This is the place from which Hegel's treatment, as a 'system of mediation', finally secures for itself the proper wealth of historical substance, which distinguishes it fundamentally from Rousseau's *Social Contract*, Kant's *Rechtslehre*, and Fichte's *Naturrecht*.

What Hegel says about Plato in his lectures on the history of ancient philosophy, when he gives an account of the contingent presuppositions of the *Republic*, remains in a deep sense valid for himself – he is 'not the man for busying himself with abstract theories and principles; his true spirit knew and presented the truth, and that could only be, the truth of the world in which he lived, the one spirit which was active in him as it was in Greece'. He had, in his *Philosophy of Right*, actually presented the genuine 'ethical life' of the modern world in substantive terms. And the words with which he concludes this passage from the Plato lecture could stand with equal justice at the beginning of the *Philosophy of Right* as the last metaphysical philosophical 'politics': 'No one can go beyond his time; but the problem therefore is to know it in its substance.'[54]

53 His *Foreword* to *GPR*, pp. viii–ix.
54 *Vorlesungen über die Geschichte der Philosophie*, in *Werke*, Vol. XIV, p. 275.

Index

Abbott, T. K., 7n
Abbt, T., 109
Achenwall, G., 142n
Aeschylus, 116
Albertus Magnus, 135, 177
Anaxagoras, 40
Aquinas, Thomas, 20n, 135, 148, 177
Aristotle, vii, 5 f., 8 ff., 12 f., 15, 17 f., 21,
    23, 30, 35n, 36, 42, 59 ff., 67, 82 f., 88,
    91, 96 f., 107, 111 ff., 114, 117, 133 ff.,
    136 f., 138 ff., 143, 147, 162 ff., 167,
    169 ff., 175, 177, 181

Bacon, F., 40
Baillie, F. B., 22n, 96n
Bauer, B., 129
Beck, L. W., 49n
Bentham, J., 45, 149, 178
Bernstein, E., 130
Besser, K. M., 129
Binder, J., 160
Bindseil, 136n
Bluntschli, J. C., 130, 187
Bobio, N., 42n
Bodin, J., 135, 147 f., 163, 174, 177
Bonald, L. G. A., Vicomte de, 40
Borden, G., 142n
Bottomore, T. B., 161n
Boumann, L., 149n
Bretschneider, 136n
Brunner, O., 139n, 146n, 163n, 185n
Busse, 160
Borgnet, A., 135n

Caligula, 62
Campbell, R. H., 14n
Cerf, W., 17n, 79n, 80n
Chamley, P., 111n
Cicero, 98, 132, 136
Commung, J., 142n
Comte, A., 52

Conze, W., 139n, 146n

Darmstädter, F., 88n
Descartes, R., 4, 7
Diderot, D., 45, 149, 178
Dilthey, W., 5
Dulckeit, G., 160, 165

Ehrenberg, H., 91n
Eiselen, J. Fr. G., 129
Engels, F., 148n, 161n
Engel J. J., 170n
Ephraim, 10n
Erdmann, J. E., 129 f., 160, 165

Falckenberg, R., 25n
Ferguson, A., 44, 109, 131, 146, 170, 177
Fichte, J. G., 11 ff., 13, 18, 27, 38 f., 42,
    68, 70, 72 ff., 79 f., 84 ff., 87 f., 91 ff.,
    94 f., 98, 100 ff., 104, 109, 119, 188
Fischer, 160
Fleischmann, E., 101n
Frankel, C., 62n, 98n
Franklin, B., 45, 149, 178
Fuelleborn, G., 135n

Gadamer, H. G.., 142n
Gans, E., 51, 57, 103n, 129, 150n, 159 ff.,
    165n, 176, 187
Garve, C., 109, 111, 135
Gentz, F., 146
Gert, B., 6n
Gibbon, E., 115
Gigon, O., 135n
Glockner, H., 4n, 31n, 57n, 76, 78n, 80n,
    114n, 115n
Görland, I., 10n
Green, D., 178n
Griesheim, 57n, 71n, 73n, 103n, 104n
Grint, L., 64n
Grotius, H., 98, 100, 132
Gutmann, J., 82n, 136n

189

Rosenzweig, F., 26n, 67n, 88n, 123n, 125n, 130, 131n, 145 f., 165, 177, 178n
Rossi, M., 131n
Rossig, K. G., 152n
Rössler, C., 129
Rousseau, J. J., vii, 17, 24, 27, 39, 60 ff., 63 f., 67 f., 72 ff., 84 f., 94, 95, 96 ff., 99 ff., 104, 107 f., 119, 131, 141n, 142, 148, 174, 188
Ruge, A., 51, 129, 160

St Simon, 52 f.
Sanderson, J. B., 28n
Savigny, 38
Scheidemantel, 142n
Schelling, F. W. J., 18, 79n, 81, 83n, 86n, 88, 91, 109, 114n
Schlegel, 40
Schlosser, J. G., 109, 134 f.
Schlözer, A. L. von, 139 f.
Schröter, M., 83n
Schulz, F., 35n
Schwartz, J., 94n
Simpson, F. H., 6n, 61n, 97n, 144n, 181n
Skinner, A. S., 14n
Smith, A., 14, 44, 108 f., 111, 119, 139, 144, 149, 184
Sohm, R., 115n

Sonnenfels, J. von, 152n
Speirs, E. B., 28n
Spencer, H., 52
Spinoza, B. de, 65, 79, 82 ff., 88, 91 f., 94, 135, 136n
Stahl, 160
Stein, Lorenz von, 130, 139, 153, 160 f.
Steuart, J., 108 f., 111, 144, 184
Stoics, 30, 98
Sulzer, 130, 145 f., 177

Thomasius, Chr., 137, 170, 183
Todd, W. B., 14n
Tönnies, F., 130, 135n, 139

Vahlen, J., 98n
Vaughan, C. E., 100n
Vogel, P., 139n

Wagener, H., 130
Wallace, W., 27n, 32n
Weigand, K., 62n, 98n
Weil, E., 131n
Weisse, Christian Hermann, 129, 176
Wolf, F. O., 60n
Wolff, Christian, 6 ff., 98, 131 f., 136 f., 141n, 147, 162, 164, 167 ff., 169 ff., 180, 184